Léopold Sédar Senghor

Twayne's World Authors Series
French Literature

David O'Connell, Editor
University of Illinois

TWAS 765

LÉOPOLD SÉDAR SENGHOR
Photography courtesy of Éditions du Seuil

Léopold Sédar Senghor

By Janice Spleth

West Virginia University

Twayne Publishers • *Boston*

Léopold Sédar Senghor

Janice Spleth

Copyright © 1985 by G.K. Hall & Company
All Rights Reserved
Published by Twayne Publishers
A Division of G.K. Hall & Company
70 Lincoln Street
Boston, Massachusetts 02111

Book Production by Elizabeth Todesco
Book Design by Barbara Anderson

Printed on permanent/durable acid-free
paper and bound in the United States of
America.

Library of Congress Cataloging in Publication Data

Spleth, Janice S.
  Léopold Sédar Senghor.

  (Twayne's world authors series; TWAS 765. French literature)
  Bibliography: p. 179.
  Includes index.
  1. Senghor, Léopold Sédar, 1906–   —Criticism and interpretation.
2. Blacks in literature.
3. Race awareness in literature.
I. Title. II. Series: Twayne's world authors series; TWAS 765.
III. Series: Twayne's world authors series. French literature.
PQ3989.S47Z89 1985   841   85–8626
ISBN 0–8057–6616–2

Contents

LÉOPOLD SÉDAR SENGHOR

About the Author

Janice Spleth is Associate Professor in the Department of Foreign Languages at West Virginia University. She received her Ph.D. in 1973 from Rice University where she held an NDEA Fellowship. During the 1977–78 academic year, she was a Fulbright Lecturer at the National University of Zaïre in Lubumbashi. She has previously published on Senghor and given numerous scholarly papers on African writers. She is one of the co-editors of the 1982 volume of the African Literature Association Annuals entitled *Interdisciplinary Dimensions of African Literature* (Three Continents Press).

In addition to her contributions as an Africanist, she was also co-editor of the 1975 volume of the *French Periodical Index* (Faxon, 1977) with Jean-Pierre Ponchie and of the *West Virginia George Sand Conference Papers* (WVU, 1981) with Armand and Mary Singer and Dennis O'Brien.

Preface

This volume is intended as an introduction to the work of the African poet Léopold Sédar Senghor. Although his poetry has been widely translated and anthologized and has received considerable attention from the scholarly community, it remains relatively little known to the educated reading public. It is our hope that by calling attention to the diversity, richness, and significance of his work, a greater audience will be created for a major figure in contemporary world literature.

The structure of this book has been dictated to a large extent by the nature of the poems themselves. The obvious personal inspiration of most of the works has required that considerable space, both in an introductory chapter and within the discussions of individual poems, be devoted to detailing the writer's life and the period of political transition in which he wrote. The immensely important role of his cultural theories in shaping his literary vision has necessitated chapters on the concept of Negritude and its influence on both the form and content of his verse. Chapters devoted to analysis of the individual poems and to discussion of critical reaction deal with all of the writer's previously collected works beginning with *Chants d'ombre* (1945) and going through *Elégies majeures* (1978). While we have occasionally referred to his prose writing, no attempt has been made to discuss Senghor systematically either as an essayist or as a political theorist, and our bibliography does not pretend to reflect his extraordinarily prolific output of articles and formal addresses or his participation in numerous scholarly publications.

Most previous criticism of Senghor's work has emphasized his role as an African poet—more specifically as the poet of Negritude— and certainly no serious critic could fail to treat this dimension of his poetry. While duly noting the relationship between Senghor's philosophy of Negritude and his poems, we have also chosen to emphasize two additional and equally important frames of reference. One of our aims is to delineate the way in which Senghor's verse documents the transition that brought Africa from colonialism to nationhood and eventually to a fuller participation in world affairs. Caught up in that transition, the poet sought not only to define a place for himself as an individual but also, in a broader context, to replace old stereotypes with new notions of race and culture. We consider this vision a modern myth, and in our examination of the poet's work, we strive to show its various facets and how, in conformity with the general characteristics of myth, it continually changes and develops. Secondly, we try to maintain a view of the man behind the archetypal embellishments, the first-person narrator of the poems who, because he represents Senghor himself, is an essential and continually fascinating element of the poetry. We cannot forget that we are sharing the inner world of a major political figure who participated in a very important way in the critical events of his era. We also sense the presence of a gifted observer who, writing over a period of four decades, leaves a priceless record of one man's lifetime of dreams, emotions, and experiences.

It seems advisable at the very start to say a word about the translations, which, unless otherwise indicated, are our own. Under any circumstances, the attempt to convey the poetry of one language in another is fraught with difficulties since the effectiveness of the poem depends not merely on its message or content but also on the interplay between meaning and form. With few exceptions, our translations have tended toward a literal interpretation of the French, but in an effort to maintain the sense of the poem, we have consistently had to sacrifice the nuances of poetic style. Because of the poet's own concept of what poetry should be, the English versions can reflect the original only imperfectly; and without its characteristic rhythm, its verbal and structural ambiguities, and its rich sonorities, Senghor's work cannot be completely transmitted in another language. For this reason, we have preferred that the French text appear first in this volume and suggest that even the reader unaccustomed to that language will want to consider the original before coming to any final conclusions about the writer. Those interested in more artistic translations of Senghor's poetry and prose are directed to the bibliography at the end of this book.

To all who have contributed their support and encouragement to the writing of this work, we express our deepest gratitude. In particular, we would like to thank our field editor, David O'Connell, for his suggestions and advice, our colleague Eleanor Gibbard for her time in reading parts of the manuscript and for her perceptive comments, and Bonnie C. Anderson for typing the final draft. Finally, we want to acknowledge the contribution of the National

Preface

Endowment for the Humanities for providing several weeks of financial support by way of a summer seminar grant at the University of Illinois.

Janice Spleth

West Virginia University

Chronology

1906   Léopold Sédar Senghor born in Joal on the Atlantic coast of Senegal just south of Dakar.

1913   Enters missionary school at Joal.

1914   Begins studies at N'Gazobil with Fathers of the Holy Spirit.

1922   Attends Libermann Seminary at Dakar.

1926   Leaves the seminary to continue his studies at the secondary school in Dakar which is today the Lycée Van Vollenhoven.

1928   Arrives in Paris to continue studies at the Lycée Louis-le-Grand.

1930   Fails entrance exams for the Ecole Normale Supérieure.

1931   Receives *licence ès lettres* from the University of Paris.

1932   Receives *diplôme d'études supérieures* after completing study of Baudelaire. Vacations in Senegal.

1933   Is accorded naturalized French citizenship.

1934   With Césaire and Damas, founds *L'Etudiant noir*. Performs a year of military service.

1935   Becomes the first African *agrégé de grammaire*.

1937   Received in Dakar with full military honors to celebrate *agrégation*. Begins teaching at the Lycée Descartes in Tours.

1938   Assigned to the Lycée Marcelin-Berthelot at Saint-Maur-des-Fossés.

1939   Serves in 23d, then 3d Regiment of Colonial Infantry. Publishes "Ce que l'homme noir apporte" in *L'Homme de couleur* (Editions Plon).

1940   Taken prisoner at La Charité-sur-Loire by Germans. Interned in various prison camps.

1941   Released from prison camp for reasons of health. Participates in various Resistance efforts.

1942   Resumes post at Lycée Marcelin-Berthelot.

1944   Teaches African languages and civilizations at the Ecole Nationale de la France d'Outre-mer. Publishes articles on African languages.

1945   Publishes *Chants d'ombre*. Elected representative to Constitutional Assembly from Senegal.

1946   Elected Deputy from Senegal to National Assembly on Socialist ticket. Marriage to Ginette Eboué.

1948   Publishes *Hosties noires* and *Anthologie de la nouvelle poésie nègre et malgache* with a preface by Sartre entitled *Orphée noir*. Founds *Bloc Démocratique Sénégalais* in opposition to the Socialist faction led by Lamine Gueye.

1949   Publishes *Chants pour Naëtt*.

1950–1951   French delegate to Fifth United Nations General Assembly.

1951   Reelected to French National Assembly but as a member of the B.D.S. with Mamadou Dia as his second.

1955   Named Secretary of State for Scientific Research in the cabinet of Edgar Faure.

1956   Publishes *Ethiopiques*. Elected mayor of Thiès.

1957   Marriage to Colette Hubert.

1958   Serves in Constitutional Assembly called by Charles de Gaulle.

1960   Elected president of Senegal.

1961   Publishes *Nocturnes*. Thwarts attempted overthrow of the government by Prime Minister Mamadou Dia.

1963   Gains approval for a new constitution and is reelected president.

1964   Appearance of collected essays, *Liberté I: Négritude et humanisme*.

1966   Promotes First Festival of Black Arts, held in Dakar.

1968   Reelected to the presidency after having suppressed or absorbed the opposition parties. A year of student and trade union unrest similar to the instability in France during the same period.

1969   Publishes *Elégie des Alizés*.

1971   Publication of *Liberté II: Nation et voie africaine du socialisme*.

1973   Publishes *Lettres d'hivernage*. Again elected unopposed to the presidency.

1977   Brings out *Liberté III: Négritude et civilisation de l'Universel*.

1978   Appearance of *Elégies majeures*. Returned to the presidency in an election which includes three competing political parties.

1981   Retires from presidency in January. Succeeded by Abdou Diouf.

1984   Invested as first black member of the French Academy.

Chapter One
Conflict and Synthesis: The Writer's Personal Drama

The African Childhood

Léopold Sédar Senghor was born in 1906 in Joal, a village situated about 75 miles south of Dakar on the Atlantic coast of Senegal.[1] Founded by the Portuguese, Joal dates from the sixteenth century and the age of adventure and exploration which opened up Africa to Europe. The poet's family name, a modification of the Portuguese "senhor," suggests that one of his ancestors might have been Portuguese or in the service of one of these early European visitors.[2] At the time of Senghor's birth, Senegal was no longer under the dominion of Portugal but of France. The village of Joal had become the site of a French Catholic mission and a center for the groundnut trade which was controlled largely by Bordeaux commercial houses. Basile Diogoye Senghor, the writer's father, seems to have adapted favorably to the new European order. A large landholder, he had become relatively prosperous through the production of groundnuts for the European market and the retailing of European goods locally. Something of the son's later success must undoubtedly stem from the father's keen ability to sense the tenor of the times. For example, in spite of the predominance of Islam in Senegal and the prevailing strength of traditional religions in the region, Basile Senghor had the foresight to arrange for his son to be christened into the Catholic faith, a step which paved the way for the boy to begin a European education in mission schools. The Western name which he gave the child, "Léopold," anticipated the needs of a young man who would later pursue his studies in France.

The environment into which Léopold Senghor was born had already been molded to a certain extent by its contact with the West, but for the poet, it was not the culture in transition that he most associated with his childhood but that of traditional Africa. While the elder Senghor maintained a residence in Joal which was useful

1

in his commercial dealings, the family's real home was in Djilor, a
smaller village in the interior on the banks of the Sine River. There,
comparatively untouched by the incursions of the French, the poet
spent the first years of his life before being sent at the age of seven
to the missionaries for schooling. The experience of these few important years later becomes the source of the African identity elaborated in his writings and memories of this period constitute the
basis for his subsequent identification with the people of the bush
and their traditions. In this light it is interesting that while church
records show the baptism of one Léopold Senghor, civil records note
only the birth of Sédar Senghor. The name "Sédar" means "he who
need never be ashamed before anyone" in the language of his father's
people, the Serer, the second largest ethnic group in Senegal.[3] It
was as "Sédar" not "Léopold" that the son of Basile Senghor seems
to have been known as a child.[4]

Although possibly distorted by the passing of time and by the
veneer which poetry must necessarily spread over reality, the description of childhood given in Senghor's works provides the best
clue to the pattern of his life in Djilor. His account takes the reader
into an exotic and faintly mysterious world which gains some familiarity in the writer's references to family ties and to the carefree,
wonder-filled days which universally characterize childhood. In "A
l'appel de la race de Saba" (At the call of the race of Sheba), the
poet evokes the activities of those pleasant evenings spent in the
courtyard of his father's home with his brothers and sisters.[5] As an
aside, it is worth noting that the family would have been extremely
large by Western standards inasmuch as Basile Senghor, as was
customary, practiced polygamy and by official records fathered
twenty-four children. The writer relates how in the course of these
gatherings he would listen to folktales like the story of Koumba
the Orphan as recounted by his nurse, Ngâ, and he describes the
playing and singing of the griots, the traditional African musicians.
The primarily autobiographical poem *Que m'accompagnent kôras et
balafong* (*Let Kôras and Balafong Accompany Me*) provides further
vignettes from the poet's memory.[6] One especially interesting episode, which seems to have served to impress upon the child a sense
of his people's history and dignity, was the occasion when Basile
Senghor received at Djilor the royal visit of Koumba Ndofène Dyouf,
the king of the region, and his entourage. From this poem it is
evident that the teachings of traditional religion remained very

strong. The child seems to have been well aware of the animist beliefs of his ancestors and had visited holy places such as Mbissel, the site of the tombs of the first kings of the Malinké dynasty from which Senghor claimed descent, and the Pangol of Simal, a sacred wood which attracted pilgrims in quest of miracles. As an adult, Senghor would later claim to have been one hundred percent animist in his youth.[7] Elsewhere in the poem, he describes his frequent forays into the area around Djilor through which he became familiar with nature and the African landscape which would later become the foundation for his poetic vocabulary. At the end of the work, he remembers with marked tenderness evenings spent in his mother's village with her brother Waly who taught him African names for the constellations and the stories behind them.

These visits to his mother's family may have led indirectly to the rather early termination of this idyllic period. Through his mother, Nyilane Bakhoum, Senghor was linked to yet another ethnic group, the Peul, also known as the Fulani. As is typical of a matrilineal society, the Serer consider the child as part of the mother's family and local people, Senghor tells us, would even refer to him as "Sédar Nyilane," using his mother's name in place of his father's.[8] The child enjoyed his trips to her village, Djilas, which retained much firmer ties with African tradition than did Djilor and where he enhanced his knowledge of traditional lore under the guidance of his uncle who, by custom, would have had a special relationship with the son of a sister. Through resentment, perhaps, of his son's affection for Djilas or because he surmised that the lessons of Tokô' Waly would not serve future needs, Basile Senghor decided, against the mother's protests, to send his son at the age of seven to the mission school in Joal. There Senghor studied the catechism and learned his first words of French. In the evenings after school he and his friends could run off to watch the local wrestling matches or listen to the poetess, Marône N'Diaye, whose songs he would later translate into French.[9]

Drenched in the exotic, the supernatural, and the bliss of childhood, this period in Senghor's life provided a wealth of poetic material to which he returned again and again. But with the school years, the era in which he would be directly exposed to the life and culture of his people was coming to a close, and he would henceforth find himself increasingly influenced by Western ways. There is, on the writer's part, a sense of recrimination directed against those forces that cut so short his sojourn in what he repeatedly termed the kingdom of childhood and that destroyed its original harmony and tranquillity. Chief among the culprits was the education process itself which, as it opened up new horizons for a selected few, also resulted in the disruption of the normal pattern of socialization with the child who received an education being separated from his peers not only in the fact of his training but often by the necessity of having to leave home to attend school. This was the case for Senghor. After having begun his studies in Joal, he was sent in 1914 to N'Gazobil a few miles away to be educated at a school run by the Fathers of the Holy Spirit. The students lived at the mission and participated in household chores, farming, and herding. Along with the usual academic subjects, lessons included Wolof, the major African language of Senegal, and French. French literature was introduced and Senghor and his classmates sometimes played at being the heroes they read about in Victor Hugo's works. During vacations, the future statesman was able to spend time with a brother in neighboring Gambia and thus add English to the list of languages he was learning. He stayed at N'Gazobil until 1922 when his studies took him even farther from home to the capital city of Dakar where he became a seminary student at the Collège Libermann.

At this point perhaps a few words are in order concerning one of the more controversial aspects of the education which African students were receiving at the time, for the education system reflected an important but questionable principle of French colonial policy: assimilation.[10] Inherent in this notion was the idea that Africa had no valid culture of its own. In order to claim a place in the modern world, the African would have to acquire—be assimilated into—Western civilization. The successful product of this process was called an *"évolué,"* one who has evolved, and the expression denotes the inferior status of those not so assimilated. In line with this policy the education offered to young Africans sought to establish the preeminence of Western values and, conversely, to discourage and belittle the practice of African customs. The curriculum took little notice of the different needs or environment of the colonial student and in most respects, resembled what was being studied in France. Consequently, the African student who adapted successfully to the French education system found himself very much alienated from his own society. This alienation was compounded in Senghor's case and for many others, as previously indicated, by the necessity of having to live away from their families in the few towns which boasted European schools. Finally, in order to continue up the academic ladder the university-bound were obliged to leave Africa altogether for the higher institutions available only in Europe. The stance of the Negritude poets would develop in reaction to the demeaning cultural assumptions upon which assimilation was based and even as a student at the Collège Libermann, Senghor was already rebelling against the concept. One of his memories of this period depicts a head-on collision between himself and the assimilationist attitude of the French system. Upon hearing one of the teaching fathers speak pejoratively of the Africans as "savages," the future architect of Negritude became incensed and retorted that the Africans, too, had their civilization, an affirmation which, although he did not realize it at the time, would become the basis for his life's work.

Only a few days after this incident, Senghor, who had originally entered the Collège Libermann in order to study for the priesthood, was called in and informed by the director that the church was not his calling.[11] For the poet whose writing would later reveal a strong religious sensitivity, this announcement proved a source of grave disappointment. It also required him to modify his plans for the future and from this point on, he would be pursuing a career as a teacher. With this new direction in mind he became a student at the Secondary School in Dakar (today the Lycée Van Vollenhoven) where he did excellent work and, in competition with his European classmates, placed first in French, Latin, Greek, and mathematics. While African students interested in such practical fields as veterinary medicine would occasionally receive scholarships to study in Europe, there was some reluctance on the part of the authorities to make awards to students in liberal arts subjects. Senghor had been so outstanding in Greek that his professor felt compelled to plead his student's case with the governor-general of French West Africa who was able to provide a partial grant to permit Senghor to go on to Paris. In 1928 he sailed for France. As fate would have it, this ultimate separation from his people would eventually prove the catalyst for effecting a reaffirmation of his African heritage.

Paris

The decade spent in Paris before the outbreak of World War II was critical to Senghor's intellectual development. As a student in some of France's finest institutions he would receive an enviable education in the humanities that would provide him with the credentials for beginning a teaching career. Ironically he would also find in Paris, the very capital of French civilization, the seeds of a reaction against French colonial domination. Students came there from all over the empire and inevitably, their encounters led to the organized expression of dissatisfaction with the current political status.

Shortly after his arrival Senghor was advised to enter the Lycée Louis-le-Grand where he spent three years preparing for entrance exams at the Ecole Normale Supérieure. During his stay at the lycée he was the only African among the so-called "exotic" students, a term which included Pham Duy Khiem from Indochina and Louis Achille and Auguste Boucolon, both from the West Indies. Once when he was given the occasion to describe this phase of his education, Senghor applauded the school for the absence of racial prejudice among the instructors, for the teaching of a clear, objective, and efficient method of analysis, and for the constant concern for the human implications, the "sense of Man," within the individual disciplines. He further recognized the impact of new friendships among fellow students on his personal growth, especially in his learning about contemporary France. Singled out for special gratitude in this respect was Georges Pompidou whom he credited with having converted him to Socialism and with having introduced him to such writers as Barrès, Proust, Gide, Baudelaire, and Rimbaud. The future president of France also gave him a taste for the theaters and museums of Paris.[12]

In 1930 Senghor was unsuccessful in the competition for entrance into the Ecole Normale Supérieure. He opted to continue his studies at the Sorbonne where in 1931 he received his *Licence ès Lettres*. In 1932, after the completion of a study on "Exoticism in the Works of Baudelaire," he was awarded the *Diplôme d'Etudes Supérieures*. He next determined to try for the *agrégation,* a competition necessary for teachers at the lycée but one which was closed to noncitizens. In Senegal only the inhabitants of the four Communes—Saint-Louis, Dakar, Rufisque, and Gorée—automatically received French citizenship at birth and were represented at that time in the French National Assembly. The rest of the country was normally excluded from this privilege. Senghor consequently undertook to become nationalized and after a first attempt at the *agrégation* in 1933, he spent a year in Verdun and in Paris fulfilling the military obligation incurred upon becoming a citizen of France. As a soldier his duties were such that he was able to spend a great deal of time at the Sorbonne preparing his exams so that in 1935 he became the first African student to be accepted at the *agrégation*. This noteworthy achievement would merit a reception with full military honors upon his short visit to Senegal in 1937. He began his teaching career at the Lycée Descartes in 1936 in Tours where he also gave lessons to workers at the Maison de la Culture, an indication of his increasingly stronger adherence to socialism. In 1938 he was named to the Lycée Marcelin-Berthelot at Saint-Maur-des-Fossés, not far from Paris.

While Senghor's education provided him with a superb literary background, the experience of living in France also produced a certain degree of culture shock. His progress through the academic maze was also marked by growing disillusionment with France, the beginning of which coincides with his failure in 1930 to be accepted into the Ecole Normale. The academic disappointment is insufficient to explain the intensity of his feelings, the actual source being somewhat more complex. Under the policy of assimilation, he had been led to believe that acquiring the outward manifestations of Western civilization was all that would be required in order to achieve equality. As a black man in Paris he was discovering that this simply was not so. One of Senghor's critics alludes to a severe "moral crisis" originating around 1931.[13] There is also a reference to "a romantic disappointment, perhaps due to the blackness of his skin."[14] During his years at the lycée, Senghor, who had once considered the priesthood his vocation, had even broken temporarily with the church. While retaining the foundations of his faith, he was unable to justify the actions of Christians in the light of Christian principles.[15] Having gradually been alienated from African society by virtue of his Western education, he was now faced with the cruel reality that neither did he belong to Europe.

He was not alone in these feelings of rootlessness for among the other university students who had come to Paris from throughout France's colonies, many shared his state of mind. Their encounters in the capital led to organized expressions of dissatisfaction with the political status quo and as a reaction against assimilation, they began to seek out and proclaim the values and traditions of their particular peoples. Senghor's generation was not the first to tackle these issues. Their movement had ample preparation in the appearance of numerous European and American groups concerned with the welfare of blacks, in the publication of journals on subjects of interest to blacks and in the growing fascination on the continent with black culture in general. In France, the period following World War I had been particularly crucial to the development of black awareness. In 1919, Paris hosted the first Pan-African Congress whose organizers included W. E. B. DuBois, the American author who early defined the black personality in *The Souls of Black Folk* (1903); Blaise Diagne, Senegal's black representative to the National Assembly; and Gratien Candace, the black deputy from Guadeloupe. In the early twenties Marcus Garvey popularized the "Back to Africa" slogan which helped to recall the ties between black Americans and Africa by proposing their return to the continent. In 1924, Kodjo Tovalou Houénou from Dahomey, who was associated with Garvey, created in Paris the *Ligue universelle de Défense de la Race nègre*. The organization later became known as the *Comité de Défense de la Race nègre,* the first president of which was a cousin of Senghor's, Lamine Senghor, a former *tirailleur.* Lamine Senghor also participated in the founding of the *Ligue contre l'Impérialisme et l'Oppression coloniale* (1927) in Brussels and was subsequently arrested and imprisoned. He died shortly after his release and was replaced as president of the *Comité* by the Malian Tiémoko Garan Kouyaté. A scholarship student at the Ecole Normale in Aix-en-Provence, Kouyaté also founded the review *Africa* and a number of other organizations including the *Comité universel de l'Institut nègre de Paris* in 1930 with Léo Sajous from Haiti. In addition to the obvious kinship with Lamine Senghor, there were ties between other figures on the preceding list and Léopold Senghor, the relationships with Blaise Diagne, Gratien Candace, and Léo Sajous being easily demonstrated.[16]

Shortly after Senghor's arrival in Paris, two extremely influential periodicals appeared which further attempted to articulate the various components of the racial issue. The first such publication was the *Revue du Monde Noir,* directed by Dr. Sajous and by Paulette Nardal from Martinique, a niece of Louis Achille and the organizer of a literary salon which drew numerous prominent blacks including Senghor. The articles in the review were by Africans, American blacks, and West Indians, many of whom had attained considerable recognition in their various fields: Claude MacKay and Langston Hughes, the black American writers; Jean Price-Mars, the Haitian ethnologist; Félix Eboué, the future governor-general of French Equatorial Africa; René Maran, the West Indian author of the novel about Africa, *Batouala,* which won the Prix Goncourt in 1922. The review existed to provide a forum for writing by blacks and on subjects related to blacks. In its statement of purpose it anticipated Senghor's insistence that along with other races, the black had a valuable contribution to make to the future of mankind as a whole. While the ideas expressed by the publication undoubtedly influenced the development of the Negritude poets, it soon ran into financial difficulties and political resistance. Coming out first in November 1931, the *Revue du Monde Noir* published only six issues. In 1932, a group of West Indian students headed by Etienne Léro published the single issue of a more militant review, *Légitime Défense.* It attacked black writers for their unimaginative imitation of white literary conventions and the entire black bourgeoisie for its submission to cultural oppression. In literature, it championed the relatively new ideas and techniques of Surrealism, itself an iconoclastic intellectual force; politically, the document revealed the communist sympathies of its authors. This manifesto helped pave the way for the rejection of the assumptions behind assimilation and for the rehabilitation of black values.

This demonstration of racial consciousness on the part of the black community in Paris was accompanied by the rising general public awareness of Africa and of black culture. In the twenties, the Black Renaissance in the United States had brought about the immense popularity of black music, entertainment, and literature, and the influence of the phenomenon was subsequently being felt in Paris. Certainly jazz, the blues, and the dances they inspired had received an exuberant welcome in France and the black American singer Josephine Baker enjoyed considerable success. Black American writers were received in the salons of Paulette Nardal and René Maran and the future poets of Negritude avidly read Claude MacKay's novel *Banjo,* which prefigured many of their own key themes. As early as 1937 we find Senghor quoting MacKay whom he later labels "the veritable inventor of Negritude."[17] There were also indications of a burgeoning interest in Africa among French art and literary figures. Picasso had discovered the Baoulé masks as early as 1906 and the inspiration of African art is sometimes evident in Cubist painting. The Surrealists, more visually influenced by Indian and Oceanic art forms, brought home the point that the thought of "primitive" cultures provided a new perspective for approaching the traditional Western concept of reality. Léro, in *Légitime Défense,* paid homage to Surrealism as a model for black writers, and later the preface to Aimé Césaire's 1947 edition of *Cahier d'un retour au pays natal* was written by André Breton, the dean of the French Surrealists. In 1927, André Gide's publication of the *Voyage au Congo* drew public attention to Africa and the shortcomings of colonialism. Further awareness of Africa was stimulated by the Colonial Exposition in 1931.[18]

It is little wonder that in this atmosphere Senghor and his fellow students became increasingly absorbed by issues related to racial identity. By 1931, Senghor had made the acquaintance of Aimé Césaire, a student from Martinique, and the two formed a close friendship. The West Indian was eager to learn about his African heritage and found Senghor, in spite of his acclimitization to France, an intriguing source of information. Together they rediscovered Africa in the studies of European ethnologists such as Maurice Delafosse and Léo Frobénius. Their research in this area bore considerable fruit. Césaire would open an impressive literary career with a work which affirmed his African origins, *Cahier d'un retour au pays natal* (1939), and Senghor, after years of alienation, would begin to assert his newly reclaimed African identity in the poems which would see publication after the war as *Chants d'ombre* (1945). This common effort on the part of Senghor, Césaire, and other black Francophone writers to define themselves in terms of their race soon became identified as the Negritude movement. In the period preceding the war, Senghor contributed to the movement in a variety of ways and helped to shape its philosophy as well as his own. Between 1934 and 1936, he collaborated in the preparation of the review *L'Etudiant noir,* which stressed the cultural implications of the racial question; there Césaire first used, in print, the term "Negritude" to formalize a tendency which had already begun to be recognized in the abstract.[19]

In 1933, Senghor organized the Association of West African Students, a group which held monthly meetings on topics related to the clash between the traditional and the modern in France's colonies. Relatively moderate in tone, it sought to rehabilitate African culture without rejecting the positive values which Europe had to offer. Interestingly, these parallel themes would become central to Senghor's own writing. On a visit to Senegal in 1937, he dealt at length with one of those themes in an address to the Dakar Chamber of Commerce on the subject of "Le problème culturel en A. O. F." Although he spoke eloquently at the time of the need for African education to respond to contemporary problems, this speech should not be taken as a defense of assimilation but, as he would express it later, an insistence that the Africans assimilate judiciously what might be useful in Western civilization instead of being assimilated by it: "assimiler, non être assimilés." Whereas this talk stressed what Europe had to offer to a new Africa, Senghor elsewhere elaborated on what the African had to contribute in return in an essay entitled "Ce que l'homme noir apporte," published in *L'Homme de couleur* by Librairie Plon in 1939. These two papers serve as complementary examples of Senghor's belief in the desirability of enriching the world through "métissage" or a sort of cultural crossbreeding. After 1936, Senghor's career began to reflect more closely his desire to learn and write about Africa. In his work for the doctorate *(doctorat d'Etat)* he had chosen to focus his research on African languages and on Serer oral poetry. To facilitate his work he took classes in ethnology at the Institut d'Ethnologie in Paris and in linguistics at the Ecole Pratique des Hautes Etudes. While Senghor was on the one hand continuing to pursue the stipulated path for a model *évolué,* he was also becoming a part of the Third World protest against the assumptions of France's assimilationist policy.

World War II and Its Political Aftermath

Up to this point in his life Senghor's primary ambition was to teach and his involvement in the Negritude movement was essentially a cultural one. The changes brought about by World War II would ignite the writer's political awareness and turn him in the direction that would lead to his becoming one of Africa's foremost statesmen.

Senghor was mobilized in September of 1939 and was taken prisoner while defending the bridge at La Charité-sur-Loire on 20 June 1940, just two days after the fall of France. He tells a dramatic story of his capture in which he and his black comrades only narrowly escaped being shot by the Germans.[20] He then passed the period of internment in seven different camps. In Poitiers, at Frontstalag 230, a guard noticed him reading a book in Greek, and he was subsequently assigned administrative duties. After clandestinely listening to a radio broadcast of de Gaulle's plea for resistance, he became involved with organizing the escape of French prisoners, an act which, because of his position of responsibility, led to his being transferred for a few months to the harsher conditions of a punishment camp. In 1942, a year when many French prisoners were returned to their homes, Senghor was also released, ostensibly for reasons of health, although the tropical disease conveniently diagnosed by the cooperative French prison doctors appears to have been merely a ruse invented to deceive his captors.[21] His internment would provide the inspiration for a number of poems in the collection entitled *Hosties noires* (1948), a memorial to black soldiers who served in the war. After resuming his teaching post at the Lycée Marcelin-Berthelot he continued his Resistance support as a member of the *Front national universitaire*. In recognition of his wartime efforts he would later receive the Franco-Alliée medal.

In 1944 at the close of the war, Senghor was appointed to the chair in African linguistics at the Ecole Nationale de la France d'Outre-Mer and the following year he obtained a scholarship to return to Senegal for the purpose of gathering information for his doctoral thesis. But the post-war changes in France's relationship with her empire were already beginning to be felt and Senghor soon found himself caught up in this new tide. First came the request from de Gaulle that he represent the colonies at the meetings of the Monnerville Commission, which was to decide on the role of the overseas possessions at the Constitutional Assembly. Senghor spoke up articulately against any return to the previous state of affairs. On arriving in Senegal to begin his research for the thesis, he was approached to serve as a candidate for the Constitutional Assembly. Reluctantly, for he did not want to abandon a successful academic career, he agreed to run as a representative from the bush—rather than the Communes—with Lamine Gueye under the Socialist (S. F. I. O.) label. Victorious, he went back to Paris to help draft a new constitution giving a greater voice to Africa. Not only would he be instrumental in determining the content of the document, but as a former teacher of French, he was also asked to verify the correctness of its language. In 1946, under the new constitution, he was elected along with Lamine Gueye to represent Senegal in the new French National Assembly.

While Senghor's election required him to leave teaching it did not curtail his cultural activities which supported, in a different register, his political stance as he sought greater equality and freedom for the colonies on the eve of independence. His first collection of poetry, *Chants d'ombre* (1945), depicted his personal experience of racial prejudice and cultural alienation in terms that pointed clearly to the failure of the French policy of assimilation. The second collection, *Hosties noires* (1948), reminded France in a powerful and poignant way of the debt owed to Africa for its contributions to the war effort. In constant opposition to the idea that the African was "tabula rasa" and to those who defended imperialism with the argument of the white man's burden, Senghor continued in various articles to stress the existence of a black civilization and to define it. Along with Alioune Diop and others who sought a forum for the presentation of studies on black culture, Senghor participated in 1946 in the founding of the journal *Présence Africaine,* the first issue of which came out simultaneously in Paris and Dakar in 1947 and which continues to be an important publication in its field. In 1948 he published his *Anthologie de la nouvelle poésie nègre et malgache de langue française* and achieved a major coup in persuading Jean-Paul Sartre to write a preface. Entitled *Orphée noir,* Sartre's essay conferred a certain validity on the whole Negritude movement by describing it in existential terms and by placing the colonial struggle in a Marxist perspective with France in the role of the oppressor.

In 1946, at the age of forty, Senghor married for the first time. In his 1978 interview with Mohamed Aziza, he explained that he had intentionally delayed marriage because he had not yet found the right bride. He believed that it was his "duty" to marry "preferably a black woman from Africa, an Arabo-Berber, or, this being impossible, a woman from the Antilles."[22] Marriage to Ginette Eboué, the daughter of Félix Eboué and Eugénie Tell, permitted him to conform at least nominally to this ideal. Although Ginette herself was born in Paris and educated in French schools, her parents were both from black Guyanese families. Her father, whose successful career as a colonial administrator had culminated in his appointment as governor-general for French Equatorial Africa, won de Gaulle's gratitude and admiration by throwing his support behind the Free French. Her mother was named representative from Guadeloupe to the French National Assembly after the war. Senghor had first heard of Ginette from her half-brothers, Henry and Robert, who were his fellow prisoners at Frontstalag 230, but he met her only after the war when she was serving in a secretarial capacity in the Ministery for the Colonies. Their wedding was a political affair with several members of the government in attendance. In 1949 Senghor brought out a third collection of poetry, *Chants pour Naëtt,* a cycle of love poems inspired by his wife. The couple would have two sons, Francis and Guy, before the marriage ended in divorce in 1955.

Probably the most significant political move Senghor made during this period was to resign from the French Socialist Party, the *Section Française de l'Internationale Ouvrière* (S. F. I. O.). He had originally begun his foray into politics as a Socialist and an early poem, *A l'appel de la race de Saba,* shows something of his affinity for the socialist ideas of internationalism and brotherhood. From his election in 1946 until 1948 he represented Senegal as a member of the S. F. I. O. Largely because of the socialists' assimilationist tendencies, he transferred his loyalties to the *Mouvement Républicain Populaire,* France's Christian Democratic party of that era. In Senegal he organized a new opposition party, the *Bloc Démocratique Sénégalais* (B. D. S.), to compete against the S. F. I. O., the incumbent party there. In the next elections he ran against Lamine Gueye, his former ally, in a campaign which took on strongly symbolic overtones. Lamine Gueye, born in one of the Communes and educated in France, had been a French citizen from birth and his constituency was composed of the educated black and mixed-blood elite and the white French residents of the urban centers. Previously these had been the only inhabitants of Senegal to have a legal voice in the government but the constitution of 1946 had extended citizenship to other parts of the colony and it was among this newly enfranchised electorate that Senghor sought his support. In contrast to his opponent Senghor travelled extensively in the rural areas where, dressed in comfortable khaki, he sat down and talked with village leaders about local problems. Ironically, Senegal's leading intellectual had formed his political base not from the assimilated urban *évolués* but from the citizens of the bush. In 1951 the two groups confronted each other at the polls with the B. D. S. defeating the Socialists. The campaign helped to make Senghor something of a legend and now he could truly claim to be the voice of the people. Other political successes followed. In 1955 in the government of Edgar Faure, Senghor served as Secretary of State for Scientific Research. In 1956 he was elected mayor of the Senegalese railroad town of Thiès. He also served in the Constituent Assembly in 1958, which paved the way under Charles de Gaulle for independence in Africa. The drama

of political battles and the poet's awareness of his own transition to
the role of political leader and statesman were recorded in a new
collection of poems, *Ethiopiques,* appearing in 1956. Also included
in the volume was a major work entitled *Epîtres à la Princesse,* the
story of the correspondence between an African envoy and a European
princess. Partially an allegory of Senghor's "métissage" concept, it
was also inspired by his courtship of Colette Hubert, a Frenchwoman
whom he married in 1957. Her family roots were in Normandy
where she and the writer would spend many future vacations. The
couple had one son, Philippe Maguilen.

Independence and the Presidency

The notion of independence for the territories of French West
Africa did not become an issue until the late 1950s, a period which
also saw the end of the Fourth Republic and the return to power
of Charles de Gaulle. As a member of the French National Assembly,
Senghor had an active role to play in the proceedings. Rejecting
the more radical viewpoint of the R. D. A. *(Rassemblement Démocratique Africain),* an inter-African party led by Houphouët-Boigny
of the Ivory Coast, the representative from Senegal headed up a
group of independents and championed a moderate position which,
while seeking greater autonomy for the colonies, avoided an outright
break with France. He also attempted to stave off what he termed
the "balkanization" of Africa, his preference being for a continued
association of the francophone African colonies with each other,
possibly a federation, which would maintain the advantages of the
Federation of French West Africa in which Senegal profited from a
particularly favorable status. Aside from protecting the interests of
his constituency, this aspect of Senghor's stand grew naturally from
a long-held belief in the importance of African unity, a natural
outgrowth of the concept of Negritude. In spite of Senghor's efforts
many of the developments leading to independence proved disap-
pointing to him personally. De Gaulle's new constitution rejected
a union in which the colonies would be truly self-governing. The
referendum of 1958, which permitted the Africans to vote on whether
or not they would remain in the French Community, provoked
Guinea's premature withdrawal from French hegemony, setting in
motion the break-up of French West Africa which would also be
weakened by administrative changes under the constitution of the

Fifth Republic. Never abandoning the theory that the colonies would be economically and politically ineffectual if allowed to come to independence without some system of mutual support, Senghor still sought to link Senegal to its neighboring states. By 1959, when independence became an inevitability, only the French Soudan was willing to remain in such a partnership and the Mali Federation was formed. Even this arrangement was short-lived and terminated in 1960. At that time Senegal became an independent republic with Senghor elected as its first president, an office to which he was to be re-elected four times before retiring in January 1981 at the age of 74. In spite of the fact that the battle for independence had been won, conditions were not precisely as he had wanted them to be and one of the characteristics of Senegal's future foreign policy would consist of a continuous effort toward harmony and cooperation with the former French colonies in Africa in order to combat the disadvantages perceived in the fragmentation of the old Federation.[23]

Despite the rigors of political life, President Senghor was able to produce several additional volumes of poetry. The struggle for independence and the birth pangs of a new nation are recorded in the elegies published under the title of *Nocturnes* (1961). The single poem, *Elégie des Alizés* (1969), depicting the labors of the writer on behalf of his people, appeared first in an edition illustrated by the Russian artist, Marc Chagall. Also published with Chagall lithographs was *Lettres d'hivernage* (1973), a cycle of love poems which focused primarily on the poet's wife but which also provided a privileged glimpse of his own inner life and personal concerns as head of state. Less intimate in inspiration are the works collected under the title *Elégies majeures* (1979), many of which celebrate people or events of some political significance. There is less tension in most of these later works than in the poems which depicted the narrator's youthful quest for identity. They represent the situation of a man who has reached maturity with a strong sense of himself and his mission. The archetypal inspiration is no longer that of the romantic quest but rather that of the prince who has returned home to his kingdom with his consort to rule there with greater insight and new wisdom. The dominant emotions of alienation and struggle in the first poems gradually give way to other emotions such as those of the solitary leader who keenly feels the weight of his responsibilities. Considering the demands placed upon Senghor in his new role, it is remarkable that he was able to continue writing poetry at all but these few volumes do little to convey the extent of the president's activities and preoccupations during his term in office. In this respect the poems cease to be adequate as a biography of the poet and for most of the details of this part of his life it is necessary to rely on the public record and the efforts of historians.

As for making any judgment about Senghor's presidency, it is really too soon to come to any valid conclusions in as much as only the future will demonstrate to what extent his policies have influenced the ultimate direction of his country. Certainly his period of government was not without serious difficulties. Since independence, Senegal has suffered considerable economic decline. Droughts, strikes, and political rivalries also added to the president's woes. On the plus side, the country long remained united and stable under a leader known for his ability to compromise. At first a one-party state, as were many of the newly independent African nations, it later permitted the growth of opposition parties, although the party of the president continued to remain popular and to win elections by considerable margins. While endorsing many of the tenets of socialism and instituting some changes in that direction, Senghor also preserved numerous capitalist ideas and institutions. Under his direction the country maintained very close ties with France, often in spite of criticism at home and abroad. With respect to inter-African affairs, Senegal managed to remain on relatively good terms with its neighbors in as much as Senghor persisted in his dream of African unity through the development and support of such organizations as the Organization of Senegal River States and its successor, the Organization for the Development of the Senegal River Basin; the Organization for the Development of the Gambia River Basin; OCAM (*Organisation Commune Africaine, Malgache, et Mauritienne*); and the Organization of African Unity. As further evidence of his continued concern for the propagation of African culture, Senghor also helped to create a national cultural policy to foster the study and development of African arts, his most celebrated accomplishment in this area being the sponsorship of the First World Festival of Negro Arts, an international fair for the recognition of black artists and writers held in Dakar in 1966. Finally, he has been active in encouraging the growth of a world-wide union of French-speaking countries on the premise that their common language and culture give them certain areas of common interest. When he retired from office in 1981, Senghor was respected not only as his country's chief of state but as an important voice in world affairs.[24]

Senghor's reputation in political circles resides not merely in his achievements as a political leader and statesman but also in the much broader influence of his theoretical writings. From the original concept of Negritude, he was able to develop a philosophy which served first as a motivating force in the quest for African equality and independence. In the post-independence era, he further molded his ideas in such a way as to help unify his people and provide a basis for his government's policies. His belief in the existence of an identifiable African culture led to his developing a peculiarly African interpretation of socialism which has left its mark on socialist theory across the continent. He has extended the idea of cultural cross-breeding inherent in his philosophy into an elaborate theory of history intended to rationalize a new world image necessitated by the changes wrought in the post-colonial era. His vision is one of unity and progress, but not strictly technological progress. He foresees mankind moving toward an eventual "universal civilization" to which all cultures would contribute. The president's major theoretical essays have been published in three anthologies, each emphasizing a different dimension of the original philosophy of Negritude. The first volume, *Liberté I: Négritude et humanisme* (1964), assembled some of the key essays on the theory of Negritude and included several articles dealing with literary subjects. In *Liberté II: Nation et voie africaine du socialisme* (1961), Senghor summarized his thoughts on the subject of socialism. *Liberté III: Négritude et civilisation de l'Universel* (1977) further developed his earlier thesis concerning harmony among the world's diverse cultures. Senghor's contributions, cultural and political, have received international recognition. By the time of his retirement, he had been awarded over two dozen honorary doctorates and numerous prizes for his written work. In 1984 he became the first black member of the French Academy.

The dramatic story of the Serer village child who grew up to become a prominent writer and world leader possesses a certain fairy tale quality. Although it would be difficult to dispute the fact that there is ample material in Senghor's life story for the creation of a modern myth, his own writings have probably helped to give these events their present readability. Much of what we know about the early years comes primarily from Senghor as he has depicted them in his poems and essays or in his interviews. As a poet he has obviously been aware of the mythic potential of his own story and has undoubtedly enhanced its telling with his art. As a politician he must surely have recognized the value of cultivating a positive, even heroic, self image, and in this there must have been numerous accomplices, both African and French, who would have deemed it useful to sustain that image. The question then arises as to whether Senghor's own eloquent and ample interpretations of the story of his life might have had the unfortunate effect of blinding biographers to other equally interesting and important aspects of their subject's history, a possibility which future historians might yet consider. Regardless of what such eventual insights may offer, they could scarcely deny Senghor's very real achievements on a variety of levels and the genuine fascination of his story. For those interested in Senghor principally as a poet, his own version of his biography considerately supplies most background details needed for appreciating the personal allusions in his poems and establishing the identity of his first-person narrator, and ultimately it is this romantic perception of his own life as a constant effort to reconcile the various conflicting cultural elements of his environment that constitutes the central drama of his creative works.

Chapter Two
The Philosophy of Negritude

An outstanding characteristic of Senghor's poetry is its coherent and unifying substructure, for almost every poem, either in its theme or form, illustrates some aspect of the poet's concept of Negritude. Many of the major works of Senghorian criticism, as indicated by their titles, have chosen to focus specifically on this attribute: *The Concept of Negritude in the Poetry of Léopold Sédar Senghor; Léopold Sédar Senghor et la défense et illustration de la civilisation noire; The African Image in the Work of Léopold Sédar Senghor; Léopold Sédar Senghor, l'Africain; L'Afrique dans l'univers poétique de Léopold Sédar Senghor;* and even *Léopold Sédar Senghor: Négritude ou servitude?*[1] Each study emphasizes some dimension of the writer's style or imagery which stems from his African origins. Beyond mere exoticism this evocation of Africa becomes, in Senghor's hands, a poetic expression of a tightly knit philosophy expounded elsewhere in his speeches and essays. As the theory of Negritude undergoes various metamorphoses in its different political and cultural roles, these changes are reflected in the poems. On one level, the poetry can be perceived as just the barest tip of a more solidly constructed conceptual iceberg.

Consecrating Negritude as a literary movement on sound philosophical grounds, Sartre, in 1948, gave Senghor the celebrated essay "Black Orpheus" with which to preface his *Anthologie de la nouvelle poésie nègre et malgache de langue française.* At that time Sartre made the astute observation that in defining Negritude, it was necessary to recognize its two different manifestations: a subjective Negritude arising from the historical reality of a situation experienced because of race and an objective Negritude having to do with the innate characteristics, or essence, of the African personality.[2] Other critics have maintained this division and even more than three decades later it continues to be appropriate. Although the two categories occasionally overlap and much of what is relevant to one affects the other, each has different implications for the poetry and poses different problems. Each attracts a different type of critical response.

Negritude as Situation

In most regards this aspect of Negritude meets with the least controversy among critics. Looking at the concrete facts of history— slavery, colonialism, discrimination—few would deny that the black race shares a collective experience of suffering or that the presence of themes of anguish and protest in the creative works of black writers and artists might well constitute a racial inheritance of sorts. Since the inception of Negritude the condition of blacks, especially in Africa, has undergone considerable evolution, changes which affect the interpretation of Negritude in its historical context and give rise to wide differences of opinion regarding its definition and even its validity. Although Sartre, in his 1948 essay, sanctioned the protest elements and the implied resistance to colonialism that he perceived in the black poetry of that era, no one could have predicted the train of events which were to follow. Over time, Negritude, as articulated by Senghor, was refitted to accommodate these successive events to the point that it becomes necessary to speak of it not as a response to a single situation but as a variety of responses to different situations.

In his study of Negritude as a political phenomenon, Markovitz divides the movement into three different stages:

> The evolution of Negritude progresses through three general historical periods. The first period begins with the gathering of young black intellectuals in Paris in the thirties and continues until the Second World War. During this time Senghor belonged to a group of students, young intellectuals and politicians who were still seeking their *personal identities*. The second period runs from the war until Senegal's independence in 1960. Senghor became a recognized African leader sitting as a representative from Senegal in metropolitan institutions. At this time African leaders dealt with the central problems of establishing *national identities* and defining the relationship between the overseas territories and France. The third period follows independence. Negritude grew into an ideology for unity, economic development and cultural growth.[3]

This analysis is framed chiefly in terms of the African involvement and stresses Senghor's participation in particular; for other regions and other writers—Césaire, for example—the sequence would vary somewhat. Markovitz is only concerned with chronological divisions, but in his subsequent discussion of the initial stage he appears to recognize two separate components: that which relates to the personal experience of the individual and the public—and often militant—protest in which the private reactions are incarnated. Although both are characteristic of the same time period, for our purposes each deserves independent treatment.

In drawing up the history of the Negritude movement, the role of black congresses and Pan-African efforts previously outlined should not be discounted, but with reference to the stages of the movement as they involved Senghor's personal participation it is sufficient to begin with the period of his student days in Paris. Most critics recognize that the nascent phase of Negritude was not its public manifestations but the individual experiences of the black writers themselves. The identity crisis suffered by Senghor at this period of his life was triggered by the recognition that in spite of his education, his race and color precluded any possibility of assimilation. The isolation, alienation, and confusion which resulted led ultimately to the writer's reaffirmation of those facets of his heritage and identity which had previously been derided or denied by his European teachers. Sartre recognized the importance of this aspect of Negritude when he chose the title for his essay, "Black Orpheus." He regarded this conscious attempt at self-discovery as an orphic descent into the inner being.[4] L. V. Thomas calls this highly individual stage of the movement "Narcissistic Negritude" in contrast with a later, more other-centered demeanor accompanied by a strong commitment first to cultural and eventually to political causes.[5] The term, perhaps pejoratively so, stresses the highly personal and emotional nature typical of the first stirrings of self-awareness.

This Orphic or Narcissistic Negritude soon demanded a public expression and in Senghor's case, merged easily with the next phase of Negritude which almost all critics characterize as aggressive or militant. Thomas uses the term "Negritude de combat" at this point;[6] Markovitz calls it "pre-establishment Negritude" to distinguish it from its more sedate successors.[7] The feelings and needs that were unleashed during the Orphic stage—alienation, protest, and the rehabilitation of Africa and its traditions—gave rise to the first poetry. Senghor's *Chants d'ombre* (1945) chronicles his own experiences of self-doubt and self-discovery. In *Hosties noires* (1948), his subject is the sacrifice of African soldiers who had fought for France in World War II, and this collection contains some of the poet's strongest attacks on colonialism and French policy. Some critics, Marcien Towa among them, tend to prefer these early works and find in them a virility and indignation which flags somewhat in the more recent collections. In this respect, Towa singles out "A l'appel de la race de Saba," written in 1936, on account of its lusty call to action and obvious Marxist inspiration.[8] For others, this more hostile face of Negritude is less appealing than its constructive and compromising nature in later works.[9] Certainly this was the stage of Senghor's career that is most strongly influenced by Marxism. It was at this stage that Negritude, at its most revolutionary, risked being categorized—with justice—as a form of racism, or as Sartre called it, an "anti-racist racism."[10] This intensity, Senghor tells us, was tempered by the lessons learned from the intemperance of Nazism.

The phenomenon of rediscovering one's African past occurred almost exclusively among the Francophone African students and it has been theorized that the reaction came in part as a response to certain defects in French colonial policy such as the failure of the French to educate African students in their local languages or the erroneous assumptions of assimilation, an objective not adopted by the British. For whatever reasons, two of Negritude's most frequently cited African critics were born in former British colonies: the Nigerian, Wole Soyinka, who declared memorably that a tiger does not have to proclaim his tigritude, and the South African, Ezekiel Mphahlele, who found particularly offensive the "return to sources" so typical of the Negritude poets.[11] Contrary to the movements in former English-governed colonies, the Francophone protest did not involve nationalism so much as the overall cultural oppression of the black race. Frantz Fanon, in an essay in his book *The Damned* (originally published as *Les Damnés de la terre,* 1961), pointed out that this tendency not to think in terms of specific states was actually an extension of the French colonial perspective that discouraged such notions and tried to lump all Africans together regardless of origin or culture.[12] In justification of this preference on the part of black students in Paris for finding their common ground in their race rather than in a particular ethnic or national group, it must be remembered that some of the strongest voices of the Negritude movement during the early days were not African in terms of their place of birth. The directors of *Légitime Défense* were West

Indian, Césaire was from Martinique, and Damas from Guyana. In fact, *L'Etudiant noir,* the review which Césaire and Senghor helped to produce, had as one of its tasks the unification of these various groups around that which gave them a common cause: their race and African heritage.

The close of World War II brought with it a climate ripe for a change in the relationship between the colonies and the Metropole. This climate established a new context, and consequently a new role, for Negritude. The early Negritude poetry loudly condemned assimilation and colonialism. But what was needed was not only an articulation of grievances, but also a constructive alternative to previous colonial policy. Senghor, by virtue of his election to political office, found himself in a position to help formulate that policy, but to be effective he was obliged to transform his ideology into a basis for dialogue. The very realities of political survival required of Senegal's deputy a more moderate stance, a talent for compromise. From 1947 on, his presentation of Negritude shifts noticeably to place more emphasis on the merits of cultural crossbreeding (Senghor's alternative to outright assimilation) and of an ultimate universal civilization which would be the product of values from many cultures. While continuing to promote the values of African civilization, Senghor nevertheless affirmed his admiration for the civilization—and language—of France. Without hostility he could depict the future in a positive, nonthreatening way as a more amenable and mutually enriching configuration of cultures, a much more comfortable posture from which to negotiate than that of the militant Negritude of the pre-war years.[13]

These assumptions, originally framed in a primarily cultural context, also provided a justification for Senghor's political orientation. Whereas he had spoken in favor of independence as late as 1947, he soon abandoned this type of rhetoric and sought instead to promote a plan for some sort of federation between France and the colonies, a political interdependence which reflected his commitment to cultural interdependence. Illustrating this concept and the important place it then occupied in Senghor's thought was the poem "Epîtres à la Princesse," published as part of the collection *Ethiopiques* (1956). The letters and their sequel, "La Mort de la Princesse," depicted the courtship of a European princess by an African envoy in terms which were clearly an allegory of the political situation as viewed by the poet. Senghor's conciliatory brand of Negritude, necessary to him as a representative to the National Assembly and a public figure, received criticism from those who felt he was too accommodating. Marcien Towa saw the theme of complementarity which figured in *Ethiopiques* as proof that Senghor had abandoned the cause of revolution and independence[14] and accused him of being a new manifestation of the *bon nègre* (good nigger).[15] Ezekiel Mphahlele was especially critical of Senghor's exclusive emphasis on peace, love, and harmony, and he reminded the world on at least one occasion that anger and violence were African characteristics as well.[16] An admirer of Gandhi, Senghor unquestionably preferred a nonviolent solution to Africa's problems. That he did so may account in part for his often criticized temperance in dealing with the French. The example of Madagascar, where efforts to bring about a more equitable situation had led in 1947 to much bloodshed (11,342 victims according to one account), had served as a timely dramatization of the tragic consequences of the use of violence as a means of procuring political gains and dictated prudence to those in positions of responsibility. If Senghor's own natural inclinations had not caused him to pursue the more moderate course, the Madagascar incident would have been enough to warn him and others like him of the dangers of overzealousness.

In a major essay on Teilhard de Chardin, Senghor has described how he rejected a scenario for the colonial struggle which would depict African and European civilizations as opposites or antagonists in perpetual conflict. He was first attracted to Marx's philosophy because it provided a dynamic, dialectical interpretation of history, one which portrayed the resolution of the world's dilemmas in terms of synthesis.[17] There were, however, aspects of socialist theory with which the African did not feel entirely comfortable. He rejected Marx's emphasis on materialistic determinism at the expense of man and his liberty, he objected to Marx's atheism, and he felt that the German philosopher had poorly understood the realities of colonialism in categorizing it as a facet of the struggle between classes.[18] Even though Senghor had initiated his political career as a member of the French socialist party, he eventually (1948) withdrew and formed his own party. He gave as his primary reason for doing so his belief that the extension of European socialism into the colonies was merely another form of assimilation, an effort to export yet another inappropriate Western concept to Africa. In spite of the weaknesses which he perceived in Marx, Senghor continued to find the approach to history appealing. In 1953, he encountered the work of the Jesuit philosopher Pierre Teilhard de Chardin, whose concept of historical evolution was similar in the important respects to Marx's dialectics, but which had the additional merit of a spiritual orientation and an interpretation of world conflict that went beyond the disgruntlement of the proletariat. It was to Teilhard that Senghor turned to draft an African variant of socialism, and the profound influence of the Catholic philosopher must also be taken into account when discussing the changing character of postwar Negritude which, as Senghor interprets it from this point on, shares Teilhard's vision of a Universal Civilization and the overriding preeminence of the principles of brotherhood and love.

Independence and accession to the presidency placed further demands on Senghor's concept of Negritude. Markovitz notes that at the outset French-speaking Africans had tended to be primarily descriptive and analytical in framing their resistance to colonialism. They did not present practical plans for action. This notable absence of pragmatism is often cited as another way in which they differed from their British counterparts.[19] Since independence, however, Negritude, originally speculative and abstract, has been used as a tool for nation-building, providing justification and direction for many of Senghor's activities. In as much as his concept of a universal civilization enabled him to value what he deemed useful and positive in Western culture, Senegal's first president had no difficulty, in spite of his advocacy of traditional values, in incorporating the benefits of science and technology into his development efforts. His emphasis on cultural crossbreeding and the spirit of exchange and compromise it fosters proved valuable on another level by helping him to promote a sense of national unity in the midst of Senegal's diverse population and interest groups. Finally, the notion of black culture which is inherent in Negritude provided a specifically African rationale for much of Senghor's political and economic decision-making.[20] Thomas calls this final phase "prospective" Negritude because it has such important implications for planning in Senegal and elsewhere in Africa.[21] Senghor has referred to it as "rectified" Negritude.[22]

Senghor's critics could not accept Negritude as an effective basis for a national (or racial) myth or as a solid theory for economic development. They contended that as the product of the drama experienced only by the French-speaking elite of the country and the foundation of poems and essays that just a very few can read and fewer still appreciate, it has only limited popular appeal or usefulness as a rallying force. A recent African novel satirizes the erudite nature of Senghor's poetry and points out that even those who might be able to read it would probably prefer a few good verses by Victor Hugo.[23] There is also the concrete fact of real economic problems in Senegal to suggest some weaknesses either in the philosophy or in its application.

These are the major steps constituting the metamorphoses of Senghor's Negritude: its initial, personal "orphic" birth, its militant, "antiracist racist" proclamation, a mediating, post-war transition into a context for negotiations between Senghor and the French, and its role after independence as a philosophical basis for political policies. In one sense, "Negritude" is an unsatisfactory term for describing this multifaceted theory of history. In actuality, it refers accurately to only one part, albeit an important one, of Senghor's more complex ideology. From his earliest writing in the 1930s, he portrays the need to recognize the existence and merit of black values as only the initial phase in a much broader scheme, for although he seems to believe in the implicit superiority of these values, he has never suggested that they be prized to the exclusion of others. Instead, his writings promote the notion of a cultural crossbreeding which will eventually lead to a new civilization enriched by the best qualities each race or people might contribute. It is this aspect of his theory that has raised Senghor's writing to the level of a doctrine for the third world with an array of cultural, political, and economic implications far broader than the term "Negritude" seems to imply. In another sense that label, however misleading in some respects, succeeds in placing the emphasis on what is constant and permanent in Senghor's thinking: his belief in the existence and value of a definable black culture or personality, the objective element in Sartre's original analysis which deals with the essence of being black.

Negritude As Essence

In simple terms, Senghor defines Negritude as "the sum total of black cultural values."[24] His preferred English equivalent of the expression is "black personality." Other black writers, such as Césaire, have been associated with the philosophy,[25] but what sets Senghor apart is his achievement in going beyond a general definition in order to elaborate more precisely just what specific qualities typify black culture and just what distinguishes the black personality from that of other races. One of the most useful works in this respect is the published text of a speech delivered to the Second Congress of Black Artists and Writers in Rome in 1959. The article, entitled "The Constituent Elements of a Civilization of Black African Inspiration" and divided into seven parts and a conclusion, systematically examines the black personality as it is related to the following areas: environment, psychology, ontology and religion, society, property and work, ethics, and art. A brief analysis of the pertinent parts of each section provides an excellent framework for understanding the nature of Negritude.[26]

The tropical agrarian environment.   Senghor bases the validity of his entire concept of a black personality on the premise that culture is the product of man's efforts to adapt to his environment. Black culture is the consequence of the black man's adaption to a tropical climate. The writer notes that the African is traditionally a farmer, one who lives "off the land and with the land."[27] Because of his agrarian environment he is extremely sensitive to nature, and much more than in a temperate climate, nature responds to the needs of man and to the labor of the farmer.

Psychology.   Largely because he lives close to nature and is more sensitive to it, the African perceives the world differently from those who live in a highly technological society. Senghor creates a simplified dichotomy between the black farmer and the white engineer, between what he calls feeling-reason for the farmer and eye-reason for the technician. This difference between the two races is also evident in their varying attitudes toward nature: the European takes an essentially pragmatic view of the exterior world which he uses for his own ends or which, in Senghor's words, "he assimilates."[28] The Black, on the other hand, being more sensitive to the world, seeks actively to be assimilated by it. Senghor brings home this point by paraphrasing Descartes: "I sense the Other, I dance the Other, therefore, I am."[29] He claims that "European reason is analytical by utilization; Black reason is intuitive by participation."[30] This, Senghor asserts, is the better method of perception. Along these same lines, he has stated that "emotion is Black just as reason is Hellenic,"[31] a stand which he bolsters by using a line from Sartre defining emotion as "the descent of the conscious into the magic world."[32] Senghor sees a relationship between emotion and magic, the latter being synonymous for spiritual in the writer's vocabulary. This spirituality, a direct result of the African's perception of nature, becomes an important element underlying his view of the world and his emphasis on community feeling.

Ontology and religion. Senghor's description of African ontology finds its source in traditional animistic beliefs where all objects are considered to possess a spiritual force. Everything in the universe, "from God to a grain of sand,"[33] has its own "vital force" which, being common to all things, imposes a sort of unity on all matter. Man, at the center of the universe, strives constantly to strengthen his own vital force through his interactions with others. This view of the universe must also be placed in the agrarian context of African society with a preponderance of nature deities and rituals associated in some way with nature or the cycle of cultivation. Religion is strongly family oriented acting to bring together not only the living members of the community but also the ancestors in order that they might survive by sharing their vital force with their descendants. Finally, Senghor interprets the magic quality of African religion as a means of effecting some interaction with the vital forces, an example of this being rites of sacrifice.

Society. Against this background of vital forces and man's duty to enhance his own vital force, Senghor justifies the enormous value placed on family and community ties in African cultures. He contrasts the nuclear family in Europe with the notion of an extended family where the greater family unit is even further enlarged and fortified by communion with the ancestors and, through the totem (an animal considered as an ancestor or somehow related to the ancestor of the clan), with the natural world. Because a family's vital force depends on the number and prosperity of family members, children have a special importance as do women, who are considered sources of vital force and guardians of the future of the extended family, the clan. Senghor further points out that even the governing bodies and other social institutions also function within some religious context.

Property and work. Senghor deplores the notion of private property. Emphasizing the primarily communal and collective nature of African societies, he points out that "ownership" of the land is an irrelevant term where the people worship the land as a deity and where cultivation is therefore imbued with a religious significance. Working the land, interpreted as an interaction between man and the forces of the universe, becomes a source of satisfaction and joy, and even the work of artisans has religious or magical trappings.

Ethics. The writer lists work, honor, filial piety, charity, and hospitality as virtues in the African code of ethics, the most important being honor. "Suicide," he tells us, "is the last requirement of honor."[34] He makes a distinction between the African ethic which is lived and the European ethic which he considers as a mere catechism to be recited.

Art. Art, like work, is a product. It is essentially functional. Everyone may participate in the creation of art, and art, because it is functional and serves a social purpose is, virtually by definition, *engagé,* or committed. The principal characteristic of art is unity. Stylistically, its two most important features are rhythm and analogical imagery. (Senghor's concept of these elements is so essential to his own poetic art that they are treated at length in the following chapter.)

As many of Senghor's poetic themes and subjects emerge out of the changing situation of Negritude, so too do other elements in the poems originate in his theory of the black personality. An image that might seem gratuitous at first reading often gains deeper meaning when reevaluated in terms of Negritude. It may illustrate what Senghor considers a characteristically African value or it may have specific significance in the dichotomy between African and European which, for Senghor, contrasts such attributes as dark and light, night and day, emotion and reason, spiritual and materialistic, natural and artificial, agriculture and technology. In some instances what might seem obscure to Western eyes becomes clearer in the light of African ontology or customs as interpreted by Senghor in his discussions of African culture. Much of what is singular or characteristic in the poetry is derived directly from the way in which it animates the premises of Negritude.[35]

There are a number of evident weaknesses in Senghor's analysis of black culture. His dependence on the relationship between environment and personality fails to take into consideration the diversity of African geography and peoples. Much of what he describes would be true of any tropical agrarian society regardless of race. Overgeneralization apart, his observations about the nature of African culture and beliefs are generally accurate and conform to the writings of contemporary anthropologists.[36] He is rather selective in what he reveals about African society and much of the criticism of his analysis relates to the way in which he chooses to depict Africans. Some have pointed out the futility of defining the black personality by making it the opposite of the white.[37] Such distinctions are at best problematic and have the adverse side effect of sustaining theories of racial differences which contribute to racism. Others have objected to the relationship between Senghor's portrayal of African life and romantic exoticism, especially the myth of the noble savage. Mphahlele has attacked the way in which this image tends to confirm many of the stereotypes Westerners have long held concerning the dark continent.[38] He emphatically rejects using such a philosophy as a foundation for an African literature and further asserts that it loses its validity by assuming a common inspiration for all African writers when, manifestly, all black writers do not write in the same way.[39] Fanon also rejects black writing grounded on a historical black heritage because he feels that the emphasis placed by the African "bourgeois" writer on conserving traditional values eventually causes his literature to become less representative of African life, not more, because African society is caught up in a process of irreversible change.[40]

As a scientific theory or even as a literary one, serious questions can be raised about the validity of Negritude. To be acceptable, scientific theories must meet certain requirements, and there is no room for what cannot be interpreted on an entirely intellectual plane. Poetry, however, knows no such constraints. Perhaps this is why Negritude, which becomes so vulnerable when presented as science, seems to be at its hardiest and most enduring when allowed to flourish in the climate of the poem. Sartre's introduction to Negritude asserts that beyond the logical description of Negritude there is an aspect which cannot be comprehended on a rational level, something which is *"poésie pure."*[41] Ironically, what threatens its philosophical solidity contributes much to Negritude's effectiveness in the poetry. Whereas Negritude in the real world may not always describe human behavior exactly or account completely for the outcome of events, it accords to Senghor's poetic world an extraordinary consistency and unity. The opposition between black and white personalities which, in his description of the African personality, receives considerable criticism, creates in the poems a play of light and shadow, of successful, effective contrasts. Time and the progress of events in his verses reflect the writer's devotion to a dynamic theory of history which resolves almost every crisis—personal, national, or racial—in a positive synthesis of opposing forces. The exoticism that threatens the credibility of his anthropological hypothesis adds a certain measure of charm to his literature. The equation of Africa with the innocent paradise of Eden, the image of peoples living in perfect harmony with nature and with each other, a world inhabited by noble warriors and pure maidens, where music and magic are always present—such a vision has had an undeniable appeal for diverse cultures throughout history beginning with the legend of the Golden Age and has a long and respected literary heritage. It is logical that in his attempt to refute negative European stereotypes of the African, Senghor should draw on the romantic tradition of the noble savage with which his readers were already acquainted and to which they were sympathetic. The noble savage has often appeared in Western literature as a means of conveying criticism of the status quo, of hypocrisy or inappropriateness of behavior in government or in some other aspect of society. In Senghor's works the figure serves a similar function in order to bring into question the conventionally accepted wisdom of his era concerning the intrinsic superiority of "modern" man in a technological society. Even a hasty perusal of Senghor's contemporaries and immediate predecessors in French literature shows that he was not alone in challenging such values. The Surrealists, for example, had previously rejected much in their own culture including its overly rational intellectual tradition, and in their search for wider horizons had proposed studying the art and mind of the "primitive."

In defending Negritude's contribution to Senghor's poetry, it should be noted that because of his preoccupation with it—both as a chronicle of the black race and as an attempt to give his people an identity—Senghor's work assumes an importance far beyond that of much modern lyric poetry, a significance that can be deemed epic or mythic. In his essay, "The Possible Nature of a 'Mythology' to Come," Henry A. Murray proposes ways in which myths for our era might be expected to resemble primitive mythic patterns. He gives the following "formal, descriptive definition of myth": "A myth manifestly consists of the essential features of an *important,* more or less natural/preternatural situation or event (that has a basic thema) in which at least one extraordinary, more or less natural/ preternatural psychic entity is involved—all this is sensibly represented in one channel or another."[42] The underlining of the word "important" is ours to stress what Murray makes clear later, that a myth concerns "important, critical endeavors (matters of physical, social, or spiritual vitality or death)—not about trivial people involved in inconsequential interactions."[43] The revolt of the black intellectual on behalf of his race against a world order which presumed his inferiority, the conception of independent statehood for the peoples of Africa and the struggle to win it, the creation of policies and aspirations on which a new nation might be founded, and finally the formulation of a new world order which denied the concept of a single, straight-line pattern of social and technological evolution and replaced it with one which allows for a synthesis of contributions from diverse peoples and cultures—these are the situations dealt with in Senghor's works, and whatever one might say about them, they certainly are not trivial. They constitute one of Murray's required ingredients for the creation of myth. In the preceding chapter, we presented the record of Senghor's own remarkable personal achievements, and to the extent that the poetry is written in the first-person singular and that the narrator can thus be considered Senghor, it does not seem to be an exaggeration to suggest that the poems also meet the second of Murray's criteria for myth, that they feature the exploits of an extraordinary psychic entity. What remains to be discussed is the "channel" of representation, the form and style of the literary works themselves, which will be discussed in chapter 3. Murray elaborates on the notion of mythic representation; he claims that it should be neither "an abstract, conceptual (scientific) model of a certain class of events, nor an accurate, factual report of a specific event."[44] Myth must be an indirect, "symbolic," representation of events. Perhaps in this truth lies an important part of the explanation for the failure of Negritude to succeed completely as a philosophy, and conversely, the very reason why it should be expected to have its most convincing expression in the poems.

Chapter Three
The Poetics of Negritude

Senghor's theory of Negritude, with its description of African society, includes an analysis of traditional literature. His writings also feature a number of essays dealing with contemporary African literature and works by Western authors. He devotes relatively little space to discussing his own poetry, but his commentaries on other poets are revealing since his approach to literary criticism involves relating his subject to a standard set of literary characteristics derived from African oral literature. Indirectly, he shows us what he strives for in his own works. As in other areas of his intellectual life, Senghor has written prolifically on literary topics. In addition to the essays in *Liberté I* (1964), other accessible studies include *La Parole chez Paul Claudel et les Négro-Africains* (1973) and an essay in *Elégies majeures* (1979) entitled "Lettre à trois poètes de l'hexagone."[1]

An immediate problem that arises in conjunction with any contemporary African writing has to do with language, and an especially pertinent question is that of how Senghor, writing in French, can consider his work an expression of African values. This paradox has provided the fodder for a seemingly endless critical debate over the extent and importance of various literary influences on the writer's work. Certainly his raw material, the French language, and his tools, the traditions of French poetry, are foreign. But in what measure is his way of manipulating them a reflection of his African heritage? Most scholars agree that in elaborating his own style Senghor has drawn heavily on techniques and concepts furnished by oral traditions.[2] At least one major Senghorian critic expresses reservations that African poetry would have much to offer a modern poet writing in French, while he nevertheless applauds Senghor's contribution to French style.[3] The writer W. E. Abraham even asserts categorically that, for him, Senghor does not write like an African poet.[4] At the opposite extreme we find Janis Pallister, who laments the tendency of Western critics to make far too much of possible French influences on Senghor and to deemphasize the role of African sources.[5] The issue does not lend itself easily to resolution.

It remains true that Senghor has chosen to write in French, a language which he admires for its intrinsic beauty and for its universal audience.[6] By doing so, he tacitly accepts both its limits and the assets it has accrued over centuries of stylistic experiment and development, but we cannot ignore Senghor's statements about how he has chosen to adapt that style for his own use and the way in which those choices conform to his other writings on black esthetics.

The Poet

Traditional African culture provides Senghor with his ideas concerning the nature and role of the poet, whom he depicts not merely as historian or entertainer but as one having exceptional spiritual power. Through words, the poet becomes capable of re-creating the world. While this description might be regarded as merely figurative at first glance, an examination of the significance of words and speech in African tradition gives it another dimension.

In his work on African culture, *Muntu,* the German Africanist, Janheinz Jahn, devotes a chapter to discussing the concept of *Nommo,* the life force which "influences things in the shape of the world."[7] He makes it clear that, in African thought, the power of words rests not in their logic or persuasiveness per se but in their intrinsic ability to create or to bring things into existence. It is believed that all changes are effected through words and that nothing can take place without them. This explains to some extent the charms and spells so typically associated with magic or voodoo. In mythology, it was through the power of the spoken word that God, in some versions, created the world, and in one essay Senghor takes pains to recount in detail such a myth in which human life is born from an egg "fertilized by the word of Amma [God]."[8] One of these first men was called Nommo and gave both language and form to mankind. Subsequently, the word has retained its creative strength and the poet, as *Maître de la Parole* (Master of the Spoken Word), shares something of the Creator's power as indicated in the following passage from *Muntu*:

According to African philosophy man has, by the force of his word, dominion over "things"; he can change them, make them work for him, and command them. But to command things with words is to practise "magic." And to practise word magic is to write poetry—that holds not only for Africa. . . . African poetry is never a game, never *l'art pour l'art,* never irresponsible. "To practise magic" is therefore a weak expression; the African poet is not "an artist using magic," but a "magician," a "sorcerer" in the African sense. He is the muntu [human being] on the captain's bridge of the world. Out of the great coherence of all things he calls "things" individually and then they are there.[9]

In a society that presumes a harmonious, well-ordered universe, it is the poet's duty, in the presence of apparent disintegration, to rediscover this essential order and to reaffirm by his words its original harmony. Senghor tells us:

. . . man is a "cosmic" being . . . He lives in and through the world. Now, under its appearance of chaos, the world is harmonious order. To live, materially and spiritually, Man must unravel this order. In order to conform to it, or, if it is disturbed, to reestablish it through the Word. The Mythology of the Word in traditional civilizations. I leave matter to the engineers. To the Poet belongs the Spirit. A man privileged among men, the Poet is one who gives orders and one who restores order; he is Father, Priest, and Magician at the same time."[10]

We see that Senghor views the traditional poet not merely as commentator but as an active manipulator both of words and, by a form of sympathetic magic, of the things which they stand for. In his theoretical writings he sometimes uses the word "poïetic," meaning creative or productive to convey this aspect of poetry.

Because most African poetry is sung, the significance attached to poetry is also accorded to song. We are told explicitly by Senghor that for many African languages the word for "poem" is actually the word for "song" as well.[11] Both poems and songs play a role in the creative process. The example invariably cited by way of demonstration is the passage in Camara Laye's L'Enfant noir dealing with the goldsmith. We are shown that in order for the raw material to be transformed into jewelry, it is not only necessary that the artisan know his craft, but also that the right words be uttered in accompaniment. Without the transforming power of the word, the act would be deemed ineffectual. Senghor, familiar with the text, seems to recall it when in Lettres d'hivernage he uses the following line: "Je chante en t'écrivant, comme le bon artisan qui travaille un bijou d'or" (I sing while writing to you like a good artisan who is fashioning a gold jewel. Poèmes, 239). He implies that, as in the case of the goldsmith's work, his song (or poem) will have the ability to accomplish the reality which he describes in the remaining lines; namely, the return of the beloved.

The poet and the poem maintain this creative or magic significance throughout Senghor's poetry. As narrator he sometimes refers to himself as "Maître-de-Langue," and on several occasions the power of the word is an important part of the poem. In "Elégie des Eaux," for example, he calls upon the water to descend and purify a world which has lost its innocence, and ultimately through the force and magic of the poet's words, the rains come: "Seigneur, entendez bien ma voix. PLEUVE! il pleut / Et vous avez ouvert de votre bras de foudre les cataractes du pardon" (Lord, hear my voice. Rain! it rains / And you have opened with your arms of lightning the waterfalls of pardon; *Poèmes,* 206). The capitalization of the word *Pleuve* exists in the original text and conveys typographically the transformation wrought by the language of the poem. The use of the imperative, a common device in Senghor's work, also has its origins in the belief that the poet can indeed cause the material world to change merely by commanding it.

Similarly, Senghor uses another traditional technique, that of "naming." The expression is set off in quotes because of the unusual meaning attributed to it. Jahn tells us that in some societies, children are not considered to exist until they are given a name.[12] The pronouncing of the name has greater significance and implies a desire on the part of the poet to honor the individual so named, to increase his prestige and consequently, his life force. The occurence of invocations is so characteristic in Senghor's work that one critic has claimed that it is his most frequent source of inspiration.[13] The technique plays a particularly important role in poems which praise the accomplishments of individuals, such as "Au Guélowâr," "Au Gouverneur Eboué," "Elégie pour Aynina Fall," and "Taga de Mbaye Dyob." "Naming" gives a special import to the use of capital letters in "Elégie pour Martin Luther King": "MARTIN LUTHER KING LE ROI DE LA PAIX" (Martin Luther King King of Peace).

More than a theme or device in a few individual instances, Senghor's concept of the role of poetry is transmitted uniformly in the structure or intention of nearly every single work. On one level, there is the writer's avowed mission as the defender of Negritude, as a prophet of a new civilization. In the poems that seek to overturn the old stereotypes, to rehabilitate Africa, and to devise a possible meeting ground for Black and White, the poet uses the magic of

words to bring about his vision of the future: "L'AUBE TRANSPARENTE
D'UN JOUR NOUVEAU" (The transparent dawn of a new day. *Poèmes*,
60). Certain poems become in this sense the incantation necessary
for the success of the statesman and philosopher. But the power of
the word is also visible in other contexts for repeatedly, the poems
have the effect of restoring harmony to the world, be it the macro-
cosm of society as a whole as in "Elégies des eaux," or the microcosm
of the poet's inner world as in *Chants d'Ombre,* in which poems like
"Que m'accompagnent kôras et balafong," "Neige sur Paris," or
"Totem" seek to restore the integrity of the narrator. Consistently,
the train of events in almost any given poem moves from chaos to
meaning, from conflict to resolution, or from depression or anger
to a greater, more positive vision. The ritual patterns of sacrifice
and reconciliation or of death and rebirth occur with unusual frequency within individual poems and in the order of the poems within
different collections. This is in keeping with Senghor's dialectical
vision of history; but it is more appropriate to say that the dialectical
interpretation of history lends itself well to rendering the dynamic,
creative potential which Senghor perceives in traditional African
poetry and in his own work.

One French writer with a style very similar to Senghor's, who
has often been listed as a source or model, is Paul Claudel. Senghor
freely admits his influence, adding that the French poet's original
attraction for him was in the resemblance between his works and
African traditional poetry. In addition to a noticeable similarity in
traits of style, which we will look into later, Claudel also has a
comparable notion of the creative function of the poet. He uses the
expression "magistère des mots" to denote the poet,[14] and in an
essay on Claudel, Senghor finds ideas about the power of the word
which parallel his own in the poem *The Muses,* where Claudel uses
a technique which calls to mind the African device of naming and
where he gives an account of Creation which has evident affinities
with Senghor's tale of Nommo. Senghor comments on the passage
as follows: "As in Catholic doctrine and its primary interpretation
by Claudel, we find the creation, transgression and its punishment.
But we also find something else: essentially, Man completing by
the word the creation of the world and completing himself at the
same time."[15] The kinship between the two poets is obvious on this
point, but they differ considerably in other respects, for while both
have a well-defined concept of a harmonious, ordered universe,

Claudel derives his from Catholicism and Senghor's stems from African ontology.

Imagery

In his study of black culture, Senghor identifies the two most characteristic features of African art as image and rhythm[16] and tells us that "the first gift of the Black African poet is the gift of the image."[17] The nature and function of imagery in Senghor's own works contributes a great deal to the originality of his style. Although his language is highly figurative, his descriptions are far from photographic. Irele has termed this aspect of Senghor's imagery "an impressionistic quality . . . which relies for effect more on the feeling it induces and the atmosphere it creates than on rational understanding."[18] As an example he refers to the poem "Nuit de Sine." Although the work overflows with images of the African night, which successfully convey a wealth of varied sensations, a painter would be hard pressed to accurately reconstruct the scene. Geneviève Lebaud, speaking of Senghor's poetry, warns that his images "function neither to describe nor to draw an outline with precise details . . ."[19] Certainly any reader of Senghor's poems would readily agree that they are not for the literal-minded. While in some instances much can be gained from the careful deciphering of a rich symbolic language, in others the poem demands that we relinquish our penchant for logical deduction and give in to the enjoyment of a mood or sensation which cannot be completely analyzed.

Senghor prefers not to distinguish between metaphor and simile but speaks of the "image-analogy." This type of image, which according to Senghor characterizes African languages and poetry, provides the means for using a concrete vocabulary in order to express more abstract ideas or emotions. A reference to the moon, for example, carries connotations of fertility; the serpent denotes wisdom. Senghor speaks almost with pity of European languages which require that the second term of the comparison, the abstraction for which the concrete stands, be directly expressed.[20] While apparently not a case of an explicit one-to-one relationship, the symbolism to which he refers—the analogies between animals and certain abstract ideas, for example—seems to constitute a commonly agreed upon set of meanings, a network of ideas lying beneath the world of visible things. The poet has often used the word "surreality" (etymologically, "beyond reality") to designate the phenomenon. The expression, while appropriate in some ways, has the questionable side effect of contributing to the confusion which already exists between Senghor's imagery and that of the French surrealists. The two are not entirely dissimilar; both have a tendency to express an idea through the juxtaposition of concrete terms and both create unusual and unexpected images. For Senghor it is important that he draws on the hidden meanings implicit in African thought in order to create analogies in the traditional sense, whereas the surrealists' imagery reveals no such underlying meaning in the universe.[21]

There are explanations which lie outside the established surrealist credo for the appearance in Senghor's work of what the surrealists might label "startling images," those whose elements would not under normal circumstances occur together. Because much of Senghor's imagery cannot be easily explained in terms of conventional poetic associations, this does not necessarily make it surrealist. Senghor depicts the African image as characteristically ambivalent, or multivalent,[22] since the figurative meaning can be no more precise than the symbol itself allows. It is perfectly in keeping with this notion that one of the major studies of *Lettres d'hivernage* focuses specifically on ambiguities in the work.[23] In addition to the open-endedness of the analogies, another area of obscurity exists in the poet's use of traditional African symbols which may be unfamiliar to the average Western reader who does not necessarily realize, for example, that the antelope horn is a fertility symbol in many African cultures. Equally puzzling are references to African beliefs and customs and the use of African words and expressions unavailable in most dictionaries.[24] To critics who consider his vocabulary unnecessarily picturesque, Senghor responds: "When we say *kôra, balafong, tam-tam,* and not harp, piano, and drum, we don't mean to be picturesque; we are calling 'a spade a spade.' "[25] The reader must also deal with challenges to his habitual notions of race and culture and the vagaries of a literary language not really equipped to sing the songs of a Black troubadour. The customary use of the color black to denote death or evil, for example, not only fails to appear in Senghor's poems but is virtually negated in compositions like "Femme noire," where black is the color of life, or in "Neige sur Paris," where the color white acquires connotations of brutality and even evil. Finally, there is Senghor's own personal set of symbols—

like the "sisters" Isabelle and Soukeïna—whose original appearance provides an invaluable context for their interpretation in subsequent works. It is not difficult to see how Senghor's imagery could be mistakenly interpreted as intentionally obscure in imitation of the irrational imagery of an André Breton. The methods, however, are different. While Breton's accidental discoveries of shocking but powerful juxtapositions may reveal to us an unexpected truth, Senghor carefully and consciously selects the images which reveal a poetic vision inspired by African beliefs.[26]

In Senghor's perception of the image, he is more closely related to Baudelaire and the symbolist poets than to the surrealists. We know that during the writer's university career he did a serious study of the work of Baudelaire and later spoke very highly of him as "the first to sing about 'the Black Venus,' " the poet who "caused French poetry to enter the black forest of 'correspondences,' of 'symbols'— where Arthur Rimbaud exploded the bomb of lucid delirium."[27] One of the most obvious links between Senghor and the symbolists is his use of synesthesia, the confusion of sensations which appears in poetry as the application of terms appropriate for one sense to another—the use of colors, for example, to describe perfumes. Senghor's technique of building a poem from a series of associated sensations is also highly reminiscent of Baudelaire.[28]

Rhythm

The second feature that Senghor invariably cites along with the analogical image as being characteristic of African poetry—and, for that matter, of African art in general—is rhythm. He tells us that the image must be put to rhythm in order to be effective.[29] His critical writing devotes considerable space to the analysis of rhythm in traditional poetry, and his own poetry consciously seeks to incorporate some of the traditional rhythmic effects. Consequently, the nature of rhythm in his poems deserves particular attention and has been the focus of much Senghorian scholarship.[30]

In his essays on the black personality, Senghor emphasizes the African's innate sense of rhythm and the prominence of music in many forms in the life of an African community. In his poems, music as subject or image shows up in a variety of ways: the songs of choruses and of the professional musicians known as "griots," the drumming or playing of other musical instruments, and, of course, the dancing. He also depicts the many roles of music in African society: it provides entertainment, it accompanies the workers in the fields, and it has a function to perform in religious rites and public ceremonies. In addition to using music as a subject in his poems, he has also provided directions at the head of many works for the type of instrument which would be appropriate for musical accompaniment. The notations are reminders that African poetry in its traditional setting is not read but performed, and Senghor has retained the spirit of oral literature in various aspects of his work. The shouts of a participating audience seem to be assumed in the use of interjections such as the "He!" of "L'Homme et la Bête," a poem inspired perhaps by the victory poems of the athletes, or the "Oho!" of "Congo." In the dramatic poem "Chaka" and in "Elégie pour Aynina Fall," an actual chorus provides the background rhythm of a refrain. In the "Postface" to *Ethiopiques,* Senghor asserts that recitation is essential to his own poetry and suggests several ways in which it might be done. It could be recited in the French manner with the rhythm being derived from the emphasis of the appropriately accented words and by following the given punctuation; it could be chanted or recited to the accompaniment of an appropriate musical instrument in the background; or it could be set to music as was done by Mme Barat-Pepper for "Chant de l'Initié."[31] The success of an oral presentation of "Chaka" against a background of drums seems to be an indication of the performance potential inherent in Senghor's works.[32]

The importance of rhythm in African societies has a metaphysical basis related to the concept of vital forces. The energy of these forces, which animate all beings, manifests itself in the form of waves whose ebb and flow appears as the weak and strong beats of music or poetry. The act of creating rhythm becomes a means of participating in the vital forces of the cosmos.[33] Senghor distinguishes between Western art, which imitates nature, and African art, which is participatory. African art is not only social, he tells us, but vital.[34] This is true of all forms of rhythm including the dance, which figures so importantly in religious ceremonies. Unless there is rhythm in poetry, words do not in themselves constitute a creative force. Senghor emphasizes that it was the *parole rythmée* (rhythmic word) by which God created the universe, not by the word alone.[35]

Considering the significance that he attaches to rhythm, it is hardly surprising that Senghor devotes so much attention to the rhythmical patterns in his own works. We are told that very early in his career he rejected the conventional verse forms of French poetry with their set number of syllables per line, their prescribed strophic constructions, and the use of terminal rhymes. During the 1930s he destroyed all of his early experimental work which conformed to the rules of classical French prosody.[36] It was in the process of translating African poetry into French that he came upon a verse form which seemed suitable for what he wanted to say.[37] This more creative, more flexible form was the verset, a line which could vary in length depending on the speaker's intention. It could theoretically encompass either an odd or even number of syllables and dispensed with the tyranny of rhyme and strophic design. An American reader will recognize in the verset a structure similar to that used by the poet Walt Whitman in *Leaves of Grass*. In modern French poetry the form is generally associated with the works of Paul Claudel whom Senghor admits as an influence and whose work in developing the possibilities of the verset must be acknowledged. We have already mentioned that part of Senghor's admiration for Claudel came from the similarity he perceived between the words of the French poet and African oral literature. Larousse defines the term verset as meaning a Bible verse, and certainly Claudel's use of the verset reflects its Biblical origins, especially the prosody of the Psalms.[38] As a consequence, both Claudel's poetry and that of Senghor often give the impression of echoing the Bible or the Catholic liturgy. Senghor suggests that the relationship may be more complex in his own case, that there may be certain similarities between African poetry and the Bible.[39] The Psalms were, he reminds us, oral poetry. Destined to be sung or chanted and bearing notations concerning musical accompaniment, a good number were much like the African works on which Senghor founded his own poems: invocations, prayers, or praise songs. Some of the stylistic resemblances between Senghor and Claudel—or between Senghor and the Biblical psalmist—should be considered more or less coincidental.

Another French writer associated with the verset form is Saint-John Perse, the pseudonym for Alexis Leger. Senghor professes a great admiration for Perse but he also notes that before reading his works for the first time, he had already written the material for two collections of his own poetry.[40] The influence of Perse on subsequent collections is unmistakable, with lines in Senghor's poem "L'Absente" resembling very closely similar verses in Perse's *Exil*. Senghor was especially intrigued with the way the French poet dispensed with what Senghor terms "tool-words" (*mots-outil*): the prepositions, conjunctions, and such.[41] He considered that this means of bringing concision to a line of verse also occurred in African poetry and used it himself especially in the later works. This feature and his increasing tendency to eliminate punctuation marks and use a rather elliptical syntax creates something of a distinction between Senghor's first two collections and succeeding poems. He also informs us that the later works were more carefully organized.[42] The effect, however interesting or successful, is different and we cannot help regretting just a little, as does Lilyan Kesteloot, that the echoes of Saint-John Perse sound so strong in *Ethiopiques* and subsequent works.[43]

Although an English version of Senghor's poetry might conceivably retain some features of the original French rhythm, most are too closely linked to the language to transfer easily to a translation. The French do not determine rhythm by means of feet as in English poetry. Rhythm is derived instead by the number of syllables in a line of verse and by the way in which accents are distributed throughout the line. The most characteristic line is the 12-syllable alexandrine, although decasyllabic and octosyllabic lines are also frequent. Lines with uneven numbers of syllables are relatively rare although some of the modern poets have used them for their unusual musical qualities. In classical poetry, the final or mute "e," not heard in spoken French, is counted as a syllable except at the end of a line of verse or before the cesura (middle pause) in the alexandrine. Rhythmic effects are achieved by repetitions and variations in the placement of accents.

While Senghor does not use the classical lines of verse in the conventional sense, he often builds his verset from an established verse or a combination of such verses, so that we might see, as in the following line, a grouping in which a decasyllabic segment is joined to an octasyllabic group with only the pause of a comma to separate them, a pause which is less substantial than the one at the end of the verset: "Je chante ta beauté qui passe, forme que je fixe dans l'Eternel," (I sing your beauty which passes, form which I fix in the Eternal; *Poèmes*, 15). Within these two principal divisions, the words are grouped in terms of accentuated or unaccentuated syllables. In Senghor's poetics, this grouping varies from two to eight syllables long. As in the preceding example, most of the longer versets are divided into two parts, not always equal in length. He explains this binary feature of rhythm as the rhythm "of the days and seasons, of ebbing and flowing, of the heart beating, of breathing, of walking, of love."[44] Within this seemingly regular structure Senghor manages to provide a great deal of diversity. He can vary the length of a line or the length of the segments of a line and, within each segment, he may repeat or vary the number and distribution of accents. The verset may occasionally be divided into three parts or not divided at all. Versets or segments with an odd number of syllables appear now and again for emphasis or to create a musical effect. The result has been likened to the polyrhythmic beat of African drumming.[45] Senghor utilizes variation in the rhythm not only to create interest and to break the monotony, but also to sustain the ideas, mood, or imagery of a particular poem.

Also related to the rhythmic pattern of the poetry is Senghor's persistent use of repetition. Sounds, words, and phrases reoccur with a frequency unheard of in conventional prosody. As a result of the reiterated rhythms and sonorities, the poem has a haunting, hypnotic quality similar to that of incantations or magic spells. This repetition contributes to the musicality of the poem, and although end rhymes are rare, the poet likes to incorporate rhymes within the line as well as interesting patterns of alliteration and assonance to create remarkable musical effects. At least one scholar, Irele, considers Senghor's manipulation of sounds lacking in appropriate subtlety and suggests that he verges "on excess in his use of effects of timber and the repetition of sound values," but goes on to justify it as another way by which Senghor has integrated a characteristic of African oral poetry into his own work.[46]

In the light of the type of evidence available, the debate over whether Senghor is a French or an African poet, or to what extent he is either one, emerges as hopelessly futile. His poetry constitutes a superb example of the cultural crossbreeding that he advocates in his philosophy of Negritude. On one hand, he displays extraordinary skill in using the French language. On the other, through a concrete, symbolic language drawn largely from nature and the activities of a traditional society and through a style reminiscent of the Bible or of epic, he has managed to endow his work with the qualities of oral literature. Many of his poems seem, as a consequence, to proceed from the same tradition as the earliest Western literature, to partake of the same spirit as the great poets "who gave us the *Iliad*, the *Song of Songs*, or the *Upanishads*."[47] In a form easily associated with myth and legend, he couches a new myth, a new vision of the African intended to alter radically our previous perceptions of history and race.

Chapter Four
Chants d'ombre

Senghor's first collection of poetry, *Chants d'ombre* (1945), met with considerable critical acclaim. Excerpts from reviews at the time, although not always without reservations concerning the poet's style, show that even in this initial work he successfully establishes himself as a poet, one who "will truly plunge us into a poetic universe, who is original and of rich humanity."[1] We know little of the content of his first literary efforts, those which he admits to having destroyed, but the poems published in 1945 identified him unquestionably as a distinctly African writer, a poet whose art enabled him "to evoke the black continent in its magic strangeness"[2] and to make known "the carnal face of the continent of passion and the eternal resting place of Night."[3] One critic was even able to predict, from his own insightful analysis, the poet's crucial future political role.[4]

The title *Chants d'ombre* (Shadow songs) also appears in the singular as the title of one of the works in a group of poems entitled *Par-delà Erôs* (Beyond Eros) and again in its last lines:

> Ecoute ma voix singulière qui te chante dans l'ombre
> Ce chant constellé de l'éclatement des comètes chantantes.
> Je te chante ce chant d'ombre d'une voix nouvelle
> Avec la vieille voix de la jeunesse des mondes.
>
> (*Poèmes,* 40)

> (Listen to my singular voice which sings to you in the shadow
> This song starred with the explosion of singing comets.
> I sing this shadow song to you with a new voice
> With the old voice of the youth of worlds.)

By calling his works "songs" the poet emphasizes his affinity with the traditional African poet whose works are generally sung or performed with a musical accompaniment, and Senghor even provides us with notations for several of the pieces to indicate the appropriate musical setting. The word "shadow" may be intended as an allusion to the poet's race or to the African night which emerges as an image of his Negritude: "Nuit qui fonds toutes mes contradictions, toutes contradictions dans l'unité première de ta négritude" (Night which melts all of my contradictions, all contradictions in the first unity of your negritude; *Poèmes*, 35). Throughout his poetry, the tropical night is endowed with positive attributes in contrast with its conventional depiction in Western literature as a symbol for death and as a hiding place for the unseen and terrifying. What Sartre calls the "solar hierarchy,"[5] the preference for day over night, corresponds to the colonial's racial hierarchy, which presumed the primacy of white over black. Senghor's imagery challenges the validity of both assumptions and by his very choice of title declares war against such stereotypes of race and culture.

The principal subject of the poems is the poet himself and the various facets of his early struggle to build an identity. The work begins with the initial recognition of his dilemma as a man between two cultures and belonging completely to neither. We then follow his efforts to redefine the image of the world and his place in it, and we arrive at the three final poems of the collection with the sense of having witnessed the achievement of a great victory. Nowhere else in future works does the poet dramatize so effectively the plight of the *évolué*. This is because these poems record his successful coming to terms with his Africanness, and while future works deal with other crises, it is only here that we see the first compelling search for equilibrium.

Most of the poems are written in the first person and derive much of their interest from the assumption that the narrator is Senghor, recounting his own feelings of alienation or elation. Because he has become something of a legend in his personal involvement with the fight for African independence and in his dramatic political ascension, his real life accomplishments contribute to the image of the narrator. Unquestionably, the writer reveals himself in his work and the assiduous biographer easily finds incidents and personal relationships which inspired individual poems. But the narrator is also Senghor's literary creation and as such, he plays many parts. Here, more than in future works, he presents himself candidly—as a displaced African student adrift in Paris; by the end of the collection, however, and in anticipation of a device that appears frequently in later works, the narrator embellishes his character to give himself a more positive self-image. He becomes the warrior, the lover, the noble vassal, and the seer. Often he acts the hero, either the hero in the sense of the questing adventurer common to medieval romances and described by Campbell in his study of myth, *The Hero with a Thousand Faces*, or the hero in a more general sense, the one who according to Webster's definition exhibits valor or fortitude, a model of noble qualities. In a century that celebrates antiheroes, Senghor's narrator is a noteworthy exception.

In addition to the inevitable association between the speaker in the poems and the facts of Senghor's own life, there is another element, exterior to the work, which contributes to its effectiveness. In spite of its obvious personal inspiration and meaning, Senghor's individual story unavoidably emerges as the dramatization in the life of one man of the more general confrontation between traditional societies and the civilization of the West. In later works Senghor will actively assume the responsibility of being the spokesman for his people. But even in these first, intensely personal poems, the poet, in his fight against assimilation and racial discrimination, becomes a symbol of all who share his conflict.

The structure of the collection does not present us with a solid chronological account of the poet's life, but an unquestionable unity is achieved by means of a repetition and variation of themes which might be termed symphonic. Leusse has even suggested that the resulting composition of the different collections constitutes an aspect of Senghor's use of rhythm.[6] Peters contends that "an argument can be made for the deliberate thematic arrangement of the poems in *Chants d'ombre*,"[7] and in this we heartily concur. There is undoubtedly a progressive and intentional order, one which resembles to a great extent the exposition, climax, and denouement of drama. The initial series of seventeen poems, from "In Memoriam" to "Libération," introduce the poet in exile and the dual themes of alienation and longing for Africa. By the appearance of the poem *Que m'accompagnent kôras et balafong*, Senghor, faced with a choice between Europe and Africa, resolutely affirms his Negritude. The commitment having been made, the last two poems represent heroic adventures in which he interprets his homeward journey.

Of the twenty poems in *Chants d'ombre*, the first seventeen consist of relatively short pieces in contrast with the last three which are longer and, consequently, more complex. Those readers who are casually familiar with Senghor's work generally know him only

through the shorter poems since these can be more easily anthologized and lend themselves more readily to a self-contained explication. Although this group reveals many of the poet's strengths,
it is regrettable that the longer poems have not been transmitted
to a wider audience and that the shorter poems must be extracted
by editors and presented without the context created by their place
in the collection. It is Marcien Towa who has astutely pointed out
that some of the major critical studies of Senghor's work often discuss
an individual poem in ways which do not take into consideration
its situation in the collection or its relationship to other poems. As
an example he suggests that the love of country expressed in "Joal,"
a poem in praise of childhood memories, can only be understood as
a sentiment provoked "by the hostility of a foreign land,"[8] a detail
which is made clear by what precedes it in the collection. Since a
systematic study of the poems as they are presented by the writer
is so essential in this respect, we have retained the original order
for our commentary, but to facilitate analysis we have grouped the
seventeen shorter poems in the following manner: 1) the initial
works that describe the poet as a figurative exile in Paris and set
the stage for the collection; 2) those poems that evoke an idealized
Africa; 3) a series of poems devoted to the confrontation between
Africa and Europe; 4) three lyrical poems dealing with the narrator's
personal alienation and despair.

The Exposition
"In Memoriam" to "Libération"

Setting the Stage.   The collection opens with several poems
which situate the poet and give direction to the work as a whole
in terms of both subject and poetic form. The first poem, "In
Memoriam," finds the narrator alone in a foreign country and dealing
with his feelings of alienation and fear. The narrator's contemplation
of a Parisian setting leads to an accumulation of images which
establish his loneliness and awareness of the racial barrier. Because
it is the day set aside by the French for visiting the cemeteries, the
day after Toussaint, his thoughts stray to his own dead in a far away
place, their absence only confirming his alienation. Ultimately, he
offers a prayer to his ancestors for the courage to overcome his
solitude and for the ability to pardon those who have contributed
to his isolation:

O Morts, qui avez toujours refusé de mourir, qui avez su résister à la Mort
Jusqu'en Sine jusqu'en Seine, et dans mes veines fragiles, mon sang
   irréductible
Protégez mes rêves comme vous avez fait vos fils, les migrateurs aux jambes
   minces.

(*Poèmes*, 8–9)

(O Dead, who have always refused to die, who have found out how to
   resist Death
On the banks of the Sine on the banks of the Seine, and in my fragile
   veins, my irreducible blood
Protect my dreams as you did your sons, the migrators with slender legs.)

The poem effectively transmits the intense emotion of the situation
and also introduces novel images and ideas from African religion
and history. Without some effort on the part of the reader to understand this cultural background, he cannot feel the full impact
of the poet's statement. The African's longing for home has to be
considered in the context of his own traditions which postulate a
world order where men have a sacred relationship with the land of
their ancestors and where the living yet maintain strong ties with
the spirits of the dead. These spirits are believed to survive but only
in the rituals and prayers of the present generation. Beyond the
easily understandable nostalgia for family and country, the speaker
feels cut off from the mystic bonds which link him to his ancestors
and the land, both of which become symbols of the poet's Negritude
in other works.

   Because he believes in the importance of the spiritual, many of
Senghor's poems are prayers addressed either to the ancestors or to
the Christian God. Such prayers usually deal with feelings of racial
separateness as in "Prière aux masques" ("Prayer to the Masks") and
"Neige sur Paris" ("Snow on Paris"). The sharply hostile reaction
to racism characteristic of much Negritude poetry is a muted voice
in Senghor's writing where it often appears, as it does in "In Memoriam," yoked to the theme of forgiveness. By virtue of its keynote
position we must assume that Senghor intended this poem to set
the stage for the rest of the collection, to broach for the first time
the issue of culture conflict but to do it in a manner that would
enable him to keep the lines of communication open with his Western reader.

The second poem in the collection, "Porte dorée" ("Golden Door"), continues to develop this theme of isolation. Once again using reminiscence as a point of departure, it also compares Europe and Africa. The poet has found lodgings in an apartment with a view of greenery which reminds him faintly of Joal, his home, but the memory of Africa only renders more painful his unfamiliarity and awkwardness in the foreign surroundings, especially in the realm of interpersonal relationships. In the last lines, he imagines a poignant scene in which, shyly, he tries to strike up a conversation with a young Frenchwoman, a confirmation of his outsider's status which contrasts with his feeling for the village of Joal and the sense of community which he will elsewhere equate with African life.

In addition to presenting the problem of alienation, which he deals with and ultimately resolves in the course of the work, the poet uses these two initial poems to set the stage in another way. In what is perhaps only a minor motif with respect to Senghor's primary intentions, each of these vignettes of the poet in Paris contains references to the speaker's lodgings which transform them into a magic place from which the poet can conjure up his special visions. In "In Memoriam," he views the streets of Paris from a glass tower, an image which Geneviève Lebaud traces to Celtic legends. Glass, she tells us, is universally held to have magic properties, and the sorcerer Merlin was once imprisoned in a castle of glass (or air).[9] Senghor repeats the concept in "Kaya-Magan" when he calls himself the "Sage / Maître de l'hiéroglyphe dans sa tour de verre" (the Wise one / Master of the hieroglyphic in his glass tower; *Poèmes,* 103). In "In Memoriam," the image operates to isolate the dwelling and emphasize the theme of alienation, but it also sets the place apart in the sense of making it special. In "Porte Dorée," the dwelling is situated "près des remparts rebâtis de ma mémoire, à la hauteur des remparts" (near the reconstructed walls of my memory, at the height of the walls; *Poèmes,* 8). Surrounded by foliage the poet is reminded of settings from his childhood and he bestows on the room the power to call up memories of the past. Significantly, the poet will immediately draw upon those memories as the material for the next series of poems to be presented. The dwelling place— the glass tower—serves as a "golden door" to the poet's past and to his poetry. But first we have two more poems which might be considered in the domain of prefatory remarks.

In the poem "Ouragan" ("Hurricane"), the narrator speaks as a poet. In the same way that a Milton might consecrate his work by first addressing his muse, Senghor apostrophizes the hot wind of the West African dry season and asks that his work might faithfully reproduce the images of the past. Here, as elsewhere, the Harmattan is associated with purification. Among the moments he wishes to recapture are the games and laughter of children, for in these early works, the Africa which he depicts can only be that of his own childhood or of his imagination. In the final lines, he takes on the guise of a traditional poet, a griot accompanying himself on the kôra and referring once again to his poems as songs: "Embrase mes lèvres de sang, Esprit, souffle sur les cordes de ma kôra / Que s'élève mon chant, aussi pur que l'or de Galam" (Fire my lips with blood, Spirit, blow on the strings of my kôra / That my song might rise as pure as the gold of Galam; *Poèmes,* 9). The motif of purification introduced with the wind returns here in the reference to the gold of Galam, the region of the upper Senegal River where gold was traded. (Senghor's exceptionally effective use of the verset to convey the movement of wind is analyzed at length by Hubert de Leusse.[10])

Following this invocation, Senghor establishes some of his own poetic principles. "Lettre à un poète" ("Letter to a Poet"), addressed to Aimé Césaire, serves (as do the first three works) to point the way to what is to come. The poem stands as a clear tribute to Senghor's friend, an important force in the Negritude movement, and Irele compares it justly to the traditional African praise poem which uses a similar pattern of enumerating attributes in its development.[11] He also suggests that Senghor's depiction of Césaire reveals his own poetic values: his preference for African subjects,[12] for example, and the syncopated rhythm.[13] These lines provide a glimpse of what we will come to associate with Senghor. The title of Césaire's well known opus, *Cahier d'un retour au pays natal,* although not cited in the poem, seems significant in terms of the letter's position as a general introduction to a collection which depicts Senghor's own spiritual return to Africa, and specifically to four poems devoted primarily to idealizing the Africa of his childhood. The notion of returning dominates the poem's last stanza where Senghor, as the African host, invites his friend of the Diaspora to come back and to share with him the sweetness and fellowship of an African evening.

Rehabilitating Africa. Having identified himself as an out-sider who is homesick and ill at ease among strangers and who seeks to revive his memories and traditions, Senghor next offers us a selection of poems about Africa. Unlike the case of *Le Retour de l'enfant prodigue* which appears at the end of the collection, the poet does not construct these poems on the basis of an actual return home. Only in "Joal" does he draw primarily upon his own memories of home, although the other pieces might well contain references to personal experiences. In looking at any of these works it is nec-essary to remember that they are conceived at a distance as a response to the poet's feelings of alienation and under the influence of readings from European ethnologists which had restored to the African stu-dent a sense of his own traditions previously lost or suppressed in the process of Europeanization. They should also be read as subtle polemic, a quiet argument that contrary to colonial dogma, the African was not merely a recipient of Western culture; on the con-trary, his own traditions represented positive values which could conceivably help to revitalize the world. A favorable depiction of Africa and its culture effectively counterbalances our previous ex-perience of negative stereotypes so prevalent in Western literature. On close examination we also discover a set of underlying assump-tions concerning the differences between African and European val-ues. A rather short little poem, "Tout le long du jour . . ." ("All The Day Long . . ."), which describes a train ride as the poet returns in his thoughts to his native land, provides a transition to this series. It also contributes an image for the confrontation of the modern and the traditional: "Tout le long du jour, sur les longs rails etroits / Volonté inflexible sur la langueur des sables . . ." (All day long, on the long narrow rails / Inflexible will on the languor of the sands . . .; *Poèmes,* 11). The rigid, straight lines of the railroad tracks bend to their will the gentle lines of the African countryside.

The first piece in this group, "Nuit de Sine," illustrates values which are for Senghor characteristically African: the sense of com-munity, the presence of nature, the strong spiritual awareness. As the title indicates, the poem captures the beauty of an African night, the Sine being the region where the poet was born. With a woman at his side, the poet enjoys the evening activities of storytelling, dancing, and singing. He describes the sights and smells of the village settling down for the evening and especially the night sounds:

"Ecoutons son chant, écoutons battre notre sang sombre, écoutons /
Battre le pouls profond de l'Afrique dans la brume des villages
perdus" (Let us listen to its chant, let us listen to the beating of
our black blood / the beating of the profound pulse of Africa in the
haze of forgotten villages; *Poèmes*, 12). The beating of the drums
and rhythm of dancing feet echo in the rhythm and sonorities of
the poet's style. In the third stanza the anthropomorphic concept
of nature common to African religions is preserved in the personification of night. Finally, the narrator finds comfort in the presence
of the friendly spirits of the ancestors before dropping off to sleep.
Van Niekerk claims that "few poems in the Négritude tradition . . . have more radiantly succeeded in portraying a part of the
African scene than 'Nuit de Sine,' " and he notes the skillfulness
of the imagery, music, and rhythm.[14] Beyond the beauty of the
poetry, Senghor uses this piece as a veritable dramatization of his
theories of Negritude: a harmonious community extending from the
children to the Ancestors, a people whose lives pulsate in tune with
the essential rhythms of the cosmos. What a contrast between this
idyllic setting and the poems written about Paris. The isolation of
"In Memoriam" gives way to a night humming with human activity
and the awkward conversation between strangers in "Porte Dorée"
is replaced by the warmth and intimacy of the woman's presence.
The poem also evokes the concept of Negritude through the poet's
choice of night as the setting. As we have seen in studying the
significance of the collection's title, Senghor, while accepting the
inevitable poetic analogy between night and the black race, strives
to transform it into a favorable one. In doing so, he disrupts the
normal triad of associations in which black, night, and negative
figure as the contrary of white, day, and positive. The reversal cannot
be consistent in his poetry where dawn is often a positive symbol
of hope, but in his efforts to infuse the image of night with pleasurable connotations, "Nuit de Sine" becomes an important reference
point.

A second poem that idealizes Africa is "Joal," a poetic recon-
struction which recalls the African village in the Sine where Senghor
spent his early school years. Remembering typical scenes from the
life of the town, the writer artfully chooses his vocabulary to favorably influence our idea of Africa. The poem centers on local
ceremonial festivities but the language is such that the setting might
well be classical or biblical. The sacrifices, processions, dances, and

athletic contests contain little of the purely African except by way
of what the imagination supplies. The expressions used evoke scenes
from Homer or from the Western myth of the Golden Age. In the
last lines this wealth of visual and auditory images is consciously
contrasted with the sterility of Europe where Joal is only a memory
of which nothing remains except an occasional bit of jazz. Throughout Senghor's work, Joal constitutes a key symbol denoting the
childhood kingdom.[15] Mezu compares its function to Anjou in the
works of Du Bellay or to the Beauce of Péguy in that it represents
everything which is dear to Senghor: hearth, family, childhood and
native country.[16]

In Senghor's efforts to rehabilitate the image of Africa and to
affirm the existence of African culture, the poem "Femme noire"
("Black Woman") becomes the basis for a new code of feminine
beauty.[17] The significance of this poem must be regarded in the
light of the larger problem of language, of the difficulties involved
in adapting the idiom of the French writer to the needs of his African
counterpart. As in the case of the analogies associated with night
and day, the conventional imagery used for describing a white woman
does not easily weather the change to another race. The African poet
forced to abandon literary traditions must recreate the language and
destroy conventions unconnected or antagonistic to the standards of
beauty of his race. The radical reorientation of perspective appears
immediately in the poem's frequently quoted opening lines: "Femme
nue, femme noire / Vêtue de ta couleur qui est vie, de ta forme qui
est beauté!" (Naked woman, black woman / Dressed in your color
which is life, in your form which is beauty!; *Poèmes,* 14). Tackling
the issue of color, Senghor asserts that black, which is associated
with mourning and death in Western tradition, is for him the color
of life.[18] He confronts the European prejudice that would exclude
specific racial features from the accepted canon of aesthetics and
proclaims them the very essence of beauty. Throughout the poem
he glorifies the black woman by means of imagery inspired by the
color black, by exotic landscapes, and by references to African culture
and history. The conclusion of the poem links it to the *vanitas
vanitate* theme of Western poetry but with a peculiarly African
nuance. While recognizing that beauty is ephemeral—and that the
poet may render it immortal—Senghor also inserts a cyclical notion
of time typical of African thought where, as in nature, death is only
a prelude to life. Since its appearance the poem has attracted a great

deal of attention, not all of which has been favorable. Mezu, who offers an excellent discussion of the poem's cultural significance, has nevertheless pointed out, with justification, that it is "neither very personal or very inspired. It is a beautiful tableau, a little cold, drawn with marvellous images but into which the detached artist has put little of himself."[19] Van Niekerk, while also admiring the poem, claims that it is difficult "not to decry Senghor's poetic insistance on, as it were, 'black sex' as so much poetic attitude . . ."[20] Peters even suggests that the poem can best be interpreted not as the portrait of a real woman but as the description of a statue, and he makes a very impressive case for his theory in a careful analysis of the poem's plastic qualities.[21] It would be impossible to argue the virtue of "Femme noire" as a passionate expression of the poet's love for a particular woman but in spite of speculation to the contrary,[22] there is considerable room for doubt that it was ever intended to be taken as such. Its symbolic value as a milestone in the development of Negritude poetry is tremendous for it implies a cultural and linguistic revolution reaching far beyond the sense of the poem. It also has its place as a source of imagery for Senghor's many other poems celebrating the beauty of women.

It is not enough for Senghor to revive the memories of an African childhood or to depict Africa and its people in such a way as to tear down the old racial stereotypes. His notion of culture requires more than this. Having been brought up among those who believed that the Black had no civilization and nothing to offer to the rest of the world, he was anxious to show that this was simply not true. In African art he found the highly visible evidence to support his case. By the turn of the century African masks and statues had begun to make a serious impression on Western artists to the extent that their influence must be taken into account in any discussion of Cubist painting. This is the context in which to place "Masque nègre," the next poem in the series. Senghor dedicates his description of a mask of Koumba Tam, the Serer goddess of beauty, to Pablo Picasso, and his depiction of the curving lines and shapes which compose the woman's features even suggests the rhythm of a Cubist canvas. The mask in African culture has a religious function, which Senghor maintains. The cheeks are described as patens, the dishes used in communion to cover the chalice and receive the host. The timelessness associated with the sleeping deity whose eyes are "closed on ephemeral things" and whose face bears no trace of expression contrasts with the narrator who, in his mortality, feels all too vulnerable to his own emotions. The poem emerges as both a hymn of praise to the beauty of African art and a tribute to the traditional gods.

Africa and the West.   The four preceding poems deal with Africa in a way which could scarcely be conceived as threatening to a Western reader. They are developed almost without direct reference to France, the last lines of "Joal" constituting a significant exception. From its beginnings African literature in French has had one dominant theme—that of cultures in conflict—and in the next group of four poems, Senghor introduces Europe as a factor in his own poetic equation. This would be the perfect point in the collection to give vent to any feelings of hostility toward colonialism or racism but these sentiments, while they do indeed occur, are rarely blatant in Senghor's work.

First in the series is the poem "Le Message" ("The Message") which laments the erosion of African traditions as a result of colonialism. The setting for this poem takes us back to the time of Africa's empires. No longer the homesick student, the speaker now assumes the role of the African warrior summoned by royal decree to hear from the Prince the message indicated in the title of the poem. The Prince deplores the catastrophes and changes in values which have corrupted traditional society. The principal medium of such changes, Western education, receives an especially strong dose of criticism. The Prince castigates the *assimilés* who have unselectively adopted French culture even to the point of ludicrously affirming that the Gauls were their ancestors. The reference comes from a story often cited by detractors of the French educational system who complained that, since reading materials were the same for the colonies as for France itself, African students might well have had to recite history lessons which told them of their ancestors, the Gauls, with blond hair and blue eyes. Senghor even casts doubts on the meaning of his own intellectual achievements under the French when he has the Prince make fun of those scholars from the Sorbonne who would rather collect pieces of paper, as he terms diplomas, than to collect gold coins as did their fathers before them. The Prince proposes that the glory of the old ways be resurrected and that the speaker heed the voice of his blood, of his race. The subject affirms that he has indeed understood the Prince's message. This meeting between the narrator and the ancestors anticipates *Le*

Retour de l'enfant prodigue at the end of *Chants d'ombre* where a similar symbolic confrontation serves to restore the poet to his people.

Immediately following this enumeration of ills perpetuated by contact with the West, Senghor gives us a poem for the French nurse, Emma Payelleville, who worked among the Senegalese. The placement of the poem in this particular grouping suggests that not everything inherited from colonization was deleterious and tacitly lauds the benefits of Western medical science. First and foremost, the lines are addressed to a dedicated individual who succeeded in overcoming the barriers of race and culture. He places her name in capital letters and using the magic of the poet's word, he prophesies that: "Ton nom brisera les bronzes poudreux des gouverneurs" (Your name will shatter the dusty bronzes of the governors; *Poèmes*, 18). The implied criticism of the colonial administration becomes more explicit in the "Neige sur Paris" ("Snow on Paris").

Only rarely is the poet's sense of isolation as a foreigner intensified by direct reference to either racial discrimination or colonial injustice. "Neige sur Paris" lists the offenses of Europe against Africa, and though ostensibly a prayer for pardon on behalf of those who have persecuted blacks, it manages to communicate strong sensations of hurt and bitterness. In the poem Senghor interprets snow as a purifying agent for Europe's sins, a function which he attributes to salt in Africa. In subsequent lines there is yet another interesting reversal of imagery when white, the color usually associated with innocence and purity, becomes linked instead with villainy:

J'oublie
Les mains blanches qui tirèrent les coups de fusils qui croulèrent les empires
Les mains qui flagellèrent les esclaves, qui vous flagellèrent

(Poèmes, 20)

(I forget
The white hands which fired the shots that crumbled the empires
The hands which scourged the slaves, which scourged you)

Senghor poetically reduces Europe, the perpetrator of destruction, indignity, and exploitation, to the phrase "white hands"; those same hands, he tells us, have condemned him to solitude and, what he considers worse, to hating. Characteristically, the poet places this last indignity on the same level as violent abuse. The Christian God addressed in these lines, incidentally, is depicted as having brown hands, not white. The power of the poem stems from the juxta-position of the history of inhumane acts engaged in by whites against blacks and the sentiment of forgiveness expressed by the speaker.

In "Masque nègre," Senghor praised the beauty of an African mask. By dedicating the poem to Pablo Picasso, he was able to allude indirectly to the influence of African esthetics in modern European art, but he did not mention this influence explicitly in the poem. "Prière aux masques" ("Prayer to the Masks") is devoted specifically to the detailing of what Africa has to offer to the universal banquet of nations. The prayer, offered not to the Christian God as in "Neige sur Paris" but to the ancestors and the masks repre-senting them, begins by invoking these spiritual protectors, in-cluding the writer's totem animal, the lion. From the present chaos—the end of the period of empire and a Europe ravaged by war—he imagines a new world order in which he prays that Africa may play a part much like the leaven which is necessary to white bread. Africa offers richness, not merely by contributing its material wealth of cotton, oil, and coffee which attracted the colonizers, but also in its spiritual essence: the zest for life, joy, and vitality which, for Senghor, are inherent in the black personality. This vision of the future parallels in many respects Senghor's essay entitled "Ce que l'homme noir apporte," which details the characteristics that dis-tinguish African culture and shows how they complement what the author perceives to be the weaknesses of Western civilization.[23] It signals the first instance in which Senghor introduces what Peters calls appropriately "the Messianic note" of Negritude poetry. "The apocalyptic day of destruction caused by the machines of white culture is to be followed by a day of resurrection achieved through the rhythmic flow of sap from a 'civilization sans machine.' "[24] The note is sounded again in the eighth stanza of *Que m'àccompagnent kôras et balafong* and echoes repeatedly throughout *Hosties noires,* the war poems written at a time when it must in fact have seemed that the machines of death would surely triumph. As Joal comes to denote those memories of Africa and its traditional values associated with the poet's childhood, at the other end of time there is, in Senghor's poetic universe, an apocalypse which will ultimately yield to "the rebirth of the World." In such a future, the values of Negritude will represent the contribution of the black to the restoration of civilization.

The most powerful of Senghor's poems on the theme of culture conflict, "Le Totem" ("The Totem"), consists of only seven poignant lines.

> Il me faut le cacher au plus intime de mes veines
> L'Ancêtre à la peau d'orage sillonnèe d'éclairs et de foudre
> Mon animal gardien, il me faut le cacher
> Que je ne rompe le barrage des scandales.
> Il est mon sang fidèle qui requiert fidélité
> Protégeant mon orgueil nu contre
> Moi-même et la superbe des races heureuses . . .
>
> *(Poèmes, 22)*

> (It is necessary for me to hide him in the most intimate of my
>   veins
> The Ancestor with the skin of storm streaked with lightning and
>   thunder
> My guardian animal, it is necessary for me to hide him
> So that I might not break open the dam of scandals.
> He is my faithful blood which requires fidelity
> Protecting my naked pride against
> Myself and the presumption of happy races . . .)

The totem, an animal—in Senghor's case, the lion—which symbolizes the virtues of the clan and which, in the mythic past, actually allied itself to the clan, becomes the emblem of the narrator's African heritage. The poet admonishes himself to hide this most essential part of his identity so that it may not prove to be an embarrassment to him. But the act of hiding the totem has a double sense for not only do we hide that which we do not wish to reveal to the mockery of others, but we also hide treasures to preserve them. Senghor gives the word both meanings since the totem also serves as his guardian animal—a play on guardian angel—which, in return for his allegiance, will be able to protect his pride in his African origins against the disdain of the whites, represented by the expression "happy" races. The short two sentences of the poem terminate in ellipses with whatever elaboration was intended left to the reader's imagination, the few terse lines offering an excellent perspective of a man trying to come to grips with both the fear of being himself and the fear of losing his identity.[25]

Viewed as a separate entity, this group of poems constitutes an eloquent denunciation of political and cultural imperialism and must surely have had great appeal for the militant African nationalists of the period. In "Le Message," the poet mocks the effects of assimilation; in "Neige sur Paris," he depicts an Africa raped and brutalized by the colonial powers. While "Prière au masques" gloriously vaunts the future dominion of African culture in epic terms, "Totem" commands our sympathy for a single individual and his present struggle to maintain his allegiance to those same cultural values. Those who consider that in other collections Senghor mitigates his position vis-à-vis French colonialism would do well to look more closely at these early works, for even here he reflects the complexity of his stance and its many nuances. The vituperous "Neige sur Paris," for example, is ultimately a prayer of pardon addressed to a Christian God, and both the subject and placement of the poem for Emma Payelleville demonstrate quite clearly that in Senghor's affirmation of his own race and cultural heritage he does not correspondingly reject all that he has acquired from Europe. The theme of cultural synthesis that is reiterated in later poems has already been anticipated here in "Prière aux masques."

Senghor's "Spleen" Poems. "Totem" brings the drama of culture conflict down to a touchingly individual level. The next group of poems maintains that lyric quality and continues to depict the anguish of the poet in exile. The mood and imagery of these lines uniformly recall the "Spleen" poems of Baudelaire. The works of the two poets are also similar in the way that they give concrete form to the expression of states of mind. Senghor's "Ndéssé ou 'Blues' " treats the poet's loneliness and lovelessness in surroundings that are far from the tropical settings of "Nuit de Sine" or "Joal." To convey the sense of his not belonging, climate provides the basis for yet another comparison between Europe and Africa. Memories of the warmth of Africa in September stand figuratively for the passion and human warmth that the narrator misses in a colder climate. The title anticipates the oppressive mood of the poem which is further intensified by images of darkness and frustration. The depiction of the poet as a creature helplessly beating his wings against the bars of a lowered sky can be traced to Baudelaire's fourth "Spleen" poem, "Quand le ciel bas et lourd . . . ,"[26] and recalls its dominant theme of ennui. The literary allusion comes as no real surprise from the student whose *mémoire* was entitled "Exoticism in Baudelaire." A repeated use of rhetorical questions—to which no one, of course, responds—deepens the feeling of isolation, and in the auditory imagery of the last line, we hear the sound of rain and the wail of Duke Ellington playing—what else?—"Solitude."[27]

"A la Mort" ("To Death") describes an encounter between the poet and death. It begins on a winter's night with a visit from death itself in the form of a pouncing jungle cat. The poet turns the experience into another opportunity to proclaim his African identity and he envisions the coming of spring when, he tells us: ". . . je manifesterai l'Afrique comme le sculpteur de masques au regard intense" (. . . I will manifest Africa like the sculptor of masks with the intense gaze; *Poèmes,* 24). Like the theme of ennui in "Ndéssé ou 'Blues,' " death is a characteristic subject for Baudelaire, and the striking seasonal imagery of his "Chant d'Automne,"[28] in which the approaching winter symbolizes death, reappears in Senghor's poem. In both works the poets turn to a woman for consolation, but in Baudelaire's case, she can only comfort him temporarily with the memories of summer, while for the African, she anticipates the promise of a future spring. Whether the spring in Senghor's poem refers to his refusal to accept death or to his faith in a life after death as depicted in African religion remains ambiguous, but what clearly separates Senghor from the "poète maudit" is the former's tendency to end his poem on an optimistic chord.

This same optimism marks the poem "Libération," which likewise begins with Baudelairian images of imprisonment, darkness, and despair, but which evolves into figures of liberation, light, and hope. The speaker, a captive, gains his freedom through his own efforts by working steadily at his prison bars with a file. The positive ending is typical of Senghor's own perspective on life; it also illustrates his habitual use of poetry to work through a crisis and to temper despair with hope—the magic of the word. Mezu identifies "Libération" as a commemoration of the writer's liberation from prison camp during World War II, and his facts are generally accurate.[29] There is some reason to believe that the other two poems in the trio might also date from the same period: their styles are similar and they both contain images which refer to prison. If we ignore any biographical reference and interpret "Libération" by virtue of its placement with respect to the other works in the collection, we find a characteristically upbeat ending for the seventeen short poems which compose this part of *Chants d'ombre* and a suitable complement for the initial poem, "In Memoriam." Whereas the poet began on a note of fear and insecurity, he arrives at "Libération" in a mood of hope and anticipation. When he leaves his prison cell behind, the closed space of the "glass tower" gives way to wider horizons. The works between "In Memoriam" and "Libération" provide an exposition of the situation which constitutes the central drama of the collection: the dilemma of race and culture confronting the narrator in "exile." They also furnish the background necessary for his attempt to deal with that dilemma in the three lengthy poems which make up the rest of the volume, and "Libération," with its lines of peace and hope, serves to prepare the way for the eventual resolution of the poet's inner conflict.

The Climax:
Que m'accompagnent kôras et balafong

It is the nature of art to create symbols out of life and to find meaningful patterns in what is otherwise the formlessness of our day to day existence. Such is the process that Senghor records in *Chants d'ombre*.[30] In the face of a situation that threatens his self concept, he rebuilds his personal map of the world in such a way as to enhance his image of himself, his race, and his culture, the idealization which takes place in poems like "Nuit de Sine" and "Femme noire" being only a taste of what we find elsewhere in his poetry. In the process of restructuring the world to reflect his place there more favorably, Senghor, like many artists, focuses on the events and meaning of his own life. *Que m'accompagnent kôras et balafong* attempts to capture these events and, in so doing, becomes the autobiography of the poet from childhood to the outbreak of World War II and, in some measure, a genealogy as well. In it he affirms his African heritage and his commitment to African culture in spite of the temptations of the West. With respect to the other poems in the collection, Peters considers it the climax "in which the poet celebrates the predicament created by a need for choice between the 'two antagonistic worlds' of Africa and Europe. Once he has chosen 'the whole peasant race throughout the world' the downward thrust begins."[31] The poem exalts Africa and attacks traditional stereotypes of the land and its people in a variety of ways and on many levels.

The first stanza captures the poet's early childhood and envelops it in bright and pleasurable images. By direct reference to paradise, by the lushness of its setting, and by the innocence which characterizes both childhood and Adam before the fall from grace, Senghor likens Africa to Eden. "One always associates innocence with childhood. Thus, in this poem, Sengor transfers this human quality to the African continent as a whole . . . As if a Black Adam and Eve had never sinned and were still living in complete innocence in the Black paradise."[32] The children bedecked with flowers, the herdsman and his flute, the festival processions, the dancing warriors and nubile maidens remind us again as in "Joal" of the classical tradition of the Golden Age where man, as yet uncorrupted by civilization, lived in serenity and freedom from want, a convention which also supported the theory of the noble savage so dear to eighteenth-century writers. In future works, Senghor maintains the association depicted here between paradise and childhood. A similar concept exists in Jungian psychology where the security of childhood, untroubled by adult anxieties, also becomes equated with Eden. In Senghor's personal drama the symbolism is more specific, with the childhood paradise signifying that part of his life not yet contaminated by Western ideas he would receive in school—that period when, not yet divided between two worlds and not yet separated from his family, he felt wholly African. Interestingly, paradisiac images often grace the childhood of a mythological hero, with separation from paradise being the first step of his adventure. Senghor successfully idealizes this poetic version of his African childhood and also finds a way to associate it with traditional archetypes.

At the age of eight, Senghor began his general education with the Fathers of the Congregation of the Holy Spirit. The second stanza of the poem identifies this as a first brush with Western ways which could not compete with the child's attraction to his own culture with its games, songs, and fables. The narrator transforms this early experience into an opportunity for choice between Africa and Europe. Using a variation of this theme of choice, in the third stanza he personifies the two cultures as two women, the African Soukeïna and the European Isabelle. The narrator again decides in favor of his African heritage and, as a poet, decides to reflect the rhythm and spirit of Africa in his writing. In the stanza which follows, the poet embodies the two cultures, the deferential *évolué* on the outside who, in his innermost being, has never forgotten that he was nurtured by African poetry and the songs of the griots, the West African musicians and storytellers.

The next three stanzas deal with the nature and history of Senghor's people, the Serers: in the poet's description of a visit of a royal figure, Koumba Ndofène Dyouf, to Senghor's father; in the dramatization of an imaginary dialogue between warriors during an important battle in Serer history; and in a tribute to the royal Princess. For a people whom the French considered tabula rasa, Senghor develops a glorious past and a claim to titles of nobility beyond the aristocracies of Europe. In the eighth stanza, the poet asks to be cleansed by the sun and the sand of his "civilized" ways so that he may march at the head of a new race of Africans, behind whom lie the days of slavery and exploitation and whose future will be founded on the true qualities of Negritude. In anticipation of just such a future, the poet consoles himself, in the last stanza, with his memories, especially those of the African night, the focal image which comes to stand for the integrity of his African identity. After the years spent in Europe under the influence of another culture and its values, he has regained that undivided sense of self he knew as a child.

In contrast with the more plaintive poems of alienation earlier in the collection, the unity of *Que m'accompagnent kôras et balafong* resides in its whole-hearted affirmation of the narrator's Africanness—past, present, and future. In the acknowledgment of its songs and fables and in his preference for its rhythms, Senghor also recognizes Africa as a source for his poetry:

J'ai choisi le verset des fleuves, des vents et des forêts
L'assonance des plaines et des rivières, choisi le rythme de sang de mon
    corps dépouillé
Choisi la trémulsion des balafongs et l'accord des cordes et des cuivres qui
    semble faux, choisi le
Swing le swing oui le swing!

(Poèmes, 28)

(I have chosen the verset of the rivers, winds and forests
The assonance of the plains and rivers, chosen the blood rhythm of my
    naked body,
Chosen the tremulsion of balafongs and the harmony of strings and brass
    which seems false, chosen the
Swing the swing yes the swing!)

While only occasionally militant, he effectively battles pejorative stereotypes of Africa by allying it with the more favorable traditions

of the Golden Age and the noble savage, by supplying it with a
dignified history and culture, and by envisioning its coming great-
ness. The poem is also important for the trappings which it attaches
to the persona of the narrator; the Edenic nature of his childhood,
his warrior heritage, his role as a vassal of a royal house—these are
images which the reader will not be allowed to forget in future
poems. In this respect, Senghor's hero closely parallels the traditional
hero of myth whose background usually includes the implications
of nobility.

The Denouement: *Par-delà Erôs* and *Le Retour de l'enfant prodigue*

In the group of poems entitled *Par-delà Erôs* and in *Le Retour de l'enfant prodigue,* the poet represents his desire to reclaim his African heritage and he does so by developing each of two traditional literary patterns: the romantic quest and the rite of passage. In *Par-delà Erôs,* he portrays the narrator as lover in a series of romantic sketches. The first two—"C'est le temps de partir" and "Depart"—contain specific references to Provence: the Mistral, the Estérel, and Etang de Berre. These allusions lead to the assumption that the poet is drawing on personal experiences but the biographers do not give us an account of any such trip to southern France that might clarify the associations in the poem and, perhaps as a result, the critics have been inclined to give this work a wide berth.

Without adequate background information there is no way to identify the woman—or women—in *Par delà Erôs,* but it is worth noting that throughout these stanzas the woman in the various episodes incarnates Africa. She resembles an African woman from the poet's past: "Toi si semblable à celle de jadis, avec ton visage sarrasin et ta tête noire . . ." (You, so similar to the woman of bygone days, with your Saracen face and your black head . . . ; *Poèmes,* 37). Similarly, he tells her: "Tu fus africaine dans ma mémoire ancienne . . ." (You were African in my ancient memory . . . ; *Poèmes,* 39). In the part called "Chant d'ombre," she is associated with the lion, the poet's totem animal, and in "Vacances" she is linked with the childhood paradise; both images symbolize the narrator's African identity. The relationship is intensified in "Par delà Erôs" where the woman and the African landscape are fused in a stanza which concludes: "Seule, je sais, cette riche plaine à la peau

noire / Convient au soc et au fleuve profonds de mon élan viril"
(Only, I know, this rich plain with black skin / Is appropriate for
the deep ploughshare and river of my virile impulse; *Poèmes,* 42).
This complex of images involving mistress, Africa, and earth haunts
Senghor's poetic universe.

Because of the woman's identification with Africa, the adventure
or adventures in *Par-delà Erôs* take on a significance which is, as
the title indicates, somewhat beyond the erotic. Several of the poems
appear to be allegories representing the poet's struggle to affirm his
identity with respect to his racial and cultural origins. In "Chant
d'ombre" the concept of quest or adventure is particularly evident.
The poem begins with a mystic flight where the poet is carried off
by an eagle in an experience described as a rebirth. He is then faced
with a challenge involving the wooing of a woman. As is characteristic of the heroic adventure, there are obstacles, and the overcoming of the woman's defenses is depicted as the scaling of a
mountain. In the process he incurs wounds, and his blood is spilled
as a symbolic sacrifice. He envisions other tasks of Herculean pro-
portions before the woman finally cedes, a woman whose beauty he
praises to the ancestors.

Sometimes, in myth or fairy tale, the "wooing and winning of
the bride," as Campbell calls it, marks the apex of the hero's journey,
its primary objective; elsewhere, it functions as merely another trial
for the hero. In "Par-delà Erôs" (which bears the same title as the
cycle as a whole) the attaining of the woman, who becomes the very
incarnation of Africa, does not constitute the end of the adventure.
While tempted to stay with her, the narrator acknowledges an even
greater calling which leads him, like the knight of old with his
lady's favor, to set out again under the standards of black and red,
the two dominant colors of African art. The mission that he accepts
foreshadows Senghor's active role in reviving African civilization and
in building the new Africa. By restoring the dignity of the black
man and his traditions, the poet will also, in a way, be reviving
the Eden of his imagination.

In the final poem, *Le Retour de l'enfant prodigue,* we again find
elements of the heroic adventure. In this instance the hero is no
longer in search of the bride and the adventure takes on the form
of what Campbell labels the "atonement with the father":

When the child outgrows the popular idyll of the mother's breast and turns to face the world of specialized adult action, it passes, spiritually, into the sphere of the father—who becomes, for the son, the sign of the future task . . . whether he knows it or not, and no matter what his position in the society, the father is the initiating priest through whom the young being passes on into the larger world.[33]

Le Retour de l'enfant prodigue provides an example of this sort of initiation as indicated even in the title drawn from the biblical story which is itself an illustration of a paternal encounter such as Campbell describes.

Like *Par-delà Erôs,* this poem also envisions the exile's return to Africa. In contrast with its predecessor, it brings the poet face to face with reality while revery and allegory become less important as the poet truly returns to the home where he spent those first golden years of his life. Unlike the young man in the parable whose father meets him bearing rich gifts and announcing the preparation of a lavish feast, Senghor's Prodigal finds death and destruction. The tone of disappointment is inescapable, for while he has succeeded in overcoming the obstacle of Space, he cannot cross the insurmountable barrier of Time. The childhood paradise which he remembers has undergone irreparable change.

The passage of time and the subsequent disintegration of the poet's paradise first become evident through the account of the death of the poet's father in the opening lines. The house where the poet spent his childhood has fallen into a state of disrepair and shows the ravages of time. Because it was built by Basile Senghor, the house is associated with him as is more indirectly the giant tree which once stood in the courtyard. Linked with the father in life, the tree was a symbol of vitality and potency; that it has been cut down is a fitting epitaph. It is a traditional function of the tree in paradise myths to serve as a link between Man and Paradise; the destruction of the tree indicates the breaking of ties between them. The felling of the tree in Senghor's poem seems to carry with it just that connotation—the realization that the childhood paradise as a real place with real dimensions has vanished with the passing years and the disappearance of physical landmarks.

With the father's death, who then will be the Prodigal's "initiating priest?" Throughout the remainder of the poem, the poet

addresses himself to the ancestors whom he calls "Fathers." Untouched by the passage of time, these are the spiritual inhabitants
of Senghor's Eden and the guardians of his Negritude. The son feels
guilty and regrets his long absence, so as on previous occasions,
reconciliation must be preceded by purification, a traditional part
of initiation ceremonies.[34] The remainder of the poem becomes a
reaffirmation of the poet's heritage and a commitment to restore
the traditional values. In this way, the poet makes his peace with
the ancestors to whom he offers total submission and who take on
further characteristics of initiators in providing the insights necessary
to cope with the demands of the Prodigal's new mission to serve as
the ambassador of his people. The narrator announces that in returning to Europe he nevertheless longs for his country. Mezu interprets this aspect of the poem and of the poet's experience as an
abrupt counterpoint to the idealization in which the poet's absence
has permitted him to indulge: the country for which he longs—
the idyllic paradise of childhood—is only a myth and has been
unveiled as such.[35] Considering the role that this myth continues
to play for the writer, it is difficult to give much weight to any
analysis which might interpret this poem as ultimate disillusionment
and demystification. By their rechanneling of his disappointment
into commitment, these lines become another example of Senghor's
ability to use the poem as a means of creating meaning from chaos.

In these last two poems, both of which utilize a form of the
traditional heroic adventure, we see the dramatization of the poet's
own crisis of identity—the alienated individual who described his
plight earlier in the collection has undergone an illuminating experience and has been reintegrated into his surroundings. By the
end of *Chants d'ombre,* the narrator is proudly and vigorously pro-
claiming his African heritage, and while recognizing that the time
of Eden symbolic of his Negritude no longer exists, he continues
to search for it, but in terms of acceptable adult ambitions. The
pattern of events as they are presented in the collection constitutes
a sort of personal mythology which governs the poet's inner universe—a memory of paradise, the traumatic experience of exile, and
a quest to regain paradise which culminates in a new view of the
world and of the poet's responsibility to it. This schema lies at the
heart of Senghor's entire poetic work where the two patterns of
heroic quest consistently reoccur with the romantic quest figuring
prominently in the love poetry and the rite of initiation serving as

a device in the expression of both the writer's own personal trials and those of the newly emerging nation.[36] As an extension of the search for paradise, Senghor's view of the future, like that of the Christian version, also develops an Apocalypse which repeatedly emphasizes the themes of sacrificial death and rebirth and leads to a new world order founded on solidarity and mutual respect among men of all races, a world rehumanized by the values of Negritude.

Chapter Five
Hosties noires

The collection of poems entitled *Hosties noires* (Black hosts, 1948) constitutes a departure from the characteristically personal poetry of *Chants d'ombre*. The change of tone results in part from the nature of the inspiration of this second collection which deals with the events of World War II. As Gaëtan Picon reminds us, the tribulations of war turned out to be something of a catalyst for the creation of new poets in French and especially for the production of what might be termed civic or circumstantial poetry from those whose works had previously been lyric in nature. The people appeared to require voices to testify to the suffering and to sing praises to the heroes.[1] Representing the war from the African point of view, Senghor touches primarily on those aspects of the conflict which involved his race or which he experienced himself. He observes the invasion of Ethiopia and refers to the war's African theater. He emphasizes the contribution of African soldiers who served in France until it fell to the Germans and who were then interned in prison camps for the duration. Some of these lines record the poet's own emotions since he was among those African prisoners of war until he was released in 1942 for health reasons. He also consecrates poems to the black soldiers who fought in the Resistance and to the Afro-Americans who helped liberate Europe. He anticipates the new political order to be established at the end of the war and the more egalitarian relationship between France and her colonies which Senghor himself would help to create. By his choice of subject matter, the poet bears witness to Africa's substantial participation in the war. By interpreting the war through the eyes of the colonized people of Africa, he gives it a significance and a perspective which differ considerably from its conventional depiction in Western literature.

In spite of the new context, these poems repeat many of the themes of the earlier collection or expand on previously developed concepts. In *Chants d'ombre,* Senghor sought images by which his own life history might be told as a heroic adventure. In *Hosties noires,*

72

the same process of idealization serves to glorify the black soldiers. Sent to fight or even to die in a foreign land where they have no traditional bonds, they also share his sense of alienation. Not only do they defend a country which is not their own, but they must do so under the stigma attached to their race by the very nation for which they fight. The virtues of Negritude also reappear. Whether among his comrades in the prisoner of war camps or in the fleeting contact with the Afro-American soldiers, Senghor emphasizes their capacity for joy, their fraternity, their humanity. The war, by throwing the two races together, provides an opportunity to show the interdependence of blacks and whites, and as we saw in "Prière aux masques," the contribution which the African can make to civilization. What was in *Chants d'ombre* generally a personal task of seeking to restore African values is here attributed to others. The theory of Negritude also provides the key for the way Senghor develops a new theme—one which made only a brief appearance earlier—the theme of war. In the midst of death and suffering, men often search for a meaning which might justify war; Senghor links that meaning with the questions of race and colonial oppression. He interprets the death of Africans as necessary for the future of mankind; but the future he envisions is one where Africa's role will be vastly different, where men will be equal, and where the values of Negritude will counterbalance the faults of the materialistic, technological civilization of the West. The title of the collection, *Hosties noires,* reflects this interpretation of death as sacrifice. The context for the expression appears in the poem "Au Gouverneur Eboué" ("To Governor Eboué"): "Voilà que l'Afrique se dresse, la Noire et la Brune sa soeur. / L'Afrique s'est faite acier blanc, l'Afrique s'est faite hostie noire / Pour que vive l'espoir de l'homme" (Behold Africa arising, the Black and the Brown her sister / Africa has become a black host / So that the hope of man may live; *Poèmes,* 72). While the term *"hostie"* commonly refers to the consecrated wafer of the Eucharist, it also signifies the animals sacrificed to the gods in ancient religions, and clearly, Senghor intends his title to convey the concept of sacrifice, the justification of death through the hope of a better future, the theme which repeatedly occurs throughout the collection and which gradually welds itself into a strong political statement that the war was not fought in vain but to prepare some very solid changes in Africa's role in the community of nations.

Along with new themes, there is a discernable difference in the role of the narrator. While several of the poems are highly lyrical, the poet is no longer speaking solely for or about himself, a development which corresponds with Senghor's increasing political involvement. He had been elected as Senegal's representative to the Constituent Assembly in 1945, and in 1946 he won a seat in the French National Assembly under a constitution he had helped to write. In the broadest sense the narrator in *Hosties noires* speaks for his people on whose behalf he delivers a message of protest against injustice, exploitation, and inequality. His poetry becomes an extension of his political function. Most of the poems in the collection indicate the place and date of composition and appear to have been written between 1936 and 1945, a period which preceded Senghor's involvement in politics. Mezu presents good evidence from the works that some of them must have been touched up after the war because they refer so explicitly in several instances to Senghor's political office.[2] The role that he usually admits to in the poetry is considerably more modest—that of the African soldier, an articulate representative of those who suffered and died in the European war. He dons this identity in the poem which constitutes his introduction to the collection, "Poème liminaire" ("Preliminary Poem"): "Vous Tirailleurs Sénégalais, mes frères noirs à la main chaude sous la glace et la mort / Qui pourra vous chanter si ce n'est pas votre frère d'armes, votre frère de sang?" (You Senegalese Riflemen, my black brothers, with your warm hands under ice and death, / Who will be able to sing of you if not your brother in arms, your bloodbrother?; *Poèmes*, 53). The term "Tirailleurs Sénégalais" historically refers not just to riflemen from Senegal but to France's African soldiers in general. When in these opening lines of the collection, Senghor introduces himself as one of them and stresses his fraternal bond of both race and military service, he is taking no poetic license, having been mobilized as a private in 1939 to serve in the French Colonial Infantry. By abandoning in this way the stance of romantic solitude so frequent in *Chants d'ombre* and choosing instead to serve as spokesman for his comrades, Senghor gives a new dimension to his message of protest and racial affirmation. By doing so he must, to a large extent, give up the lyrical expression characteristic of so much of *Chants d'ombre,* a development that causes a little wistfulness on the part of his readers.[3]

Dated April, 1940, and addressed to the African soldiers who died in France, "Poème liminaire," in addition to establishing the voice of the narrator, sets the tone for the collection and provides its rationale, a memorial to the black victims of the war. The poem also expresses Senghor's complex feelings about the conflict. He views with considerable irony the participation of the Africans whose reception in France parallels the narrator's own encounters with prejudice. He labels as inadequate France's gratitude for their services in that those who would honor the fallen dead continue to perpetuate degrading racial stereotypes, one of which he notes in an often-quoted line: "Mais je déchirai les rires *banania* sur tous les murs de France" (I will tear up the *banania* grins on every wall in France; *Poèmes,* 53). He is referring to the familiar advertisement for a breakfast drink displaying the caricatured features of a grinning black face. In reaction to such clichés, Senghor takes up the task of making heroes of the African soldiers, a subject, he claims, which European poets, even in their quest for the most unconventional topics, would never have put to verse: "Car les poètes chantaient les héros, et votre rire n'était pas sérieux, votre peau noire pas classique" (For the poets sang about heroes, and your laughter was not serious, your black skin was not classic; *Poèmes,* 53). On the other hand, the bitterness implicit in the preceding lines does not prevent the poet from expressing genuine admiration for France in a stanza which praises the French as freedom-loving people and shows real sympathy for the plight of the war-torn nation. *Hosties noires,* taken as a whole, is unquestionably Senghor's most scathing indictment of racial discrimination yet he tempers his criticism with a characteristic sense of balance and an acknowledgment of his feeling for France, which delights French readers and irritates militant blacks.

The rest of the collection, a selective, chronological account of the war, consists of two major subdivisions, *Ethiopie* and *Camp 1940,* which are separated by the fall of France to the Nazis. The last poem, "Prière de Paix" ("Prayer for Peace"), set outside the two main sections, provides a fitting finale to the work by examining the implications of the war for the future of Africa.

Ethiopie

Linking the individual poems of *Ethiopie* is the certain progress of the war. As it moves from the Fascist incursions into Africa and Spain to the very heart of France, the poet's involvement becomes increasingly more direct. The distant rumblings of battle in Ethiopia as depicted in "A l'appel de la race de Saba" ("On the Appeal from the Race of Sheba") provide the stimulus for the vision of an imagined armed foray against colonialism, but, by the last poem of the series, "Prière des Tirailleurs sénégalais" ("Prayer for the Tirailleurs of Senegal"), the speaker, now a soldier, prepares for the very real possibility of death on the battlefield and strives to justify his sacrifice and that of his fellow Africans.

The prelude to war. One of the events to signal the onset of the war, the invasion of Ethiopia, inspired the title *Ethiopie* and also the subject of the first poem in the series, "A l'appel de la race de Saba," Saba or Sheba being the realm of the Ethiopian queen known to Western readers from her visit to the biblical King Solomon. By placing his treatment of it first in the collection, Senghor obviously recognized the African conflict as an initial phase of World War II, but the poem itself deals with the Italian initiative as merely one more instance of colonialism on the continent, an affront which Senghor interprets as a personal challenge to his pride in his African heritage. In the seven stanzas of the poem, each introduced by the phrase "Mère, sois benie" ("Bless you, Mother"), he addresses himself to his mother—either his own or, metaphorically, Mother Africa—whom he depicts as angered and sorrowful over this latest violation and disappointed in a son, the poet, who seems to have forgotten the needs of his homeland. In his own defense, the son proves that he can still recall images of his childhood, the time of his life when he felt wholly African and which has therefore remained the symbol of his African self. The litany of images supplements or, for the most part, repeats those which we saw in *Chants d'ombre*: the beauty of the African night, the memory of his family, the songs of the griots. The poet vows fidelity to those images, and in a ceremonial sacrifice to the Ancestors, he prays for the strength to overcome his assimilation, his "civilization." He further reassures the mother that she need not be troubled about the fate of Africa and conjures up an apocalyptic vision of the future in which he is joined in an uprising against colonialism by an armed force drawn from many races and from different corners of the globe. The connection between the evocation of the peaceful scenes of childhood and the final spectacle of the colonized masses moving against the colonial masters is logical in that the first justifies the second. By means of earlier works, Senghor has carefully built up the association between his identity as an African and his years spent in a primarily traditional setting. We know that in these memories resides the certainty of the value of his Negritude. The poet uses this reference to his personal struggle to strengthen an argument against the existing political situation. The message of the poem, a call for independence even at the expense of armed revolution, is an unusually strong one for Senghor. Marcien Towa, in *Léopold Sédar Senghor: Négritude ou servitude?,* has made much of the militancy of this one work. While he normally criticizes Senghor for failing to be sufficiently committed to the overthrow of imperialism, this particular instance provokes his admiration.[4] Not only militant but leftist as well, the theme of revolution bears traces of Senghor's brief flirtation with socialism as does the nature of the army he envisions: Africans of different tribes and religions are joined in his imagination by members of the European proletariat—laborers, dockers, miners.

Continuing to follow the gathering war clouds, Senghor introduces a poem which refers to the 1937 bombing by the Germans of the Spanish town of Almeria. Allusion to the incident is central to the poet's account of a voyage by sea from Marseille to Dakar in "Méditerranée" where the bombing figures as a symbol of the violence of the peoples who inhabit the northern shore of the Mediterranean. In contrast, the poet and his fellow passenger, a countryman, turn their thoughts to Africa, which carries only peaceful, pleasant memories and sensations. The friendship of the two black men stands out sharply against the brutal background of the Spanish conflict in what develops into a quiet but powerful study in comparative cultures.[5]

In an apparent departure from the chronology of events associated with World War II, the next work in the collection deals with World War I. On the brink of a new conflagration, we are asked to remember the previous one and the extent of the African involvement in the past. It may not always be noted in the history books that among the fatalities of World War I were 30,000 African soldiers. The poem "Aux Tirailleurs sénégalais morts pour la France" ("To the Senegalese *Tirailleurs* Who Died For France") takes as its point of departure the relative public ignorance of their role and pathetically salutes those who lie buried and forgotten in cold graves under the soil of a foreign land. The irony of their death sings in the last line which quotes the epitaph often carved on the tombs of French soldiers who died in battle: MORT POUR LA REPUBLIQUE. The colonial soldier has given his life for the republic—not his own

country, but that of the colonizer. What tied these lines to the
events of the year when they were composed, 1938, was the upsurge
in the recruitment of African soldiers in preparation for a new war:

'On fleurit les tombes, on réchauffe le Soldat Inconnu.
Vous mes frères obscurs, personne ne vous nomme.
On promet cinq cent mille de vos enfants à la gloire des futurs morts, on
    les remercie d'avance futurs morts obscurs
Die Schwarze schande!

(Poèmes, 62)

(They are putting flowers on the graves, they are warming up the Unknown
    soldier again.
You, my dark and unsung brothers, nobody calls your names.
They are promising five hundred thousand of your children to the glory
    of future deaths, they are thanking them in advance for future dark
    and unsung deaths
Die Schwarze schande!)

The poet anticipates a second sacrifice of African troops and in the
process reminds his readers at the time of publication ten years later
that Europe owes a debt to two generations of Senegalese Riflemen.

    Despair and hope.   Death continues to be a major theme
throughout the remaining poems of *Ethiopie* and in all three poems,
there is a figurative association between death in war and death in
nature. In "Luxembourg 1939," this analogy serves only to intensify
the poet's feelings about death as he anticipates the coming of war.
In "Désespoir d'un volontaire libre" ("Despair of a Free Volunteer")
and "Prière des Tirailleurs sénégalais" he develops the nature imagery, treating death not as an end of life, but as a prelude to rebirth
in the cycle of seasons. He comes to view the death of soldiers in
battle, specifically African soldiers, as the sacrifice upon which a
better post-war world may be built. In spite of the increasing near-
ness of the war and its inevitable cost in human lives, *Ethiopie* moves
in a crescendo to a relatively hopeful finale.

    "Luxembourg 1939" describes a visit to the Luxembourg Gardens,
a beautiful park on the Left Bank which is normally a haven for
university students. On the eve of the German occupation, the park,
like the rest of Paris, prepares for the attack. The poet's plaint that
the nearly deserted garden sports neither its usual array of flowers
nor its habitual throngs of children and young people becomes more

than just an accurate observation as the poem progresses, for the absence of living things reinforces the poem's despair at the approach of death. The garden that has always been a gathering place for the young—Senghor recalls his own student days—reminds the poet of the young soldiers destined to die in the war. The autumnal season, the dead leaves, the gravelike trenches further establish the uncharacteristic pessimism of the poem which, in conclusion, mourns: "L'Europe qui enterre le levain des nations et l'espoir des races nouvelles" (Europe which inters the leaven of nations and the hope of new races; *Poèmes*, 64). In speaking of the death of hope, the poet leaves the reader with a totally unqualified sense of impending doom.

From a general reflection on death as an abstract idea, Senghor turns, in "Désespoir d'un volontaire libre," to the narration of a specific incident. Based on an actual situation, the tale describes not a victim of the hostilities but the suicide of an African soldier as recounted by the newspapers from which is quoted the reaction of the soldier's superior officer: "I don't understand it," said the sergeant-major. "A Senegalese—and a volunteer!" Senghor's version tries to explain why a volunteer would choose to kill himself and transforms the incident into a variation on the persistent theme of racial discrimination, the suicide becoming an affair of honor. Senghor imagines what the young man might have been thinking which would have led to his death. He supposes that the soldier was trying in vain to justify his service in the war under those who treated him without respect and who considered his offer to fight for a foreign country as the action of a mere mercenary, this last affront being only one more in a line of indignities which included taxes, forced labor, punitive whippings, and the feeling that his fellow soldiers had died for nothing. Seeing no relief from his persecution, he leaps to his death.

Senghor depicts the soldier as a man who believes that his honor has been irreparably offended. Elsewhere, in one of his essays on Negritude, he discusses the concept of honor in African ethics:

More important than the duties toward one's neighbor are those to oneself. It is not only a question of requiring and receiving marks of *téranga* (honor, respect), but also and especially of affirming and protecting one's *person*. This is essentially affirmed through *courage* and *generosity* which are noble virtues. But the person can be insulted and, sometimes, Destiny denies us any effective response. Under those circumstances, we have only one solution: to abandon our vital breath in order to save our personal life, our soul. *Suicide is the last requirement of Susceptibility, daughter of Honor.*[6]

With no alternative in sight, Senghor's code would appear to permit suicide for the cause of honor but what makes this poem so tragic is that, while the young soldier has lost all hope, Senghor can find a meaning in the war's present dishonor and suffering which would provide a justification for them. The poet sees what the soldier cannot: "Il ne voit pas que les morts et les terres hautes des morts masquent les champs là-bas qui verdoient dans l'ombre / D'or et d'étoiles constellés, comme arrosés du sang à leurs pieds et des cadavres gras bien nourris" (He does not see that the dead and the land piled high with the dead hide the fields beyond, which grow green in the shadow / Studded with gold and stars, as if watered by the blood at their feet, and nourished by the stout corpses; *Poèmes,* 65). Earlier in the poem, the boy compared the bodies of the dead to "sterile seeds," but the poet stresses instead, like Walt Whitman, the green fields nurtured by the bodies of the dead and implies that there is, after all, significance in their sacrifice. Whether Senghor finds some satisfaction in the eternal cycle of nature or whether the flowering green fields denote symbolically a new political future remains ambiguous, but in the following poem, "Prière des Tirailleurs senégalais," nature imagery is clearly used to convey a message of social and political import.

Like the two previous poems, this last piece in the series *Ethiopie* treats the theme of death. As in "Poème liminaire," the poet speaking as a simple soldier "among the humblest soldiers," becomes the voice of his comrades formulating a prayer to God as they prepare to die. Central to the meaning of the poem, the image of harvest occurs at several levels. In the second stanza, the soldiers regret that they might not survive the spring and the writing of the poem to see the end of summer, the maturation of the crops and the harvest festival with its traditional dancing and rites of passage. But the war itself is also a form of harvest, "la machine à recruter dans la moisson des hautes têtes" (the recruiting machine in the midst of the harvest of high heads; *Poèmes,* 66). In the agricultural cycle the cutting of the ripe crops only serves to prepare the ground for the planting of new ones, and in the third stanza Senghor extends the implication of rebirth to the image of war as harvest when he depicts it as preparing a better world characterized by the absence of racial prejudice: "Que l'enfant blanc et l'enfant noir—c'est l'ordre al-phabétique—, que les enfants de la France Confédérée aillent main dans la main" (That the black child and the white child—this is the alphabetical order—that the children of Confederated France may go hand in hand; *Poèmes*, 69). The soldiers interpret their sacrifice as the material necessary to ready the soil for this new crop. In the eternal rebirth of nature, Senghor finds a way of giving meaning to the war and the fatalities it inflicted on the African regiments, a significance which was particularly appropriate in the light of the struggle to improve Africa's political situation in the period following World War II when the collection appeared.

In conjunction with this primary theme, there is another, com-plementary theme, that of the affirmation of life in the face of death. Certainly the symbolism of the cyclical movement of nature denies the dominion of death; the poet also stresses the zest for living of his comrades whose prayer is to savor fully the time which is left to them. This appreciation for life with all its sensations, and the strong empathy with nature which is evidenced in the poem, il-lustrate the temperament which he believes distinguishes the African from the European, a development of the concept of Negritude which becomes more pronounced in the second sequence of poems in *Hosties noires, Camp 1940.*

Camp 1940

One evening in 1941, Georges Pompidou, the future president of France, answered a knock at his door to find himself face to face with an Austrian soldier. The soldier was not there to arrest him but to turn over to him for safe-keeping some poems written in the prison camp where he was a guard by a former classmate of Pom-pidou, Léopold Senghor. A number of these poems figure in the subdivision entitled *Camp 1940,* which covers a period from 1940 and Senghor's captivity after the surrender of France, until 1944 and the liberation of Paris. The poems continue to emphasize the black involvement in the war: the response of Africa to de Gaulle's plea for support, the life of the African prisoners of war, the par-ticipation of blacks in effecting the coming of peace. Some of these works might well be categorized as poetry of circumstance, but here and there, a more lyric, personal quality prevails.

De Gaulle's challenge and Eboué's response. On 14 June 1940, France surrendered, leaving the fate of her African troops in the hands of the victors. On 18 June, Senghor, a prisoner of war, began his internment in a series of camps situated at La Charité-sur-Loire, Poitiers, Amiens, and then near Les Landes. Feeling abandoned by the French, he held out hope for the efforts of Charles de Gaulle who, having refused to surrender to the Germans, had fled to Britain to become the head of the Free French movement. As early as 18 June 1940, he had launched an appeal for resistance which Senghor recognizes in the poem "Au Guélowâr" ("To the Guélowâr"). The term "guélowâr" refers to the nobles descended from the Malinké warriors, the caste which provided the rulers of the kingdoms of Sine and Saloum; the shared consonance makes the epithet particularly appropriate for the French hero addressed in the poem, Charles de Gaulle.[7] The poem, written from the camp at Amiens in September 1940 and narrated in the first person plural, carries a dual message. It conveys the soldiers' sense of helplessness in the face of events by comparing them to birds fallen from the nest or wild animals which have been declawed. The Africans feel strongly betrayed by those for whom they had been fighting; neither the church nor the government, whose magnanimity is compared to that of hyenas in an extension of the use of animal imagery, seems to focus on the plight of the blacks, and the poet is extremely bitter. But the second theme of the poem is, miraculously, that of faith in the Republic and hope in the future inspired by de Gaulle's refusal to capitulate. The poet can even envision a new city being raised up "in the equality of fraternal peoples."

While much of France's African territory supported the Nazi-occupied Vichy regime, Félix Eboué, governor of Chad, became the first African leader to swing his support behind de Gaulle. A black from the West Indies, he won Senghor's admiration, which the poet expresses in "Au Gouverneur Eboué" ("To Governor Eboué"). The poetic model for this particular work might well be the praise poem of traditional African literature, an oral form used to celebrate an individual's valor or success. Senghor compares Eboué to a rock and a lion with the intention of lauding both the fidelity and the courage of this important political figure who would become his father-in-law. The poem is dedicated to Eboué's two sons, Henri and Robert, whom Senghor had met in the prison camps. This poem also speaks of the African participation as a contribution to the safeguarding of the future of mankind. The emphasis on the war as preparation for a better future, here and in "Au Guélowâr," will be reiterated throughout the rest of the collection.

   The prison camp poems.   The poems inspired during the period of Senghor's captivity reveal a variety of tone, perspective, and poetic form. In the poem which bears the same name as the group of poems, "Camp 1940," he describes the barrenness and misery of Front-Stalag 230 and the nature of camp life. "Taga de Mbaye Dyob" ("Taga for Mbaye Dyob"), using the *taga* or praise song formula and numerous traditional motifs and images, honors one of Senghor's fellow prisoners. "Assassinats" ("Assassinations") is another eulogy for the African soldiers in France; "Femmes de France" ("Women of France") acknowledges the role of the French women whose letters provided encouragement for the prisoners of war. Assuming a more personal tone, Senghor describes his own suffering as a captive in "Ndessé," the title being Senghor's translation of the word "blues," and in "Lettre à un prisonnier" ("Letter to a Prisoner"), he compares life in the prison camp among comrades to his mode of life after being released from captivity, free but sullied by racial discrimination. In spite of this diversity, the principal themes of most of the poems are so similar as to constitute repetitiveness, and the poet's central message varies little from that in *Ethiopie*. While in the previous sequence of poems Senghor speaks frequently of the debt which France owes to those Africans who died in the war, in *Camp 1940* he points to the suffering of the Africans as prisoners of war and especially to the support which they provided for their white comrades. The period of captivity constitutes part of the sacrifice which should be rewarded by the creation of a more egalitarian society.

   In a sense, the prison camp develops into a microcosm of just such a society, the relationship of the two races becoming a second major theme. Turning the tables on the concept of the white man's burden, Senghor argues the dependency of the whites on the blacks, for the latter, in the poems, look after the white prisoners, bear their burdens, comfort them, and distract them. In both "Camp 1940" and "Taga de Mbaye Dyob," Senghor even suggests that except for the needs of their white companions, the Africans would long since have found a means of escaping. The description of the Africans mirrors Senghor's ideal of the black personality and highlights the music, laughter, spontaneity, and fellowship among the black soldiers, qualities which provide necessary sustenance in the time of trial. In "Ndessé," the poet, in trying to deal with his personal despair and humiliation, returns to the memories of his childhood, the source of his African identity, in search of the comfort and pride he finds in his own Negritude. Elsewhere, he contrasts the virtues of Negritude with war and its machines of death which he considers manifestations of Western culture, and in "Assassinats," the confrontation is explicit as he addresses the black martyrs; "Le chant vaste de votre sang vaincra machines et canons . . ." (The vast song of your blood will conquer machines and cannons . . . ; *Poèmes,* 75). For Senghor, the prison camp poems represent a testing ground that proves the value of what the African has to contribute to the universal civilization of all races.

These poems succeed only to the extent that the premises related to Negritude which they illustrate are palatable for the individual reader. Van Niekerk labels "Camp 1940," "one of the truly great poems to have come out of World War II" because of its compelling description of the poet's life as a prisoner of war. "The whole gamut of his captivity experiences are recalled here: the destruction of the hopes of young men, the miserable living conditions and the hate-ridden and hungry inmates, the humiliations, the dreams of warm African nights, but also the resignation of people who believe in the saving mercy of destiny."[8] Obviously, for one critic at least, the poet's symbolism is so closely woven into a faithful, moving account of the prison setting that it in no way distracts from the effectiveness of the poem. In referring to the same work, Mezu finds Senghor's presentation of the black soldiers, characterized here by "the candor of their laughter," not merely extremely idealized but in paradoxical conformity with the usual Western stereotype of blacks. Senghor's African soldiers, Mezu tells us, are always smiling: "Thus, the poet instead of 'tearing up the *banania* grins on the walls of France' seems incapable of getting rid of them himself; he finds them everywhere and multiplies them around him."[9] Mezu's point is well taken and demonstrates the unfortunate way in which Negritude's racial dichotomies, by their very predication of inherent racial characteristics, have a tendency to misfire in such a way as to support rather than to dissipate racist assumptions.

Ostensibly for reasons of health and due to the influence of several notable French figures, Senghor was removed from the camp in 1942 and finished out the war near Paris where he wrote "Lettre à un prisonnier." Addressed to a comrade he had left behind in the camp, the letter recalls with relish the sense of community with which the poet endows prison life and the association with the black soldiers whose songs and stories revived memories of his childhood. He creates an opposition, not between life in the prison camp and life as a free man, but between the fraternity of his black comrades in captivity and the renewed isolation of a black man living in a white man's world. He speaks of his black skin as another sort of prison and as a cage of solitude. To his former fellow prisoners he describes his plight: "Vous ignorez les restaurants et les piscines, et la noblesse au sang noir interdite / Et la Science et l'Humanité, dressant leurs cordons de police aux frontières de la négritude" (You do not know the restaurants and swimming pools, and the nobility denied to black blood / And Science and Humanity, setting their police cordons along the frontiers of negritude; *Poèmes*, 81). The period of captivity which should have enhanced the narrator's appreciation of liberty has merely provided a powerful metaphor for alienation.

The end of the war. As autumn denoted the coming of war in "Luxembourg 1939," seasonal imagery in "Chant de Printemps" ("Spring Song") heralds the coming of peace. Presented as a dialogue between the poet and a young woman who may well be only the personification of the poet's inner voice, the poem offers alternative reactions to the war.[10] The woman, referring both to the bombing of Dakar and of Europe, focuses on the destructive force. The poet anticipates the coming of peace and the new order prepared by the war: "la vie qui fait vagir deux enfants nouveau-nés au bord d'un tombeau cave" (the life which makes two newborn babies cry at the edge of a hollow tomb; *Poèmes*, 85). Rebirth images representing the fecundity of nature are reinforced by the poet's avowal of desire, newly awakened by the forces of Spring.

Senghor introduces a new theme in this poem which reappears with variation throughout the remainder of the series—the interpretation of war as divine punishment. In his depiction of war's havoc, the blood of the Europeans flows "redder than the Nile," a reference to Moses' turning that river to blood in his efforts to persuade the Pharaoh to release the Israelites from bondage; the Egyptians were further to know the power of God on that occasion when He sent the angel of death to kill their first-born sons. Senghor asks if the war's destruction and bloodshed are not other examples of God's wrath. He represents the African soldiers not as objects of God's chastisement but as His instruments against Europe: "Est-ce sa faute si Dieu fait de ses fils les verges à châtier la superbe des nations?" (Is it her [Africa's] fault if God makes of her sons rods to chastise the pride of nations?; *Poèmes*, 85). In Senghor's imitation of the figurative style of African languages, bombers become eagle-fortresses and the flaming cities are compared to dry grass which has been set on fire at the end of the dry season, a common sight in the African savanna. The lightning which sometimes causes such fires becomes the metaphor for the bombardment itself. "Aux soldats négro-américains" ("To The Black American Soldiers") introduces this fire as the thunderbolt of Jove and refers to the burning of Sodom and Gomorrah: "Frères, je ne sais si c'est vous qui avez bombardé les cathédrales, orgueil de l'Europe / Si vous êtes la foudre dont la main de Dieu a brûlé Sodome et Gomorrhe" (Brothers, I don't know if you are the ones who bombed the cathedrals, Europe's pride / If you are the lightning by which the hand of God burned Sodom and Gomorrah; *Poèmes*, 87). He imagines that the black American soldiers participating in the liberation of France might also have crewed the bombers that fired the cities. While assuming that Europe has committed sins for which the war serves as God's method of chastisement, he remains vague about the exact nature of those sins, but "Prière de paix" ("Prayer for Peace"), the final poem of the collection *Hosties noires,* identifies these transgressions as Europe's exploitation of the black. "Aux soldats négro-américains" and "Pour un F.F.I. noir blessé" ("For A Wounded Black F.F.I."), a vignette of a black hero of the Resistance, illustrate the truly comprehensive nature of the black contribution to the war effort. Senghor also notes the sense of brotherhood he feels with the black American soldiers who exhibit characteristic attributes of Negritude.

Images of martyrdom and purification return again in "Tyaroye," a poem not directly inspired by the events of the war but rather by the massacre of unruly Senegalese troups by the French at Thiaroye, a transitional camp for the repatriation of former prisoners of war located on the outskirts of Dakar. [11] The poet asks: "Et votre sang n'a-t-il pas ablué la nation oublieuse de sa mission d'hier? / Dites, votre sang ne s'est-il mêlé au sang lustral de ses martyrs?" (And has not your blood cleansed the nation forgetful of her former mission? / Tell me, has not your blood mixed with the purifying blood of her martyrs?; *Poèmes*, 88). Asking further whether this sacrifice will have been in vain, the poet responds with a resounding "no!" and another reference to the new world to be created in the future as a result of their efforts. The last line of the poem and that of the series *Camp 1940* is addressed directly to those who died: "Dormez ô Morts! et que ma voix vous berce, ma voix de courroux que berce l'espoir" (Sleep, O Dead! and let my voice cradle you, my angered voice cradled by hope; *Poèmes,* 89). This line, not merely a statement but a commitment, terminates the series on a word which strongly marks the entire collection: "hope."

The beginning of peace. Rounding out the collection is a five-stanza poem entitled "Prière de Paix." Having come to regard the war as evidence of God's displeasure with the white race, Senghor, on behalf of persecuted blacks, turns to God to ask forgiveness for France and an end to the war's suffering. As in "Neige Sur Paris," the poem becomes a vehicle by which the poet may list all the offenses that he wishes pardoned: the destruction of his homeland, the humiliation and persecution of his people, the slave trade. He notes particularly the inconsistency between Christian principles and Christian behavior on the part of the colonists and even the missionaries. To bring his argument closer to home, he offers a timely parallel between France and Africa by using terms such as occupation, resistance-fighter, torture, and deportation to depict the plight of colonized peoples. He also compares Africa's struggle for human dignity to the democratic ideals of the French Revolution. It is impossible not to sense, in this extensive list of grievances, some irony in the poet's contention that his prayer is one of pardon; he has made such an excellent case for the prosecution. Nevertheless, untempered hostility does not characterize Senghor's writing. He claims that while hating evil, he has a weakness for France. He recognizes that country's losses in the war and ends the poem by asking God's blessing on France and on all people everywhere that they might, in the wake of this global conflict, join hands fraternally under the rainbow of His peace. The rainbow, the sign God gave to Noah after the flood as a promise that earth would never again know similar disaster, also appropriately symbolizes the harmony of men of all colors.

This poem, which describes so graphically Africa's grievances against the French, has ironically received an unusual amount of negative criticism on the grounds that it is not sufficiently and uniformly hostile to France and because of its conciliatory frame-

work. Senghor has been repeatedly lambasted for his use of the
notion of pardon in conjunction with the enumeration of Europe's
sins against the colonies and for the emphasis on universal brotherhood.[12] He is also depicted as trying to present his case against
colonialism without endangering his political effectiveness. Mezu
claims that the poem is weakened because we cannot tell whether
it is the poet or the politician speaking, and he also announces a
"new ambivalence" on the part of the poet which will dominate
future collections.[13] Moore calls the poem a triumph for assimilation
rather than for Negritude.[14] Such criticism somehow implies that
Senghor's poem would be improved if only he were to repress the
complexity inherent in France's relationship with her colonies and
in his attitude toward that relationship, that the work would profit
from a narrowly focused single-minded expression of rage. Such a
position would be totally uncharacteristic of Senghor. The use of
the terms "ambivalence" and "assimilation" are clearly appropriate
in speaking of "Prière de la paix," but in our opinion, they need
not be applied pejoratively. As early as 1937, in his speech to the
Dakar Chamber of Commerce, Senghor had affirmed his admiration
for French culture,[15] and by 1945, he had distinguished between
the active verb "to assimilate," which he regarded as positive, and
the passive "to be assimilated," which he rejected.[16] "Prière de la
paix" only illustrates this selective assimilation of French values
encouraged by the writer in his essays. The poem does not really
represent a new stand in his poetry either, since the concept of
forgiveness for France appeared earlier in both "In Memoriam" and
"Neige Sur Paris" and the theme of a universal civilization also
appeared previously in *Chants d'ombre*. Far from representing a be-
trayal of the poet's values, this concluding work of *Hosties noires*
serves to confirm ideas he has long held. Those who would want it
to develop otherwise may be indulging in a bit of wishful thinking
which is more political than literary in inspiration. As the poem
now stands, the writer's success in reshaping his various and sometimes incompatible allegiances into a homogeneous view of the
future constitutes no meager victory for man's imagination in the
face of the world's absurdity.

Conclusion.   Unquestionably, *Hosties noires* has its political side.
Nearly every poem argues, however indirectly, that the only fitting
memorial to the black victims of the war would be an improvement
in the status of the colonies and the elimination of racial discrim-

ination, changes which by their very nature would require government action. The audience for the poems would hardly have been the unlettered African veterans of the war or even the Senegalese representative's bushland constituency. Writing in French, Senghor must surely have intended his work to stir up a sense of injustice among those who could accomplish the most to rectify the situation, the French themselves. Dedications to politically influential figures—de Gaulle, Pompidou, the Eboués—and the generally mitigated tone of the poems beg to be considered the diplomatic gestures of an astute politician seeking to enlist support for his cause. The overt idealization of the African soldier, which has prompted one critic to remark that in Senghor's work "all black soldiers are strong and loyal,"[17] must also be considered as a useful rhetorical device in line with the poet's political objectives rather than an imbalance in his perception.

Considerably more than a political maneuver, *Hosties noires* has its place in the development of Senghor's poetic universe. At the end of *Chants d'ombre,* in *Le Retour de l'enfant prodigue,* the poet discovered that the paradise of childhood was no longer accessible to him. While it continues to serve in the poetry as a potent memory and a source of inspiration, he knows that it does not exist in the here and now. At the close of the poem he projected his quest elsewhere, vowing service to the cause of his people, the new goal of both Senghor the poet and Senghor the politician. In his imagination time stands polarized, with the paradise of childhood at one end and the vision of a better future for Africa at the other. In *Hosties noires,* Senghor transforms the war into a step in the direction of a new world whose creation fulfills his objective. It functions symbolically as do the simulations of death in traditional rites of passage to signify the end of an era and a purification of old sins. The sacrifice indicated in the title becomes the source of greater strength for the community. The transition from the despair of autumn to the hope of spring, from "Luxembourg 1939" to "Chant de Printemps," supports the notion that, for Senghor, the death and destruction of war are but a prelude to regeneration. Day, dawn, and the final image of the rainbow depict the state of the world after the war and signify man's entry into a new period of history to be characterized by racial harmony and based on the full participation of African culture.

Chapter Six
The Senghorian Woman

Poems about women or on the theme of love figure prominently in Senghor's work. In *Chants d'ombre*, the poem "Femme noire" crowned the poet's early efforts to rehabilitate the image of black women in literature, and in *Par delà Erôs*, he depicted his search for identity in terms of a romantic quest. "Chant de Printemps," one of the poems dealing with the end of the war in *Hosties noires*, used the hope for the future implicit in young love to convey the poet's faith in a new world order. Several subsequent collections center primarily around women and love: "Chants pour Signare," "D'autres chants," "Epîtres à la Princesse," and *Lettres d'hivernage*. These works contain some of Senghor's best poetry as the poet seems to acknowledge when he tells us that "I would burn all of my prose texts to save a single one of these love poems."[1] While the last collection will be discussed separately later, the two collections of "Chants" and "Epîtres à la Princesse" invite treatment together in that they represent two complementary facets of Negritude, both of which are depicted as love stories.

The first person narrator who characterized *Chants d'ombre* and never really disappeared in *Hosties noires*, returns in the love poems, which seem likewise to have their origins in the poet's personal life. "Chants pour Signare," published in 1961 as part of the collection entitled *Nocturnes*, was a revision of an earlier work, *Chants pour Naëtt*, written when Senghor was married to Ginette Eboué, the "Naëtt" of the title, but from whom, by the date of the second publication, he was divorced. The changes in the second version involved only minor adjustments of style and content, the latter including a certain abstraction of the black woman who is the focus of the poem. In 1957, Senghor married Colette Hubert of Normandy, and to an extent, their courtship is the subject of "Epîtres à la Princesse," published in 1956 in *Ethiopiques*.

The biographical element in these works inevitably cedes to the poems' symbolic intent; in this regard, Senghor's depiction of women differs little from that of his fellow African writers. With practically no women authors to give realism and psychological depth to women characters in the Francophone African works of this period, they tended to figure only in supporting roles or to clarify the personality of the male protagonist. Writing whose principal theme was culture conflict often reduced women to personifications of the vices or virtues of either the modern or traditional viewpoint. Senghor's women exist almost solely as love objects or as culture symbols. The black woman in his poems almost always embodies the values of Negritude, itself a variation of the theme of traditional Africa. The couple in "Epîtres à la Princesse" prefigures the union of black and white cultures, Senghor's concept of cultural crossbreeding, with the male protagonist this time representing Negritude and the woman, Western civilization. It would be inaccurate to suggest that the women in the poems have no individual personalities but they have very little to offer by way of character development or as a psychological study. Senghor's depiction of African women has received some justifiable criticism in this respect: "His enthusiastic images of African women are of limited usefulness in the understanding of woman's actual situation in Africa because these images are so uniformly, and cloyingly, idealized."[2] With this caveat in mind we must deal with the Senghorian woman as she exists, a vehicle for the poet's ideas.

The Image of Woman in "Chants pour Signare" and "D'autres chants"

In spite of the different publication dates, the cycle of twenty-one short love poems in "Chants pour Signare" (*Nocturnes,* 1961) and the little group of poems in the same vein entitled "D'autres chants" (*Ethiopiques,* 1956) share a family resemblance in subject matter and form as well as in the depiction of the woman they address. Throughout both collections, the woman in the poems becomes a personification of the poet's African ideal and comes to be associated with a set of characteristic types of images and connotations. She is described physically in terms of the African terrain and especially the childhood paradise; as Mother Africa she is occasionally a maternal figure, and sometimes she is presented as a divinity on the same plane as the ancestors. Above all, she is the poet's mistress and a human lover capable of arousing passion.

Senghor's own interpretation of the African concept of woman renders her an especially appropriate symbol for Negritude. She represents the continuity of the race and the preservation of traditions: "Woman, being the permanent member of the family and the giver of life, has been dignified as the source of vital force and as guardian of the clan's future."[3] This role assumes greater significance when we remember the religious implications attached to the propagation of the clan in African tradition: one must have children to assure one's survival after death in their prayers and sacrifices. In addition to this social function, the female, by her very temperament, projects more than the male, the values of Negritude for she is more sensitive to the cosmic forces and more easily touched by the emotions of joy and sadness.[4] So keenly attuned to her environment, woman illustrates the relationship with nature which Senghor believes typical of black culture and which he sees as the key to the revitalization of civilization. While the symbolic value which Senghor assigns to the black woman is solidly rooted in African philosophy, it also has origins in the French literary tradition which, throughout the ages, has used the image of a woman to crystallize male ideals. Senghor's cycles of love poems to a woman who manifests the virtues of Negritude recall the sonnets of the Pléiade with their overtones of neo-platonism. Similarities of treatment also suggest a debt to Baudelaire's poems to Mme de Sabatier.[5]

One of the most interesting consequences poetically of Senghor's persistent association between the woman and Africa is to be found in his penchant for portraying her in terms of landscape imagery. It is the background against which she is presented, and its vegetation and terrain provide the metaphors with which to describe her. In other instances, her image is imposed upon the face of the land. There appears to exist for Senghor a certain correspondence between the two which renders them inseparable and, in some instances, even indistinguishable. This parallel occurs even on the thematic level with separation and longing characterizing the love relationships in the same way that exile and nostalgia for home dominate *Chants d'ombre*. When the lover must go away in "Chants pour Signare," he expresses his regret at leaving both the place and the loved one: "Je regretterai le pays natal et la pluie de tes yeux sur la soif des savanes" (I will miss the native land and the rain from your eyes on the thirst of the savannas; *Poèmes,* 170). Here the woman and the land manage to retain their separate identities, but elsewhere in the cycle the African setting exists only to furnish images with which to describe the woman: "mon amie, couleur d'Afrique," "les baies de tes yeux," "la forêt bleue de tes cheveux," "le palmier souriant sous l'Alizé," (my beloved, the color of Africa, the bays of your eyes, the blue forest of your hair, the palm tree smiling beneath the trade wind.) This merging of the woman and the land also characterizes the poet's descriptive vocabulary with reference to places which, in a similar manner, tend to display female attributes as in this passage where, in "Chant de l'initié" ("Song of the Initiate"), he describes an African landscape:

Soleil de son sourire! et la rosée brillait sur l'herbe indigo de ses lèvres.
Les colibris striquaient, fleurs aériennes, la grâce indicible de son discours
Les martins-pêcheurs plongeaient dans ses yeux en fulgurances bleu natif
    de joie
Par les rizières ruisselantes, ses cils bruissaient rythmiques dans l'air
    transparent

(Poèmes, 190–91).

(Sunlight of her smile! and the dew sparkled on the indigo grass of her
    lips.
The humming birds, aerial flowers, ornamented the inexpressible grace
    of her discourse
The kingfishers plunged into her eyes in native blue flashes of joy
Throughout the shimmering rice fields, her lashes rustled rhythmic in the
    transparent air.)

This type of personification could very well have its origins in the anthropomorphism of African religion which also traditionally assigns female gender to the land. There is also the belief that the clan obtained its original right to cultivate the land in the union between the deity of the place (female) and the totemic ancestor of the clan (male); "First of all, black African animism has it that the Earth . . . is a person, a spirit. The Ancestor of the clan, the first clearer and occupant of the land, concluded with this spirit, a pact sanctioned by sacrificial ritual."[6] In an earlier poem, "A la mort" ("To Death"), Senghor profits from the myth as a source for the following lines:

Je sais que l'Hiver s'illuminera d'un long jour printanier
Que l'odeur de la terre montera m'enivrer plus fort que le parfum des
    fleurs

Que la Terre tendra ses seins durs pour frémir sous les caresses du Vainqueur
Que je bondirai comme l'Annonciateur, que je manifesterai l'Afrique comme
le sculpteur de masques au regard intense

(Poèmes, 24)

(I know that winter will be illuminated by a long spring day
That the odor of the earth will rise up to intoxicate me stronger than the
perfume of flowers
That the Earth will proffer her hard breasts to quiver beneath the caresses
of the Victor
That I will leap like the Harbinger, that I will manifest Africa like the
sculptor of masks with the intense gaze.)

When the poet describes the earth as one would a mistress, the
image is more than literary convention since it is derived from
traditional lore.

While Africa often functions as a lover in the poems, she also
appears with maternal connotations. In "Par delà Èros" the poet
announces his return to Africa by saying: "Et je renais à la terre qui
fut ma mère" (And I am born again to the land that was my mother;
Poèmes, 39). In addition to the fairly obvious connotation of "Mother
Africa," the place of his birth, the dominant female figure of the
childhood paradise was Senghor's own mother and through this
association, she retains the identification with Africa which prompted
the poet in "A l'appel de la race de Saba" and "Ndéssé" to turn to
her at times when he needed reassurance of his own African identity.
Interestingly, the mistress often plays a similar role in the love
poems; the beloved is generally an extremely maternal figure who
nurtures, soothes, and consoles the narrator and even exhibits the
same traits of character as the mother in the poems. We find a sort
of poetic trinity composed of Africa, Mistress, and Mother where
one serves as metaphor for the other and each represents the object
of the poet's quest as he searches for confirmation of his Africanness.

Rather on the fringe of landscape imagery, but universally characteristic of Senghor's treatment of women, is his use of the light
image. Certainly a means of translating human warmth and sympathy, it also symbolizes spirituality and purity. In "Chants pour
Signare," light imagery must also be considered a structural device
with light and dark signalling the presence or absence of a beloved
and setting as well the mood of the individual poems. The sun,
moon, and stars, as well as the artificial light of candles and lamps

come to indicate the appearance of the beloved in a varied and intriguing use of imagery. The same device occurs with reference to divinities; the Christian God is often compared to sunlight, and the spirits of the ancestors are depicted against the light of the stars. This divine or supernatural implication of light images adds to their significance when applied to the descriptions of women who, surrounded by a halo of light, tend to assume a distinctly religious attitude. Despite the eroticism of certain passages, the poet's depiction of the woman can also be distant and respectful. In some cases, it is even worshipful and the choice of vocabulary sometimes bears religious connotations as when Senghor calls her "the Angel of the Prodigal Son" or "the Virgin of black silk."

One of the most frequently noted features of Senghor's poetry is his eroticism, both in his descriptions of women and of the act of making love. Some such passages seem to have their origins in European literary conventions; the source for the following idea can be found in Renaissance sonnets: "Si cependant j'étais la lumière qui dort sur tes formes fluides de statue" (If however I was the light which sleeps on your fluid statue forms; *Poèmes,* 150). Ronsard and Du Bellay also dreamed of metamorphoses that would bring them closer to the beloved in a similarly sensual way. It is also possible to draw parallels between Senghor's sensuality and the frank sexuality of African art, both of which reflect the importance of fertility in African culture. Since only through his progeny can a man assure the continuity of the clan, the equivalent—more or less—of the concept of life after death in Christianity, love, as the medium for the propagation of the life force, assumes a different and far greater importance than it is normally accorded in Western literature. In his reading of the early Negritude poetry, Sartre viewed the importance placed on sexual imagery in a cultural context. He interpreted what he called the "sexual pantheism" of these writers as an expression of their peasant's relationship to the world: "To plant is to impregnate . . . the earth . . . Techniques have contaminated the white worker, but the black remains the great male of the earth, the sperm of the world. His existence . . . is the repetition from year to year of the sacred coitus."[7] Similarly, Sylvia Washington Bâ warns that "the constant fusion of images of fertility, femininity, maternity, physical love, and physical force in Senghor's poetry must be understood in the context of black African cosmogony if one is to avoid the pitfall of construing his sensuality as eroticism,"[8] and

Senghor himself prefers to consider African art forms "sensual" rather than "erotic."[9] Regardless of the inspiration for Senghor's imagery, the expression "Black Eros" continues to be used in reference to his work and not without cause. Van Niekerk even ranks it "amongst the best erotic poetry produced in the French language since the war."[10]

The Use of the Quest Theme in "Chants pour Signare"

"Chants pour Signare" is a group of poems on the subject of the poet's love for the woman indicated in the title. The term "signare," as defined by Sylvia Washington Bâ, signifies "a word of Portuguese origin (senhora) used to refer to well-born Senegalese women, originally the term used to designate a mulatto mistress of a white man."[11] This more general word replaces the name "Naëtt" of the 1948 edition, Chants pour Naëtt, and results in further depersonalization of the ideal figure who emerges from the poems. As the poet evidently considers the second version his more polished work and in order to be consistent, we shall concentrate on this edition which is also the more accessible of the two. In its present form, the work is not merely a random selection of love poems bearing similar themes, for however loosely defined, there exists an observable pattern, perhaps a plot, which unites them. The first three poems act as an introduction to the cycle, describing the couple and their separation. In the following stanzas, the poet writes principally from Europe and there are references to a crisis, possibly the war years. The woman appears as a memory of the past or a dream of the future. Gradually she becomes the object of the poet's attempt to regain her, a sister-soul whom he seeks across Time and Space and behind her many disguises. In the last poems his efforts to win her take on the characteristics of the traditional romantic quest.

By its themes of separation and nostalgia, "Chants pour Signare" has a great deal in common with Chants d'ombre, although the longing for Africa is replaced by the poet's yearning for a woman associated with Africa. An analysis of the first poem in the cycle reveals additional similarities. Here we are introduced to the lovers in their African setting:

Voici la fleur de brousse et l'étoile dans mes cheveux et le bandeau qui
    ceint le front du pâtre-athlète.

J'emprunterai la flûte qui rythme la paix des troupeaux
Et tout le jour assis à l'ombre de tes cils, près de la Fontaine Fimla
Fidèle, je paîtrai les mugissements blonds de tes troupeaux.

(Poèmes, 169)

(Here is the bush flower and the star in my hair and the band which circles
  the brow of the herdsman-athlete.
I will borrow the flute which provides the rhythm for the peace of the
  herds
And, all day long, sitting in the shadow of your lashes, near the Fountain
  Fimla
Faithful, I will graze the blond lowing of your herd.)

The proximity of the fountain, the poet as herdsman, the sound of
the flute, even the wildflower ornaments—all of these are elements
of the childhood Eden and imitate with surprising affinity these
lines from the initial stanza of *Que m'accompagnent kôras et balafong*
which recall the poet's youth:

Et toi Fontaine de Kam-Dyamé, quand à midi je buvais ton eau mystique
  au creux de mes mains
Entouré de mes compagnons lisses et nus et parés des fleurs de la brousse!
La flûte du pâtre modulait la lenteur des troupeaux

(Poèmes, 26–27)

(And you Fountain of Kam-Dyamé, when at noon I used to drink your
  mystic water in the hollow of my hands
Surrounded by my companions naked and slim and adorned with bush
  flowers!
The shepherd's flute modulated the slowness of the herds)

The flute, especially, holds mysterious powers for the poet. He
heard its music as he stood on the threshold of his father's house
in *Le Retour de l'enfant prodigue,* and in "Chant de l'initié," its notes
have the power to draw him magically into the golden era and bring
him across the awesome barrier of time. The musical accompaniment
indicated for this initial poem in "Chants pour Signare"—Senghor
has assigned all of the "songs" to an appropriate musical instrument—is "for flutes," and we are once more in the childhood
paradise.

The woman's presence in the garden and the constant theme of
love are unaccustomed additions to the childhood memory but not

inexplicable in terms of literary tradition, for we find here all the
necessary ingredients for transforming the paradise myth into the
setting for a pastorale: a pair of chaste lovers in a rustic tableau
which becomes a tropical Arcadia, the traditional projection of man's
dreams of a more harmonious society and a refuge from the com-
plexities of the real world. As indicated by Frye, the pastorale
sometimes occures in the early stages of romance; having discussed
the first stage, the birth of the hero, he then continues:

The second phase brings us to the innocent youth of the hero, a phase
most familiar to us from the story of Adam and Eve in Eden before the
Fall. In literature this phase presents a pastoral and Arcadian world, generally a pleasant wooded landscape, full of glades, shaded valleys, mur-
muring brooks, the moon, and other sexual imagery. . . . The archetype
of erotic innocence is less commonly marriage than the "chaste" love that
precedes marriage; the love of brother for sister, or of two boys for each
other. Hence, though in later phases it is often recalled as a lost happy
time or Golden Age, the sense of being close to a moral taboo is very
frequent, as it is of course in the Eden story itself. [12]

While the heroic adventure is less evident in this cycle than in
Chants d'ombre, the poems can nevertheless be said to share the
archetypal pattern. The relationship becomes stronger with the greater
prominence of the quest theme in the last poems in which the
winning of the woman turns into an obsession.

   Light imagery, often associated with the Senghorian woman,
serves in "Chants pour Signare" as a cohesive structural device that
indicates the woman's real or imagined presence. This first poem
in the collection opens appropriately at dawn: "Une main de lumière
a caressé mes paupières de nuit / Et ton sourire s'est levé sur les
brouillards qui flottaient monotones sur mon Congo" (A hand of
light caressed my eyelids of night / And your smile rose on the
mists which floated monotonously on my Congo; *Poèmes,* 169). The
poet passes the whole day with the beloved but nightfall will signal
their separation. In the next two poems the time for departure grows
increasingly near and the light of the woman's presence becomes
dimmer and dimmer until, as the sun sets, she also disappears into
the shadows, leaving her lover alone in anticipation of a new dawn.
Not dawn, but the painful image of the unfamiliar European night
rises to meet him in "Mais ces routes de l'insomnie . . ." ("But
these sleepless roads . . ."). Gone are the familiar activities of "Nuit

de Sine" and the hypnotic rhythm of the drums, but this particular night has one redeeming aspect, for it brings a vision of the loved one, not clothed in sunlight but, in his imagination, set like a new constellation amid the stars of the southern sky. At the end of the poem there appears a reversal of associations, the poet preferring to prolong the night with its dreams of the beloved and dreading the reality of daylight in an alien country.

As the narrator in *Chants d'ombre* longed for the place and time of his childhood, he projects in "Chants pour Signare" his nostalgia for the person of the absent loved one who is herself a part of the paradise setting. The separation of the lovers, which Frye considers the next stage in the progress of the romance, is intensified by the coming of war. The poet refers to himself as a warrior and putting aside the flute for more appropriate instruments, sings of his own impending death. With the war posing an additional barrier, the poet must be content with the presence of the mistress in his dreams, his memory, and his imagination, and the next few pieces, similar to the love sonnets of Ronsard or DuBellay, lyrically interpret the poet's love for his lady.

In addition to their both being love poems, Senghor's poetry and the Renaissance sonnets also share the Petrarchist imagery, especially in the persistent play of light and shadow; in Senghor's continual association of the woman with Paradise, there is also an echo of the Platonic concept of the woman as the personification of the Ideal. In spite of her ties with this Western literary tradition, Senghor's beloved remains completely African, and the way in which she represents Africa for the poet becomes the unifying theme varied and elaborated on from poem to poem. From Africa's history, its music, and the lushness of the rich, tropical setting, Senghor selects images with which to surround and enhance the woman. One of the most successful of these creations appears in the following lines, a tropical variation of Baudelaire's "Invitation au voyage":

Et nous baignerons mon amie dans une présence africaine.
Des meubles de Guinée et du Congo, graves et polis sombres et sereins.
Des masques primordiaux et purs aux murs, distants mais si présents!
Des tabourets d'honneur pour les hôtes héréditaires, pour les Princes du
    Pays-Haut.
Des parfums fauves, d'épaisses nattes de silence
Des coussins d'ombre et de loisirs, le bruit d'une source de paix.

Des paroles classiques; loin, des chants alternés comme les pagnes du
    Soudan.
Et puis lampe amicale, ta bonté pour bercer l'obsession de cette présence
Noir blanc et rouge oh! rouge comme le sol d'Afrique.

(*Poèmes*, 175–76)

(And we will bathe my beloved in an African presence.
Furniture from Guinea and the Congo, grave and polished, dark and serene.
On the walls, pure and primordial masks, distant but so present!
Stools of honor for hereditary guests, for the Princes of the High Country.
Wild perfumes, thick mats of silence
Cushions of shade and leisure, noise from a source of peace.
Classic words; in the distance, responsive songs like the cloths of the
    Sudan.
And then the friendly lamp, your goodness to soothe the obsession of this
    presence
Black white and red oh! red like the soil of Africa.)

The "luxe, calme et volupté" of Baudelaire's exotic Dutch interior
is reconstructed here in an African setting. Senghor uses much of
the French poet's vocabulary and assigns a similar role to sensorial
imagery, including the reference to perfume so particularly characteristic of Baudelaire. Both poets have opted for a marked musical
effect to support the dreamy mood of the poems. In spite of what
it might owe to Baudelaire, Senghor's tableau responds to his own
specific conceptual requirements and fits well in the cycle of love
poems, an imagined, womblike retreat whose rich decor provides
an idealized African setting for the poet and a woman who incarnates
Africa.

A rather intriguing affinity between the mistress and the paradise
of childhood occurs in the poem "Ton visage . . ." ("Your
face . . .") which ostensibly describes the poet's memory of an
evening outing by boat. The reflection of the starlight on the water
provides the setting for a poetic interlude. The interesting feature
of this poem is its treatment of time as we see it in the first lines:
"Ton visage beauté des temps anciens! Sortons les pagnes parfumés
aux temps passés. / Mémoire des temps sans histoire! C'était avant
notre naissance" (Your face beauty of ancient times! Let us take out
the cloths perfumed in times past. / Memory of times without
history! That was before our birth; *Poèmes*, 176). The reference to
antiquity or prehistory is not exactly new in conjunction with the

poet's Eden; he has previously associated the pure state of precolonial Africa, uncorrupted by Western Civilization, and the innocence of childhood. Senghor refers to the woman elsewhere as "la porte radieuse à l'entrée du temps primordial" (the radiant door at the entrance to primordial times; *Poèmes,* 180). In "D'autres chants," he introduces a similar dreamlike episode with the lines: "Je ne sais en quels temps c'était, je confonds toujours l'enfance et l'Eden / Comme je mêle la Mort et la Vie—un pont de douceur les relie" (I do not know in what times it was, I always confuse childhood and Eden / As I mix Life and Death—a bridge of sweetness joins them; *Poèmes,* 146). The temporal setting of childhood and the poet's idealized version of it must necessarily remain, as in myth, somewhat vague. The expression "avant notre naissance" moves from the realm of myth to that of psychoanalysis. The memory of life in the womb suggested is reiterated in a later poem in the cycle where we find the introduction: "Dans la nuit abyssale en notre mère, nous jouions aux noyés t'en souvient-il?" (In the abyssal night in our mother, we used to play at drowning, don't you remember?; *Poèmes,* 180). The darkness and tranquility, the suggestion of water, and the maternal reference appear to describe the world of the fetus. As we have previously indicated, Africa in Senghor's poetry carries specific maternal connotations; in consequence, the theme of exile can be likened to the birth trauma or to a separation of the child from his mother's presence. Appropriately, the poet uses the image of the womb to denote a scene which he wishes identified with the childhood paradise. [13]

A repeated symbol of the poet's Africanness is the mask and the bond that it represents with the ancestors. Two poems in *Chants d'ombre,* "Masque nègre" and "Prière aux masques," are inspired by masks and there are several instances in the love poems where Senghor further cements the symbolic function of the woman by comparing her face to a ritual mask. In "Ton visage . . ." and "Tu as donc dépouillé . . ." ("You have thus divested . . ."), the word "Eternal" qualifies the image, because the woman, like the ancestors signified by the mask, defies the passage of time and therefore acquires a supernatural dimension. This association also anticipates another development in the cycle: an increasing depersonalization of the poet's Ideal Woman who becomes less one individual than an essence superimposed on many women.

As in *Chants d'ombre*, the last part of the cycle is dominated by the theme of return as the poet, either forced by his own desires or merely permitted by circumstances, sets out to regain the woman. The first evidence of his resolve occurs in "Tu as donc dépouillé . . ." where he consults the sages of Africa concerning how to win her. He concludes that the best strategy lies in his own talent as a *dyâli* or poet. For a moment, it appears as if the wanderer need only to return to Africa in order to regain that lost sunlight, the presence of the beloved, and indeed, he would like to imagine her standing on the dock awaiting his arrival: "Croire qu'il y a la Jeune Fille, qui m'attend au port à chaque courrier / Et qui espère mon visage dans la floraison des mouchoirs!" (To believe that there is the Young Woman, who waits for me at the port with each mailboat / And who hopes for my face in the flourishing of handkerchiefs; *Poèmes*, 179). But the poet's quest does not terminate so easily; the woman he seeks proves elusive. The capital letters used here for "Young Woman"—not, incidentally, in the version of this poem which appeared in *Chants pour Naëtt*—transform the waiting figure from a real woman into a poetic idealization. She becomes, here and in the rest of the selections, a sister-soul, known first in the primordial era of the poet's Eden, who has since assumed many different guises; whatever name he gives her—Nyominka, Soyan, the poetess of Amboise—she is the reflection of the poet's own spirit, his double. In this respect, she has strong affinities with the Jungian concept of the anima, for the female ideal who serves as an incarnation of Negritude represents that part of the poet himself which he regards metaphorically as "feminine." This idea emerges from his own characterization of black culture as emotional and intuitive (feminine) in contrast to the mechanical and rational (masculine) viewpoint of Western civilization. A feminine personification of Negritude can be considered the projection of the poet's "feminine" attributes, the sort of manifestation implied by the term "anima."

This sisterly quality in the depiction of the woman should not be construed to mean that the love theme is strictly platonic. The poem "Etait-ce une nuit maghrebine?" describes an unmistakably romantic incident, but the actual identity of the woman seems relatively unimportant when in the last lines he tells her: "Tu seras la même toujours et tu ne seras pas la même. / Qu'importe? A travers tes métamorphoses, j'adorai le visage de Koumba Tâm." (You will always be the same and you will not be the same. / What difference does it make? Throughout your metamorphoses, I will worship the face of Koumba Tâm; *Poèmes,* 185). The woman as symbol is further emphasized in the reference to Koumba Tâm, goddess of love, whose presence the poet seeks behind the ephemeral nature of the mistress.

In "Chants pour Signare," the poet never fully succeeds in finding again the object of his desire. The last poem of the cycle provides another echo of the traditional quest, for the narrator now envisions himself a genuine knight, a horseman of one of Africa's great empires, who would carry off his woman in a hail of blades and bullets. He concludes the poem on a note of supreme devotion to the beloved—as either a real woman or a personal ideal—with the last line bearing an image of paradise which the poet complains would be empty for him in the absence of the woman.

While Senghor continues to employ the same devices and themes that he used in *Chants d'ombre,* the figure of the woman provides a fresh center of interest for the illustration of the idea of Negritude and the ensemble of poems, each one adding a new dimension to her portrait or to the love story, is delightful. The poet proves beyond question what he had so effectively broached in "Femme noire": that he could adapt the French language to sing the praise of a black woman. The exotic setting of these verses, which serves as a door to our imagination and especially to our sensuality, provides a new and decidedly successful ingredient for the time-honored convention of the love-poem cycle. In judging the value of the two collections as poetry, critics have generally tended to favor "Chants pour Signare" (or *Chants pour Naëtt*) over "Epîtres à la Princesse" and have proclaimed the love songs some of Senghor's best verse. Gerald Moore writes: "His (Senghor's) poetry is often at its best when he abandons the search for reconciliation and is content to register a single emotion without too much care for the consequences. The love poems of *Chants pour Naëtt* . . . have this quality of abandon and seem to derive a lot of their rhythmic energy from it."[14] Peters considers that "the 'Chants pour Signare' indeed contain some of the finest poems of Senghor's career"[15] and that "Senghor seems to be at his best as a love poet preoccupied with the private relationship between him and the loved one."[16] Peters believes that the return to political and ideological issues in the "Epîtres" causes these more prosaic poems to be less successful.[17] Leusse also prefers the love poems for Sopé which, he says, touch us more profoundly and are more direct and personal.[18] In a sense, such comments are not so much an evaluation of the works in question as recognition that, although each is addressed to a central figure who is a woman and a lover, the two collections represent somewhat different types of poetry. In "Chants pour Signare" the lyric elements dominate the didactic, but in "Epîtres à la Princess" the writer gives primary emphasis to his message, not his feelings.

The Concept of Negritude
in "Epîtres à la Princesse"

"Epîtres à la Princesse," published in 1956 as part of *Ethiopiques,* is shorter than "Chants pour Signare" and more clearly narrates a story. Told by means of his letters to her, this series of poems and its sequel, "La Mort de la Princesse," which contains one of her letters, describe the courtship by an African envoy of the European Princess of Belborg. There is no question about their love for one another but mutual responsibilities retain them in their respective lands, and before she can join her suitor, the Princess perishes in what is described as the apocalyptic destruction of Europe.

Once again, the theme of absence predominates and the distance between two continents separates the lovers. The situation is somewhat altered by the fact that the woman is neither African nor even identified with Africa, but a representative of European culture of whom the poet may say: "Mon désir est de mieux apprendre ton pays de t'apprendre" (My desire is to learn more about your country to learn about you; *Poèmes,* 135), and also, "Tu m'ouvres le visage de mes frères les hommes-blancs" (You open the faces of my brothers the whitemen for me; *Poèmes,* 137). She shares with the African the legends and stories that represent her traditions, and the landscape imagery used to describe her strengthens her identification with northern Europe. Although we have only one letter from her, that which is quoted by the poet in the sequel, we know about her from his descriptions, mostly memories of times they shared together. Her personality being more clearly defined than that of the amorphous Signare, the Princess emerges as a woman with a keen mind and a rather independent character.

It is the poet, in this instance, who represents Africa and who appears as its ambassador or as an administrator over its people. Chiefly through his presentation of himself, we realize that the setting is medieval. Expanding on the image created in the last poem of "Chants pour Signare," the poet, once again a knight with numerous horsemen at his disposal and surrounded in his tent by wise and noble men, bears weighty responsibilities. In spite of the historical trappings, we sense in this role the overtones of Senghor's own political career and in the courtship of the Princess, a glimpse of his private life. There develops a broad gap between the events of the poem and any real-life inspiration for its material, and the tragic denouement of the drama transcends the biographical allusions and provides a further illustration of the philosophy of Negritude. The proposed union of the lovers anticipates the new era of racial harmony which, as Senghor envisions it, will balance the values of both cultures. When the union of the couple does not take place, the poet uses the opportunity to imagine what could happen if modern society refuses the spiritual offerings of Africa.

The last letter warns the Princess to leave Europe and take refuge with him in Africa against an impending upheaval that serves as a pretext for contrasting the worst implications of technology with the most positive values of traditional societies. Europe will become the victim of its own invention, he prophesies. Having imposed upon the world the weapons of colonial exploitation and the savagery of World War II, it will be unable to survive the impact of the inevitable atomic war: "Ce sera l'an de la Technique. De leurs yeux ils cracheront un feu blanc. Les éléments se sépareront et s'agrégeront selon de mystérieuses attirances et répulsions. Le sang des animaux et la sève des plantes seront de petit lait. Les blancs seront jaunes, les jaunes seront blancs, tous seront stériles" (It will be the Technical Age. From their eyes they will spit a white fire. The elements will separate and come together according to mysterious attractions and repulsions. The blood of animals and the sap of plants will be whey. The white men will be yellow, the yellow men will be white. All will be sterile; *Poèmes,* 140). Those who have not learned to live within the rhythm of nature are menaced by the total disruption of the natural order. The threat of sterility carries horrible implications for the African whose spiritual welfare depends on the clan and its propagation.

In contrast, the envoy describes his own culture as being exceptionally sensitive to the rhythms of the earth:

Ma noblesse est de vivre cette terre, Princesse selon cette terre
Comme le riz l'igname la palme et le palétuvier, l'ancêtre Lamantin l'an-

cêtre Crocodile
Et Lilanga ma soeur. Elle danse elle vit.
Car comment vivre sinon dans l'Autre au fil de l'Autre, comme l'arbre
    déraciné par la tornade et les rêves des îles flottantes?
Et pourquoi vivre si l'on ne danse l'Autre?

(*Poèmes*, 141–42)

(My nobility, Princess, is to live this land according to this land
Like the rice the yam the palm and the mangrove, the ancestral Manatee
    the ancestral Crocodile
And Lilanga my sister. She dances she lives.
For how should one live if not in the Other swept along in the current of
    the Other like the tree uprooted in the storm and the dreams of
    floating islands?
And why should one live if he does not dance the Other?)

Senghor depicts the oneness with nature and with others which he
believes characteristic of the African, the "raison-toucher," which
causes him to sense the invisible currents inherent in all living
things, the rhythm reflected in music, dance, and love. It is in the
restoration of this harmony that the poet hopes to see the salvation
of what is salvageable of the technological culture of Western
civilization.

Once, the poet found himself faced with a choice to make between
Europe and Africa, between Isabelle and Soukeïna; he chose his own
people and his maternal soil. In this poem, the initiative is placed
on the European whose choice is to accept the offerings of Negritude
or to face the inborn consequences of a culture which has learned
to manipulate nature without learning to exist with it and in it.
The Princess, conscious of her own duties, refuses to leave her people,
and as a consequence, she dies in the disaster. While the poem is
a triumph for the values of African culture, it expresses the poet's
despair concerning the ultimate fusion of the two cultures and his
doubt as to the possibility of obtaining a perfect union of their
respective values except as it has been accomplished in the life of
the poet himself, for at the end of "La Mort de la Princesse," the
poet promises to retain the memory of his European Princess. By
carrying with him the mark of his European experience, he becomes
an interiorized version of the union of two peoples which he is
seeking in the poem.

While "Epîtres" lacks the overall spontaneity and intimacy of "Chants pour Signare," the former also has its lyric moments. Even Peters, who expresses a general preference for the "Chants," concedes that the third Epistle "closely resembles the lyric strain of the love songs,"[19] and Mezu terms certain lines of the same stanza "rich, carnal and voluptuous in contrast with the dryness and abstraction of 'Femme Noire.' " This, he tells us, is so because the poet is writing about a woman he knows and loves.[20] For us to judge the "Epîtres" by the same criteria as the love poems is to fail to recognize the poet's intent. Considered as a primarily didactic poem whose function is to dramatize Senghor's concept of cultural crossbreeding, the work is ingenious. Who else but Senghor could have thought to frame the clash of Europe and Africa in a love story?

While "Chants pour Signare" and "Epîtres à la Princesse" both use images of women as cultural symbols, they each express different aspects of Senghor's efforts to affirm the values he perceives in a traditional society. "Chants pour Signare" in many ways parallels the essentially inner-directed search for self of *Chants d'ombre,* its objective being the proclamation of the values of Negritude and the poet's consequent commitment. "Epîtres à la Princesse" takes the Africanness of its narrator and the worth of his culture as its starting point and deals with the larger implications of Negritude for the future of mankind. Both ideas were present in the early poetry and in Senghor's articulation of his theories, and certainly the differences between the two collections result in part from the different women who inspired them. Nevertheless, the period from 1948, the publication of the original version of "Chants pour Signare," until 1956 when "Epîtres à la Princesse" appeared in *Ethiopiques,* saw a transition in Senghor's work from a purely personal struggle for identity to a rising awareness of a political mission, a realignment of the poet's concerns generally reflected in the other poems of *Ethiopiques.*

Chapter Seven
The Epic Poems in *Ethiopiques*
Background and Introduction

Ethiopiques (1956) appeared at the end of the first decade of Senghor's political involvement and in both its tone and subject matter reflects the concerns which marked this period in the poet's life. The years following the war saw important changes in French colonial policies and brought increasing autonomy to African and other Third World peoples. Senghor, although not himself a radical on the issue of independence, sought consistently from his seat in the French National Assembly to better the position of the colonies within the constitutional framework. Election to the Assembly required the establishment of a solid political base in Senegal and it is this aspect of his political career—his role vis-à-vis his constituency—more than his contribution to the collapse of French colonialism which appears to have inspired these particular poems. As a record of the impact of prospective nationhood on African politics and as a glimpse into the state of mind of an African political figure during this critical era, *Ethiopiques* must be regarded as a document of historical interest as well as literary value.

The general tone of these works is one of elation, with many of them culminating in some kind of victory depicted in terms of growth or fertility imagery. In this respect, they reflect the writer's own political successes. Elected first as one of Senegal's delegates to the Constitutional Assembly, he subsequently attained a seat in the French National Assembly under the 1946 constitution which he helped to draft. Initially a candidate of the Socialist Party (S.F.I.O.), Senghor withdrew in 1948 and founded the Bloc Démocratique Sénégalais (B.D.S.), through which, in 1951, he defeated an established political figure, Lamine Gueye, to become Senegal's leading statesman. Emerging eventually as an important spokesman for all of France's African colonies he was, in 1955, awarded a cabinet post under Edgar Faure. In January of 1956, the year in which *Ethiopiques* was published, Senghor and his party were once again victorious at the polls.

The 1951 election appears to have been an especially important influence on the poems, not merely because it marked a success for Senghor, but because of its role as a political turning point for Senegal as well. Under the previous French constitution, the electorate had been limited to the citizens of the Communes—Dakar, Saint-Louis, Rufisque and Gorée—who were largely members of the assimilated elite. The 1946 constitution, for the first time, gave the people of the bush the right to elect Senegal's representative to the National Assembly. The candidate of the Communes, Lamine Gueye, failed to perceive the importance of this newly enfranchised electorate among whom Senghor and his newly organized opposition party carried out a vigorous, hard-fought campaign. He regarded his election as a victory for the people, a triumph of his concept of Negritude over the old notion of assimilation.[1]

Senghor's political role, especially his perception of himself as a delegated representative of the people, affects the narrative voice in the poems of *Ethiopiques:* "Senghor is once more the hero of his own poetry, but not now as a person in a predicament or a man discovering solidarity with his fellows, but as their symbol speaking for them with an air of confidence, as personal and impersonal as an hereditary monarch."[2] Although he continues to speak in the first person, the increased role of metaphor and allegory creates a greater distance between the narrator and the person of Léopold Senghor. With less frequent reference to the sincerely personal feelings of nostalgia, love, and suffering, the resulting poems, while not lacking in emotion, come across as extremely abstract in comparison with the earlier collections.

In addition to the two sets of love poems previously discussed— "Epîtres à la Princesse" and "D'Autres Chants"—*Ethiopiques* includes the lengthy dramatic poem "Chaka" and a suite of relatively short poems on a variety of topics which, as a group, give the collection its name. Jonathan Peters refers to these works as "epics,"[3] a term which appropriately recognizes their national, racial character. Many of these pieces also rely on the quest pattern so generally characteristic of the traditional epic, and nearly all of them feature the narrator in an unquestionably heroic stance. In the case of "Le

Kaya-Magan" and "Chaka," Senghor has even gone directly to African history and legend for his inspiration.

The poem "Chant de l'Initié" poses unique problems for the critic trying to give a more or less chronological treatment of Senghor's works. It appeared first in a 1947 issue of *Présence Africaine* and was then collected with *Chants pour Naëtt* for publication in 1949. When the latter was republished as "Chants pour Signare" in the 1961 collection *Nocturnes,* "Chant de l'Initié" was included. Because of its association with the love poems, it has at least on one occasion been interpreted as belonging to that series. Although the broad symbolism of the poem allows for a variety of different readings, its original independent publication and its dedication to the editor of *Présence Africaine,* Alioune Diop, seem to indicate that it was intended to stand alone, apart from poems of a clearly intimate nature. We have chosen not to include it in our discussion of *Chants pour Naëtt* but to treat it with the poems of *Ethiopiques,* which date from about the same period and to which it bears a striking resemblance in tone, imagery, and structure.

The Rite of Passage
as an Organizational Device

One of the theories concerning the possible origins of myth argues for a relationship between myth and ritual: the hero's trials and tribulations reflect the ordeals of the initiate in rites of passage and the victory of the hero parallels the triumph of the forces of spring over the sterility of winter so often depicted in seasonal ceremonies.[4] At this point in Senghor's poetry, the relationship between his heroes and traditional ritual figures becomes a well-developed poetic device, with numerous individual poems drawing obviously on ritual symbolism. The use of this particular pattern—with its attendant imagery—appears so frequently that one critic has complained of what he calls a certain "staleness": "The pursuance of different topics (often however the topics are also quite similar) with essentially the same imagery, cannot fail in the long run to have a somewhat mawkish effect."[5] Of the epic poems of *Ethiopiques,* at least some ritual features appear in "L'Homme et la Bête," "Congo," "Messages," "Teddungal," and "L'Absente"; "Chant de l'Initié," although not a part of the collection, easily deserves to be included with this group for which it might well have been a model. Since the parallel development of all of these works would render a sequential analysis more than a little repetitious, a comparative approach seems to be in order. This allows us, first of all, to isolate certain recurring features of structure and imagery and to document their ritual origins. Such a juxtaposition of the poems also has the added advantage of showing that in spite of the obvious similarities what others have interpreted as monotony yields on closer examination a subtle variety of detail similar to the role of repetition and variation in Senghor's use of rhythm.

Initiation rituals are almost always characterized by some sort of ordeal, and among the poems written from 1947 to 1956, several are organized around just such trials or tests in which the hero/ initiate emerges the victor. In the initial poem of *Ethiopiques,* "L'Homme et la Bête" ("The Man and the Beast"), the protagonist encounters and overcomes the Beast, a creature who symbolizes some negative force. The setting for the combat is an infested swamp where the Man struggles knee-deep in mud and encumbered by the vegetation. He is wounded but eventually prevails:

Et l'Homme terrasse la Bête de la glossolalie du chant dansé.
Il la terrasse dans un vaste éclat de rire, dans une danse rutilant dansée
Sous l'arc-en-ciel des sept voyelles. Salut Soleil-levant Lion au-regard-qui-
    tue
Donc salut Dompteur de la brousse, Toi Mbarodi! seigneur des forces
    imbéciles!

> (*Poèmes,* 98–99)

(And the Man brings down the Beast in the glossolallia of the danced song.
He brings it down in a vast burst of laughter, in a shining danced dance
Under the rainbow of the seven vowels. Hail Rising-Sun Lion with-the-
    look-that-kills
Thus, hail Tamer of the bush, You Mbarodi! lord of imbecile forces.)

Most efforts to decipher the poem depend heavily on the above lines and a couple of other references to thought and language.

The ritual origins of the work are fairly obvious and have been noted by the critics. Papa Gueye N'Diaye points out that "in warrior societies, Man does not accede to the condition of Man, that is to virility, in the etymological sense of the term, and to sociability until having undergone his initiation: killing an animal reputed to be dangerous."[6] For N'Diaye, the poem is an allegory in which an initiation is used to depict the birth of the world:

> The poet makes himself the contemporary of Adam, who watches the birth of the world. A poem about Thought taming a hostile Creation, it contains a triple symbol, with the emergence of Man from animality and of Reason from instinct. But this emergence seems to take place in Africa itself, where, Man appeared for the first time.[7]

Jonathan Ngate has perhaps explored the ritual elements of the poem in greatest detail. Using specific references to anthropological texts and to fictional depictions of circumcision ceremonies, he concludes that "Senghor's poem offers us the spectacle of the generic initiate in the process of passing through one of the stages of life . . ."[8] He does not give the symbolism of the work the same interpretation which we find in N'Diaye's analysis but considers that the emphasis of words and ideas at the end of the poem stems rather from events normally associated with the circumcision rite. Such ceremonies usually culminate in a period of education when the young man learns the history of the family or clan and shares others of its secrets; thus, "he brings down the Beast of ignorance."[9] Although the symbolism of the poem seems to invite an array of interpretations, its ritual structure is generally accepted. Most of the critics also note the importance of language as a factor in the eventual defeat of the Beast. Considering Senghor's concept of poetry as a means of giving form and significance to the universe, it seems appropriate that he has placed at the head of his collection a poem about the triumph of Man through speech. Along these same lines, we observe that the narrator is clearly distinct from the Man, the protagonist. Sylvia Washington Bâ, in her analysis identifies the narrator with the sorcerer introduced in the first stanza, "the one who utters most secret things," and points out that the "evil spirits are actually repulsed by the combined magic of the incantation and the potion."[10] Man's victory over chaos and evil depends on the voice of the poet, on the magical power of the word. This characteristically Senghorian idea seems essential to any valid reading of the poem.

Trial by combat or the killing of a ferocious animal are not the only ways in which a young man might be tested. In several of Senghor's poems, the hero proves himself by accomplishing a journey fraught with obstacles.[11] This basic structural device appears with several variations in "Chant de l'Initié," "Congo," and "Teddungal."

In the six stanzas of "Chant de l'Initié," the narrator pursues a pilgrimage through the dangers of the forest and across the scorched savanna to a sacred place where he experiences a rebirth and identification with the totem animal. Circumstances of publication have mandated that this poem appear on two different occasions immediately following the love poems first issued as *Chants pour Naëtt*. Jonathan Peters associates the two and describes "Chant de l'Initié" as "a kind of prothalamium announcing the union of the poet-lover and his loved one . . ."[12] Van Niekerk maintains that this is not a cycle of amorous poetry but represents Senghor's "effort to return to the sources of his African culture."[13] In the light of the fact that the poem was initially published separate from the love poems, this seems a more appropriate reading of a work in which the dying to the old and the birth of the new symbolized in the rite of passage might well serve as a vehicle depicting the poet's own search for self.

A dangerous journey by boat with the hero at the helm is the unifying thread in "Congo." The narrator appears again in the first person and takes up the familiar role of lover; he also assumes a new role, that of the African boatman, and the course of his pirogue is depicted as an act of lovemaking. The Congo River, another incarnation of Africa, is personified as female—mother, mistress, goddess. After an initial invocation of the river, the poem reaches its climax as the boatman navigates the rapids, and it ends on a return to tranquility. What seems at first glance a hymn to the Congo evolves into another opportunity for dramatizing the poet's encounter with his own Africanness. References to places in the poet's past—Joal, Dyilor, Ermonville—suggest that the true setting of the poem is not on the banks of the great river at all but rather in the region of the poet's imagination. The poem succeeds on a number of levels and has been singled out by critics as one of Senghor's best.[14]

"Teddungal," where the poet describes a political campaign, also uses the journey as a structural device. The narrator travels through arid and dangerous land and ultimately experiences a sudden, powerful transformation accompanied by images of flowering plants. The hero and his comrades are described as "blancs initiés" (white initiates). The poem, whose title signifies "honor" in Toucouleur,[15] is addressed to Boubou Sall, a political ally from Podor in the North of Senegal.[16] The campaign depicted here, the first real test for the B.D.S. in 1949, renders the initiation theme especially appropriate. Although this extremely hard-fought election was lost to the opposition, the margin of victory was so small that it demonstrated the viability of the new party and its potential among the Islamic peoples of the country. In spite of his Catholicism, Senghor managed to create a strong base of support among the Muslim teacher-leaders, the mourides, and their followers. (Another poem in the collection, "Les Messages," salutes another Muslim ally, Cheik Yaba Diop.)

Each of these poems, in addition to providing some obstacle for the protagonist to overcome, contains symbols of the ritual death required by a rite of passage. The very nature of their physical settings simulates the first stage of such a ceremony as described by Mircea Eliade:

Everywhere the mystery begins with the separation of the neophyte from his family, and a "retreat" into the forest. In this there is already a symbolization of the death; the forest, the jungle and the darkness symbolize "the beyond," the Shades.[17]

The descriptions of the forest settings in the poems of *Ethiopiques*, dark and threatening in aspect, carry the significance which Eliade attributes to them here. The corresponding symbolism of rebirth also appears in the poems. In "Chant de l'Initié," we find rebirth as a specific part of the initiate's progress. The idea appears first with reference to the grasslands of the savanna which have been burned in preparation for the planting of new crops: ". . . feu de la Mort qui prépare la re-naissance / Re-naissance du Sens et de l'Esprit. . . ." (. . . fire of Death that prepares rebirth / Renaissance of Sense and Spirit; *Poèmes*, 192). The savanna, he says, is like himself and in the next stanza he too undergoes a new birth, dying suddenly "pour renaître dans la révélation de la Beauté!" (to be reborn in the revelation of Beauty!; *Poèmes*, 193). Similarly, in "Congo" the poet concludes by saying that the boat, having passed the difficult stage of the rapids, will be reborn among the waterlilies of the foam. The waterlily, itself a rebirth symbol, also appears to welcome the triumph of the Man in "L'Homme et la Bête." Senghor, a careful student of African customs, was of course aware of the rebirth implications of initiation rites which he himself discussed at length:

> In the Kingdom of Sine and, in general, among the Serers, initiation classes replaced age groups in conformity with the natural evolution of African societies. The classes are formed at the time of circumcision, a ceremony which takes place around puberty. In reality, circumcision is only the opportunity for a veritable education. It is a question of preparing young men for their function as adults. Rather, it is a question of a veritable religious initiation with trials, self-denial, rites and ceremonial, of an initiation which is founded on the mystery of Death-Rebirth.[18]

The ritual references in Senghor's poetry are hardly coincidental but based on his awareness of their significance in African tradition. As a preface to "Chant de l'Initié," he even retains lines from a Wolof poem about circumcision.

Another significant part of the rite of passage is the manifestation of the totem animal which Eliade describes as follows: "In certain places it is believed that a tiger comes and carries the candidates into the jungle on its back; the wild animal incarnates the mythical Ancestor, the Master of the initiation who conducts the adolescents to the Shades."[19] While Eliade's comments are necessarily general in nature, we know that they apply to the Wolof circumcision ceremony to which Senghor referred in "Chant de l'Initié." In that rite, we are told that the "first major ceremony in which the whole village is involved occurs with the appearance of a monster *(mam)* who comes to eat the boys."[20] In "Chant de l'Initié," there is just such an encounter with the poet's totem animal, the Lion: "Au Pélerin dont les yeux sont lavés par le jeûne et les cendres et les veilles / Apparaît au Soleil-levant, sur le suprême pic, la tête du Lion rouge / En sa majesté surréelle. O Tueur! O Terrible! et je cède et défaille" (To the Pilgrim whose eyes are washed by fasting and ashes and sleepless nights / Appears in the Rising-Sun on the highest peak, the head of the red Lion / In his surreal majesty. Oh Killer! Oh Terrible One! and I yield and faint; *Poèmes,* 193). In "L'Homme et la Bête," whose very subject indicates an encounter between a man and a beast, the poet dedicates the victory to the Lion whose essence the man seems to share: ". . .Salut Soleil-levant Lion au-regard-qui-tue / Donc salut Dompteur de la brousse, Toi Mbarodi! seigneur des forces imbéciles" (. . . Hail Rising-Sun Lion with-the-look-that-kills / Hail Tamer of the bush, You Mbarodi!

lord of imbecile forces; *Poèmes,* 98–99). The word "Mbarodi" refers to the killer lion.

In "L'Homme et la Bête," "Congo," and "Teddungal," each poem culminates in nature images which denote renewal and prosperity— a flowering lake, waterlillies, a harvest. The passage of the protagonist takes him from a hostile or infertile environment to one which is rich in growing things. Such transitions place these poems in the tradition of the school of thought which sees the rite of passage as a variation of a fertility rite. In this regard, "L'Absente" seems to have a similar inspiration. Putting aside his association with the totem lion and his political function, the narrator becomes again the poet-lover, and in the dusty days of the dry season, he sets out to sing the praises of the Absent Princess. As he sings he makes her presence real, and with her arrival comes the greening of the savannas. Armand Guibert interprets the poem on four different levels: "both short-term and long-term political victory; the Beloved, described physically, with her charms and jewels; Negritude proclaimed as a mystic force; and finally Poetry, the supreme form of culture."[21] From a historical perspective, it is tempting to give greatest weight to the political interpretation of the poem, to see it as Senghor's ultimate ode in anticipation of African independence. Within the general symbolic context, all or any of Guibert's readings could easily be justified. It is as if the poet had created a single tissue of images capable of encompassing all of his most fervent hopes and dreams and had then submitted it to the magic of one mighty incantation. The victory evoked through the poet's words is yet another example of what Jahn refers to as the use of "Nommo" in African thought. As elsewhere in *Ethiopiques,* the imagery of renewal announces a change of major significance, with the magic power of the poem in this instance, causing the transformation from aridity to fertility and, for the people, from want to prosperity.

Other Heroes

Throughout his works, Senghor has depicted the narrator of his poems as a hero, and the triumphant protagonists of "L'Homme et la Bête," "Congo," "Teddungal," and "L'Absente" continue the tradition. An interesting variation on this tendency occurs in "Le Kaya-Magan" and "Chaka," where Senghor's narrator assumes the identity of a heroic figure from African history. This device lends further nobility to the narrator who, through the use of the first person and by references to typically Senghorian preoccupations, maintains his identification with the poet; it also reaffirms the existence of the essential objectives of Negritude in the struggle against assimilation.

Sylvia Washington Bâ has discovered a possible historical source for the Kaya-Magan in a ruler of the former kingdom of Ghana: The king of Ouagadougou who in 790 conquered the territory of the empire of Ghana that had existed since 300 and had known forty-four sovereigns.[22] N'Diaye adds that he was the empire's first black ruler.[23] The resemblance to any real figure is of only marginal importance, however, in the poetic function which Senghor attributes to him: "The extension of his empire is interpreted in Senghor's poem as a civilizing, creative force culminating in the harmonious and beneficial merging of people and races."[24] It should be added that the civilization he creates is the African civilization, the culture of Negritude; the harmony he represents is African unity.

The Kaya-Magan introduces himself as "la personne première" (the first person). He is the source of a whole race and claims both masculine and feminine characteristics: "Donc paissez mes mamelles d'abondance, et je ne mange pas qui suis source de joie / Paissez mes seins forts d'homme, l'herbe de lait qui luit sur ma poitrine" (Then feed on my breasts of abundance, and I do not eat who am source of joy / Feed on my strong male breasts, on the milk grass which gleams on my chest; *Poèmes,* 102). Senghor's choice of an androgynous figure as a symbol of unity for emerging Africa has interesting implications, for androgyny appears frequently in creation myths, as Eliade has noted:

But the phenomenon of divine androgyny is very complex; it signifies more than the coëxistence—or rather coalescence—of the sexes in the divine being. Androgyny is an archaic and universal formula for the expression of *wholeness,* the co-existence of the contraries, *coincidentia oppositorum.* More than a state of sexual completeness and autarchy, androgyny symbolizes the perfection of a primordial, non-conditioned state. It is for this reason that androgyny is not attributed to supreme Beings only. Cosmic Giants, or mythical Ancestors of humanity are also androgynous. Adam, for example, was regarded as an androgyne. . . . A mythical Ancestor symbolizes the *commencement* of a whole new mode of existence: and every beginning is made in the *wholeness* of being.[25]

The use of the androgynous king allows Senghor to place the emphasis in "Le Kaya-Magan" on the concept of unity and wholeness which Eliade considered an essential feature of androgyny. This is represented in the poem by the king's ability to reconcile opposites: night and day, North and South, East and West. He also joins together in his being a diversity of races. Although the personification of Africa in Senghor's poetry is usually feminine as in "Congo," there is no question about the predominant masculinity of his androgyne, and Eliade assures us that "androgyny extends even to divinities who are pre-eminently masculine, or feminine."[26] The use of the first person pronoun and the masculine character of Kaya-Magan give us reason to suspect that the poet identifies himself with this figure and the creative and unifying role which he attributes to it.

Like "Le Kaya-Magan," in which the poet created an African Adam, he represents the hero of "Chaka" as a sort of African Christ. Described as a dramatic poem for several voices, it is divided into various speaking parts and has stage directions provided. The poem is based on the exploits of the Zulu leader, Chaka, who led a bloody reaction against the white intruder in South Africa during the 19th century. The legend, related by Thomas Mofolo, describes a man who sacrifices his own fiancée in order to obtain power from the sorcerer Issanoussi. The Zulu's lust for blood becomes an obsession and he is finally killed by his brothers. The story of Chaka (or Shaka) and Mofolo's work have inspired several contemporary African writers.[27] Senghor's version deals with Chaka in his death agony and the poem becomes a justification of the warrior's atrocities by making him an early martyr to African liberation and unity.

Senghor has been criticized for attributing such sophisticated motives to Chaka in fairly obvious defiance of legend and historical fact. Guibert makes the following remarks: "Without belittling the right of the poet to inventiveness, one can consider that it would have been better to have created the myth from scratch rather than to disguise Gilles de Rais as Vercingetorix."[28] It is easy to lament Senghor's choice of martyrs but structurally, the legend provides the poet with the elements necessary to tell his story of salvation. Beyond that outline, the historical personality of Chaka is obliterated and what remains is a spokesman for Negritude who shares certain obvious traits with the poet and who animates a death-rebirth cycle similar to that of other poems in the collection.

In explaining Chaka's motivation, Senghor endows the Zulu with ideas similar to his own. Chaka's description of his people's oppression is chiefly an expression of resentment against their cultural exploitation similar to Senghor's feelings concerning assimilation:

Je voyais dans un songe tous les pays aux quatre coins de l'horizon soumis
    à la règle, à l'équerre et au compas
Les forêts fauchées les collines anéanties, vallons et fleuves dans les fers.
Je voyais les pays aux quatre coins de l'horizon sous la grille tracée par les
    doubles routes de fers
Je voyais les peuples du Sud comme une fourmillière de silence
Au travail. Le travail est saint, mais le travail n'est plus le geste
Le tam-tam ni la voix ne rythment plus les gestes des saisons.
Peuples du Sud dans les chantiers, les ports les mines les manufactures
Et le soir ségrégés dans les kraals de la misère.

                                   (*Poèmes*, 121–22)

(I saw in a dream all of the countries at the four corners of the horizon
    submitted to the ruler, the square, and the compass
The forests mowed down the hills destroyed, valleys and rivers in irons.
I saw the countries at the four corners of the horizon under the grid laid
    out by the double tracks of iron
I saw the peoples of the South like an ant-hill of silence
At work. Work is holy, but work is no longer gesture
Drum and voice no longer give rhythm to the gestures of the seasons.
Peoples of the South in the dockyards, the ports the mines the factories
And in the evening segregated in kraals of misery.)

The tools of geometry are the tools of technicians and their rigid lines contrast with the natural, fluid movement of forest, hills, and rivers, all of which would be destroyed or changed by the march of technical progress. The old rhythm also would be destroyed by labor, which was not born of a harmony with nature or linked with the fundamental rhythms of the universe expressed in the beat of the African drum. These contrasts are easily recognizable illustrations of the distinctions which Senghor places between African and Western Civilization. He defines this difference in "L'Apport de la poèsie nègre au demi-siècle," an essay published in 1952.

We know that the attitude of Man before Nature is the Problem par excellence, whose solution conditions the destiny of men. Man before Nature, that is the *subject* in face of the object. It is a question, for the

European, *Homo faber,* of knowing nature in order to make it an instrument of his powerful will: of *using* it. He will assess it by analysis, will make of it a *dead* thing in order to dissect it. But how can one use a dead thing to make Life? It is, on the contrary, in his subjectivity that the Black, "porous to every breath of the world," discovers the object in its reality: rhythm. And there he abandons himself, docile to this living movement, going from subject to object," playing the game of the world."[29]

Chaka's vision of the future is based on the assumption of this fundamental cultural distinction, and the horror he expresses at the prospect of seeing his own culture destroyed is Senghor's defense of Negritude.

Not only does Chaka become a spokesman for Senghor's ideology, but he reflects certain personal elements of the poet's own experiences. Chaka uses the expression "royaume d'enfance" several times in the poem and describes his childhood environment as pastoral, marked by the sound of flutes and the lowing of the herds. The conflict between Chaka's vocation as poet and his obligations as statesman is a dilemma which he also shares with Senghor, whose decision to enter politics had meant something of a transition from his chosen career of education and literature. The writer must therefore have expressed his personal regret in Chaka's statement: "Je devins une tête un bras sans tremblement, ni guerrier ni boucher / Un politique tu l'as dit—je tuai le poète—un homme d'action seul" (I became a head an arm without trembling, neither a warrior nor a butcher / A politician, you have said—I killed the poet—a man of action alone; *Poèmes,* 120).

As in *Hosties noires,* the death in Chaka becomes only a purification necessary to the birth of a new order. He equates the murders he has committed to the burning of the fields which prepares the ground for the planting of new crops and the death of his fiancée to the grinding up of wheat to produce flour. Chaka's own death is depicted as martyrdom by the coryphaeus: "Tu es Zoulou par qui nous croissons dru, les narines par quoi nous buvons la vie forte / Et tu es le Doué-d'un-large-dos, tu portes tous les peuples à peau noire" (You are the Zulu by whom we grow up sturdy, the nostrils through which we drink strong life / You are the One-endowed-with-a-broad-back. You carry all the black-skinned peoples; *Poèmes,* 127). Chaka consents to his role of savior and dies so that a new era might dawn, the last lines being abundant with images of light.

"A New York"

In *Hosties noires* Senghor had discovered a fraternal bond with the Black American soldiers who, in spite of their separation from Africa, seemed to him to manifest the characteristics associated with Negritude. In his quest for new settings for his poems, the writer profits from a brief visit to the city of New York to expand the notion of Negritude with reference to the Afro-American and to explore further the question of what black culture can contribute to a modern technological society. The poem, in three parts, contrasts the poet's perception of Manhattan, which represents the achievements of Western civilization, with a visit to Harlem, where he finds traces of Africa. The final stanza envisions the possible spiritual union of the two.

At first overpowered by the city with its long-legged golden girls and awesome skyscrapers, he soon comes to realize its shortcomings. The cold smiles of the women, the dark streets where tall buildings blot out the sun, the hardness of steel and stone, and the polluted air which cannot support life contrast poorly with the narrator's memories of the natural scenes of a village setting. He notes the absence of human companionship or even the natural human odors. The poet of "Nuit de Sine" finds especially disconcerting the sounds of a Manhattan night and its antiseptic lovemaking devoid of any desire for children, a particularly incomprehensible idea in view of the importance which Senghor assigns to procreation in his interpretation of African thought. In contrast to the harsh, sterile face of this part of the city, a visit to Harlem explodes in rhythm, color, and life. The night, made more animate by the undulating movements and soft, sensual forms of human beings, regains its association with dancing and music, and the scene abounds with emotion. The difference which Senghor distinguishes between the city's two cultures illustrates his theory that the two react to nature in characteristic ways: the Western tendency is to use nature and to mold it to its needs and the African seeks to conform himself to the rhythms of nature.

In the last stanza, the poet pleads with the city to open itself to the temperizing influence of Negritude, and he imagines the superimposing of the magic of Harlem on his image of the rigid, soulless city: "New York! je dis New York, laisse affluer le sang noir dans ton sang / Qu'il dérouille tes articulations d'acier, comme une huile de vie / Qu'il donne à tes ponts la courbe des croupes et la souplesse des lianes" (New York! I say New York, let the black blood flow into your blood / May it remove the rust from your steel joints, like an oil of life / May it give your bridges the curve of hips and the suppleness of vines; *Poèmes,* 115). The symbolic blending of the two cultures is created by a happy synthesis of images from the two preceding stanzas, each of which describes a different part of the city. "A New York" demonstrates in a new context a device we've seen a number of times before: the rewriting of cultural values in such a way as to challenge old stereotypes and to poke holes in the notion of the merit of technological progress.

"A New York" differs significantly from most of the poems which precede it in *Ethiopiques.* In contrast with the others, it does not focus primarily on the writer. Although it is recounted in the first person, the central drama is not experienced by the narrator, but by the city. The speaker tells of having undertaken a journey, but the transformation he envisions does not change him personally. To the extent that a transformation is depicted, this work shares a common pattern with poems like "L'Homme et la Bête," "Congo," "Teddungal," and "L'Absente." As in these works, the imagery evolves from sterility to ultimate vitality. Alain Baudot, in one of several perceptive readings of the poem, suggests that structurally it resembles a fairy tale: "situation (heroine in danger); remedy (hero); solution (happy ending)."[30] The happy ending reminds us that most of the works in this volume end on a note of jubilation.

The one exception perhaps is "Epîtres à la Princesse" which, like "A New York," preaches the virtues of Negritude to a highly technical civilization bent on self-destruction. But the future that Senghor imagines for the African ambassador and his European princess is not as fortunate as that anticipated for Harlem and Manhattan. The hero, in effect, fails to save the heroine. In spite of the death of the Princess, do we really have an unhappy ending? Africa triumphs in the end and so this poem, like "Chaka" and "A New York," becomes a resounding affirmation of the values of Negritude. Not only does *Ethiopiques* provide several variations on a theme in which the narrator as a hero or initiate individually triumphs over obstacles or proves his own worth, but it also offers two works that depict a view of history in which Negritude plays a similar heroic role in the survival of mankind.

Chapter Eight
The Elegies in *Nocturnes*
The Originality of Senghor's Elegies

As early as 1957, Senghor introduced what was for him a new poetic genre, the elegy. *Nocturnes* (1961) collected five of these poems that had appeared individually elsewhere between 1957 and 1959. In classical literature, the elegy denoted a specific meter rather than a certain type of subject, and we have examples of elegies from that period on topics as diverse as love, politics, patriotism, and personal matters. Through the natural course of literary evolution, the French use of the term "elegiac" has come to be attributed to lyric poems of a melancholy or plaintive nature. This differs somewhat from its use in English writing where it generally relates to poems on death or for the dead. Although Senghor deals with the subject of death in many of his elegies, his concept of the genre seems to derive from the French interpretation that views the elegy more broadly as a lament, often for the passing of time or for the ephemeral nature of things. In their subject matter, Senghor's elegies are the legitimate heirs of the carpe diem elegies of French Renaissance poetry and the *Meditations* of Lamartine. Despite their obvious Western antecedents, they also introduce the unmistakable stamp of African influences. In the dramatic poem, "Elégie pour Aynina Fall," with its choruses and refrains, and elsewhere in the introduction of traditional chants and ceremonies, the borrowings from oral literature are immediately evident. A further indication of the writer's debt to African sources can be found in his manner of depicting the theme of death so frequent in these works. As we have noted before, his poetry rarely describes death as a final state but frames it instead within a cyclical concept of time and nature as the sacrifice upon which some better day may be founded. The elegies retain and strengthen this notion, and in a sense, they even participate in it. Like the Master-of-the-word to whom he compares himself, the poet, by formulating a verbal image of the future, insures that such a day will indeed come to pass.

The critical reaction to the elegies published in *Nocturnes* has not always recognized the originality of these later works. The reviewer for the *Times Literary Supplement* suggests that "M. Senghor has failed to make a new exploration of experience and his poetry has lost some of its relevance. Or can it be that the barrel of Negritude itself is running dry."[1] Jonathan Peters seems disappointed that "apart from the celebration of personal repose the elegies of *Nocturnes* add little dimension to Senghor's philosophical development."[2] The distinction that he does concede to these poems is the significant suggestion that "the era of rebirth and reconciliation is finally at hand."[3] Peters's reference to the political events that provide the background for the collection is indicative of their importance and it is difficult to imagine a discussion of the elegies that fails to establish the character of this period and its influence on both the public and private life of the writer. While many of the devices used in this collection have appeared before, they occur this time in a wholly new context that must be duly weighed in any consideration of the poems. Published as they are just at the moment of Senegalese independence, several of them might even be categorized as national anthems of a sort, with the narrator-protagonist assuming yet another of the classical roles assigned to the archetypal hero, that of founder of the nation.[4]

The years during which the elegies in *Nocturnes* were written coincided with the period of intensified demands for self-government in France's African colonies. Senghor's own vision of the future of French West Africa had come to emphasize the consideration of two essential points: first, the preservation of ties with France and second, the establishment of some type of federal union among the individual French-speaking nations. At the conference of Cotonou in 1958, he found his desires for retaining ties with France opposed by the vast majority of his fellow delegates who proclaimed unconditional liberation as their primary goal. This event constituted a personal defeat for Senghor and for the moderate point of view he represented. The period from 1958 to 1959 also saw the drafting of a new French constitution, one which redefined still further the relationship between France and her colonies. It was an issue of utmost importance to Senghor that the document offer an alternative to outright secession. The creation of a French Community, an association of former colonies similar to the British Commonwealth, provided just such an option. Being satisfied on this point, Senghor helped to win acceptance of the proposed constitution in Senegal and then moved to join the French Community. On the issue of political federation among the African states he was less fortunate. His fears that French West Africa might be broken up into several autonomous units—whose chances for economic viability would be problematic—proved to be well-founded, and his efforts to promote federation, especially the short-lived Federation of Mali, were ill-fated from the beginning. While the year 1960 brought nationhood and independence to Senegal, with Léopold Sédar Senghor as its first president, the conditions surrounding independence were not those which Senghor himself had hoped to create and he could see all too well the problems that would result from the overeagerness of others for autonomy and from the failure to construct a mechanism for preserving African unity.[5]

The sheer weight of Senghor's political burden at this point in his career and his accompanying periods of frustration and disappointment give the elegies a tone and perspective that, in spite of their characteristically Senghorian rhythm and imagery, generally distinguish them from the works of the previous collection, *Ethiopiques* (1956). These were largely dawn or spring poems, their tone marked by the elation typical of beginnings. Invariably, any obstacles were overcome and the poems ended on a note of triumph and hope. As has been suggested, this pattern may to some extent be attributed to the writer's sense of achievement early in his political career. By contrast, the elegies are characterized by images of midday and summer and, consequently, reveal the regrets both of middle age and of the tempestuous political period. There is also less of a tendency on the part of the poet to hide himself behind allegory, a new development in his persona that Irele describes as a more introspective style: "The grave and often somber atmosphere of the *Elégies* in the later volume show how a reflective tone has come to control the earlier self-dramatisation, how the poet's self-awareness has now diffused itself in a more intimate identification with the elements of his imaginative universe."[6] These more personal verses reveal the human side of the political leader and statesman with his fatigue and responsibilities. The form seems to reflect the poet's change in attitude. The elegies are meditations that generally lack the sense of closure typical of the epic poems of *Ethiopiques*. One no longer has the sense of a successfully completed task. The problem remains when the poem is finished. In spite of the absence of that

sonorous note of triumph which heralded the end of the poems in
the previous collection, the writer still contrives to end each piece
with some ray of hope and an optimistic outlook for the future.

Poems of Leadership and Nationhood

The first work in the series, "Elégie de Minuit" ("Midnight
Elegy"), clearly illustrates the elements which distinguish these
poems from their immediate predecessors. The poet speaks in the
first person rather than as a hero of legend or myth, and abandoning
the epic quests of *Ethiopiques,* he confides to us his own personal
anguish. In the course of four stanzas, he describes a sleepless night
which leads him ultimately to reflections on death. In his insomnia
the electric light becomes unbearable, and he tells us that "la splen-
deur des honneurs est comme un Sahara" (the splendor of honors is
like a Sahara; *Poèmes,* 196). This plaint provides a basis for interpreting the poem as a variation on the theme of the solitude of
leadership and as a cry of suffering under the burden it imposes.
For Abiola Irele, in his analysis of the elegy, the poet intends to
convey "a moment of crisis in his life, springing from the discour-
agement of political responsibilities (as the poem indicates) and his
solitary combat against his anguish."[7] In the first stanza, the poet
intensifies the emptiness he experiences by contrasting it with the
idyllic period of childhood. The fruition of the politician's dreams
for the future of his people does little to restore his own lost paradise,
for in the words of Gerald Moore, "the Presidential Palace in Dakar
represents a more drastic exile from the Kingdom of Childhood than
even his Parisian exile did."[8] Mezu emphasizes the broader implications of the emptiness depicted by the poet; he terms it "metaphysical" and "almost Pascalian," and he compares Senghor to King
Solomon to whom he ascribes the idea that "nothing in this world
is eternal, nothing can appease the thirst of man."[9]

In the poet's state of despair, neither lover nor poetry can provide
consolation. Romantically, he contemplates death as an escape, but
fearing that hell might be an extension of this sense of absence, he
turns in prayer to God. He asks that he might find his final repose
beneath the soil of Joal in order to be reborn to the lost Kingdom
of Childhood. The afterlife that he describes delicately intertwines
ideas from Christian theology and from traditional African thought.
In the last lines, the poet dreams of sleeping peacefully in the arms

of the woman he loves. Whether he means by this a final rest or a blissful sleep after a night of wakefulness is not exactly clear. One interpretation of this poem views it essentially as a commentary on the poetic process: "The direct but antithetic imagery of 'Elegy of Midnight' deals with the aridity and the creativity of the poet. Poetry springs from childhood, into which the poet must be born again. But it also springs from the sleep of death."[10] The narrator refers to himself consistently throughout as "the Poet," and other allusions lend considerable credence to such a reading.

That this is also one of Senghor's more erotic poems has not escaped notice. Guibert, in particular, has undertaken to analyze the role of the sexual imagery and the place of the woman in the elegy. He considers that the references to the speaker's virility in the second and third stanzas constitute a necessary counterpoint to his evocation of death, and he views the woman's absence as an important feature of the emptiness to which the poet alludes.[11] It is certainly true that in the vision of peace which finally replaces the desert of the earlier stanzas, the woman's presence plays a role: "Que je sois le berger de ma bergère par les tanns de Dyilôr où fleurissent les Morts" (Let me be the shepherd of my shepherdess in the flood plains of Dyilôr where the Dead thrive; *Poèmes,* 198). It is also with a reference to her that the elegy closes.

Solitude, nostalgia, poetry, love—all of these subjects are treated importantly in a poem that, like a Cubist painting, reveals its subject from a variety of perspectives, none of which can legitimately claim to be dominant. Interestingly, the critics we have cited do not refer to Senghor's original inspiration for these lines as he has revealed in an interview: "I now succeed in reconciling my two lives: the private life and the public life, the poetic life and the political life. . . . In order to lead this double life, it is necessary to have a constitution of iron. Since 1945, I have never been confined to bed for more than twenty-four hours, except on the occasion of an eye operation, when I remained for a week in a clinic. An incident which gave me the inspiration for 'Elégie de Minuit.' "[12] This insight into the poet's personal life might help to explain his extraordinary sensitivity to light in the poem and specifically, two of the most effective images in the first stanza: his description of the Christian missionary staked out in the sun and the figure of the lighthouse lamp burning implacably day after day.[13] The poem gains in meaning if we consider that it represents a moment of special

significance in the writer's life, a moment when the fragile balance
he has achieved between his "two lives" may have become especially
precarious.

In "Elégie des circoncis" ("Elegy of the Circumcised"), the poet
again returns nostalgically to the past for inspiration. The traditional
rite of passage that elsewhere in Senghor's work serves as a structural
device or appears only as a passing reference figures as the central
image of the poem. The apprehensions of the initiate in the first
stanza are dissipated in the second stanza by the rhythm of the music
and dancing that constitute an essential part of the ceremony; in
the course of the rest of the elegy, the narrator attributes similar
powers to his own poetry in overcoming his present anxieties and
those of the people whom he now leads. In his task he invokes the
powers of the Master of Initiates: "Maître des Initiés, j'ai besoin je
le sais de ton savoir pour percer le chiffre des choses / Prendre
connaissance de mes fonctions de père et de lamarque[14] /Mesurer
exactement le champ de mes charges, répartir la moisson sans oublier
un ouvrier ni orphelin" (Master of Initiates, I have need I know of
your wisdom in order to decipher the secret of things / To take note
of my functions as father and lamarch / To measure exactly the scope
of my responsibilities, to distribute the harvest without forgetting
worker or orphan; Poèmes, 200). With its symbolism of life from
death, the circumcision rite becomes an appropriate metaphor for
the transition of the people to nationhood. As the traditional com-
ing-of-age ceremony helps to give meaning and form to the life of
the initiate upon reaching adulthood, so too does the poet's vision
of the ceremony and its function help to bring his perspective on
current political developments into focus. Again, we find intentional
comments on the function of poetry woven into the elegy. The poem
becomes a form of verbal magic able to facilitate such transitions
both through the intensity of its rhythm, which "chases away anguish," and through the act of articulating the poet's vision. The
very existence of the poem provides evidence of the creative potential
of the poet's imagination and implies the possibility of the fulfill-
ment of his vision. In the same way that the initiate in the circumcision ceremony must ritually triumph over death and so reaffirm
the eternal cycle of nature, the poem is compared in the last line
to the phoenix, the legendary bird capable of being reborn from its
own ashes.

The elegy opens with a plaintive invocation of Night which is repeated with some variation in the second and fourth stanzas: "Combien de fois t'ai-je invoquée ô Nuit! pleurant au bord des routes / Au bord des douleurs de mon âge d'homme? Solitude! et c'est les dunes alentour" (How many times have I invoked you O Night! crying along the sides of the roads / On the borders of the suffering of my adulthood? Solitude! and there are dunes all around; *Poèmes,* 198). The significance of such an appeal to night derives from the elaborate set of connotations created in previous poems, in the nostalgic African setting depicted in "Nuit de Sine," for example, or in the line from *Que m'accompagnent kôras et balafong* in which the poet also addresses Night: "Nuit qui fonds toutes mes contradictions, toutes contradictions dans l'unité première de ta négritude" (Night that melts all my contradictions, all contradictions in the primary unity of your negritude; *Poèmes,* 35). Throughout the course of his work, Senghor has repeatedly returned to this particular image and accorded it a symbolism that greatly intensifies its meaning in the elegy. Irele recognizes the special status of the term in Senghor's symbolic vocabulary when he analyzes its function here: "There are three progressive levels of significance in this invocation to night: as scene-setting for the evocation of the initiation ceremony; as nostalgic recall of the poet's early life and antecedents; and as symbol of those values that constitute his poetic universe."[15] Later in the poem, the poet contrasts the fond memory of Night and the cruel reality of the present which he terms "Midi-le-Mâle" (Midday-the-Male). The innocent nights of childhood are countered by maturity when too much illumination threatens our illusions and lays bare the weaknesses of the adult world. Peters interprets this elegy as an initiation of the poet into that phase of manhood associated with leadership.[16] These verses, despite the optimistic ending, do much to reveal the solitude and burden of responsibilities that plague the individual in a position of power.

Whereas the "Elégie des circoncis" shows us the poet's magic placed at the service of his people, "Elégie des Eaux" ("Elegy of the Waters") wields that same power in the greater interest of all mankind. By virtue of his poetic vocation, the poet claims the ability to call forth the water that will restore life to a world scorched and flaming under the wrath of God. Like its predecessor, this poem begins with a reference to the childhood paradise and contrasts those joyous summers with present summers when God in his anger has sent fire as a punishment to the proud cities of the world—to Chicago and to Moscow—in the same way that he once destroyed the wicked Biblical city of Gomorrah. This idea recalls several poems in *Hosties noires* where World War II was depicted as a form of divine vengeance. To quench the flames, the poet calls forth the waters that will also purify and provide for the revitalization referred to in the last line: "Et renaît la Vie couleur de présence" (And Life is reborn, the color of presence; *Poèmes*, 206). The rebirth of civilization anticipated by the writer recalls his concept of a Universal Civilization in that the elegy provides for the survival of the world's diverse people and cultures. This particular work also constitutes a strong indictment of the superpowers and repeats the poet's earlier warning against nuclear disaster in "Epîtres à la Princesse." It is interesting that the subject should have been in the poet's mind just at the time of independence. The poem provides an insight into the fatalism of those new Third World nations whose futures must have seemed questionable in the light of the fragile peace that presided over their birth. Senghor's verbal magic constitutes a feeble weapon against an impending holocaust, but the effort is characteristic of his own personal optimism and sense of duty. Much later, he will continue to feel an obligation to try to alert the great powers to the threat posed to humanity by their nuclear arsenals. [17]

Rounding out the collection of elegies in *Nocturnes* is the "Elégie pour Aynina Fall." Although Senghor uses the term "elegy" to denote this funerary praise song, it differs considerably from the other elegies in that it does not deal directly with the poet and, in terms of structure, as indicated by its subtitle, it is not a lyric poem in any sense but "a dramatic poem for several voices." Through the speeches of two choruses and their leader or coryphaeus, he mourns Aynina Fall, a leader of the African railroad workers' union who met his death at the hands of assassins. Van Niekerk finds this one of Senghor's less convincing efforts. He tells us that "this poem is too obviously politically inspired and pursues too patently panegyrical motives for it to succeed poetically."[18] Peters also seems unimpressed and implies that the writer has chosen a weak conclusion for his collection.[19] On the other hand, Reed and Wake, who stress that the elegies are "the poetry of the leader,"[20] easily justify the placement of this final piece: "It is perhaps not entirely without design that the 'Elegy for Aynina Fall' is placed last, for it suddenly releases Senghor's poetry from its creator and expands the notion of leadership to include all men."[21] It is also worth mentioning that in addition to its role as a eulogy for one man, the poem also carries a broader symbolic significance which warrants its inclusion among a collection of hymns dealing primarily with African independence and nationhood for Senegal: as one of its principal themes, it treats the notion of African unity so strongly—and so futilely—advocated by Senghor in the years prior to independence.

In the first of the poem's two parts, the poet emphasizes the attributes of the union leader and describes the circumstances of his death. After a brief introduction by the coryphaeus, the two choruses—one male and one female—vie with each other in praising the fallen hero. The women describe his virtues in terms of metaphors which reflect a feminine perspective with its characteristic tenderness, while the men draw attention to his strength and ferocity. The coryphaeus returns to give an account of the actual assassination but couches his narrative in the figurative language of oral literature. The assassins thus become jackals and baboons that, although clearly lesser creatures, succeed in bringing down a more worthy opponent in the king of beasts. So that such a man might not die in vain, Senghor turns to the death-rebirth cycle of nature in order to transform this death into a sacrifice capable of producing new vitality and greater unity among African peoples: "Il a versé son sang, qui féconde la terre d'Afrique; il a racheté nos fautes; il a donné sa vie sans rupture pour l'UNITE DES PEUPLES NOIRS" (He has shed his blood, which renders fertile the soil of Africa; he has redeemed our sins; he has given his life without ceasing for the Unity of black peoples; *Poèmes,* 210). The use of capitals in this way generally serves in Senghor's poetry to invoke the magic power of the word and the creative potential inherent in the poem.

It is not until part two that the text of the poem introduces the motif of the railroad. Because the railroad, suggested by its association with Aynina Fall, links the capitals of France's former African colonies, it becomes a further basis for making him a symbol of African unity. A locomotive acts as the funeral chariot of the dead hero and we feel in the rhythm of the poem the regular cadence of a moving train. The final repetition of the name "Fall" that brings the movement of the poem to a close imitates the sound of a train braking as it comes finally to a halt. This is not intended to mark the end of a life; on the contrary, death is depicted as a new beginning with Fall described as the first to arrive. In these closing lines the

two choruses come together for the only time in the poem to proclaim that they are united "like the ten fingers of the hand." In a
typically Senghorian fashion death loses its character of finality under
the power of the poet, who renders the fallen hero immortal by
transforming his life into an eternal symbol of black unity.

"Elégie des *saudades*"

In addition to those elegies inspired in some way by the subjects
of nationhood and leadership, Senghor, who profited so much in
the past from returning to his African sources, offers some reflections
on his possible Portuguese antecedents in "Elégie des *saudades."* The
term *saudades,* which occurs several times in the poem, is defined
by Senghor as a Portuguese word for "nostalgia."[22] The philosopher
has long proclaimed the values of cultural crossbreeding and his
speculation concerning his Portuguese heritage constitutes a new
direction of development for this concept. Less solemn than the
other works in the collection, this poem allows us to see the poet's
imagination from another standpoint as he returns to that century
of romance and adventure when Portugal's flag dominated the great
rivers of the world. Throughout several stanzas, he imagines that
he is his own Portuguese ancestor braving the challenges of the dark
continent and experiencing the exotic mysteries of uncharted seas.
The rich imagery of the third stanza, the emotional appeal of the
fourth, and the exquisite dialogue with the flower-women of the
Fortunate Isle create a truly marvelous fantasy and show us what
Senghor can do with words when liberated from the restriction of
his own theses. In spite of the lure of his vision he concludes: "Mon
sang portugais s'est perdu dans la mer de ma Négritude" (My Portuguese blood has become lost in the sea of my Negritude; *Poèmes,*
204).

The inclusion of this particular poem in the collection serves to
provide additional details for the writer's portrait during this period.
In various ways critics have emphasized the spirit of reconciliation
and the general absence of racial militancy within the elegies. Peters
asserts that "the racial overtones that were clearly marked in the
epic poems of *Ethiopiques* virtually disappear from the landscape of
the 'Elégies' of *Nocturnes. . . .* The opposition of black and white
values is relinquished in favour of a measure of humanism."[23] The
accustomed dichotomy of black and white does not emerge, and in

the "Elégie des *saudades*," the poet opens up the possibility that even within himself the cultural debt may not be merely French and African but multifaceted. This broadening of the poet's personal horizons is also echoed on a public level by the change in the politician's perspective as dictated by his new office. His previous role as deputy from Senegal to France had polarized his field of activity between the two nations; from this point forward, he must represent his people to the whole world. Portugal, like France and England, was an important colonial power in Africa. Two of Senegal's immediate neighbors, the Cape Verde Islands and Portuguese Guinea, are former Portuguese colonies, and for any African leader, the problems of Angola and Mozambique would naturally be of utmost interest.[24] By including a poem that recalls the extent of the Portuguese legacy in Africa, Senghor supplies evidence that his own focus on the continent is beginning to expand. In future works, such as the "Elégie de Carthage" and the "Elégie pour la reine de Saba," he will continue to fill in the map of Africa so as to show, not merely those regions of greatest familiarity to him, but the contributions of other peoples and cultures as well.

The reorientation of the statesman's viewpoint in "Elégie des *saudades*" confirms what we have seen elsewhere in the collection: for both Senghor and Senegal, the period commemorated in the elegies of *Nocturnes* represents an important stage in development. As a part of the chronicle of African progress toward both cultural and political independence, these poems celebrate—in the traditional patterns of initiation ceremonies, purification rites, and sacrifices—that precise moment when the modern African nation came into being. As a record of the poet's life, they also reveal an important transition: the leader who assumes both the honors and the duties of his country's head of state differs enormously from the victorious questing hero of *Ethiopiques*.

Chapter Nine
Elégie des Alizés
and Lettres d'hivernage

Senghor's next published volume, *Elégie des Alizés* (1969), was followed soon after by *Lettres d'hivernage* (1973). Both works were
initially presented in handsome editions illustrated with lithographs
done by Marc Chagall. Although the elegy later appeared as part
of the collection entitled *Elégies majeures,* it seems more appropriate
for several reasons to treat it here. Chronologically, it belongs at
this point in the writer's life, and thematically, it is a companion
piece to the love poems in *Lettres d'hivernage.* Compared with the
other pieces in *Elégies majeures,* it is also more personal in nature,
and like *Lettres d'hivernage,* it often focuses primarily on the poet.
To the extent that these two works reveal the writer—or his persona—they contribute another dimension to his identification with
the archetypal hero, for characteristically in myth, the hero, having
overcome his obstacles and won his bride, eventually returns home
to rule his kingdom, often with special insights gained from his
adventures. It is at precisely this point that Senghor himself has
arrived, and in both *Elégie des Alizés* and *Lettres d'hivernage,* we are
confronted by a poet-narrator who is a prominent head of state, the
man who has led his nation successfully through its first decade of
independence. The notion that the hero has returned home to Africa
also figures here. In both works, Senghor is extremely conscious of
the environment and relies heavily on images derived from the
changing pattern of the seasons in a tropical country. This pattern,
if not unfamiliar to him, would have only moderately affected the
rhythm of his existence during the many years spent in France. Now
that he has taken up permanent residence in Dakar, his concept of
time, his choice of activities, and even his moods are all obliged to
conform to that climate and its particular cadences. The prominent
role played by nature imagery in these two works is immediately
evident in the poet's choice of titles.

Elégie des Alizés

In conformity with the loosely structured poetic form which Senghor had used earlier in *Nocturnes, Elégie des Alizés* consists of ten stanzas of various length. It represents the writer's first published book of poetry since *Nocturnes* in 1961, a period of literary silence which he acknowledges in the initial lines of the poem. With the responsibilities of the presidency, even the time for the production of this slim volume was apparently very difficult to find. As early as 1967, Hubert de Leusse published an incomplete version of the poem with only four stanzas, but it took two more years before the appearance of the current version.[1] In keeping with his practice in previous works such as "Epîtres à la Princesse," Senghor's narrator describes himself not as a modern political leader, but as a traditional tribal chief, a shepherd or farmer continually battling the elements rather than the balance of trade. He also retains the role of poet-magician which characterized even his first poems: "Ma tâche est d'éveiller mon peuple aux futurs flamboyants / Ma joie de créer des images pour les nourrir, ô lumières rythmées de la Parole" (My task is to awaken my people to flamboyant futures / My joy to create images in order to nourish them, Oh lights of the Word put to rhythm.)[2] The poem deals with the trials of the nation and with the poet's efforts on behalf of his people.

In the course of the poem, the various stanzas, like the illuminated pages of a medieval book of hours, depict the narrator's struggles and triumphs metaphorically in terms of the challenges or opportunities provided by nature at different times of the year. To appreciate the poet's use of the seasonal cycle as a structural device, it is necessary to have some knowledge of the Senegalese climate. David Gamble, in his study of Senegambia, offers the following outline:

Feb.–May: The hot season. No rain. A hot east wind blowing, drying the soil, and withering the vegetation.

June: First rains. Characterized by tornadoes due to the meeting of the monsoons, and the east wind, causing whirlwinds and storms. Considerable dust storms may be raised before the rain, which often comes in short, violent thunderstorns.

July–Sept.: The rainy season.

October: End of the rains. Very humid conditions. Rains terminate
            with further violent storms.

Nov.–Jan.: The temperature falls gradually. The north wind begins to
            blow, while a dry sea breeze is felt in the coastal zone.
            Sometimes high clouds give a little rain. The sky becomes
            dull and hazy.[3]

Correspondingly, Senghor describes the tornadoes of July and the
subsequent floods of the rainy season with their "pourritures spon-
gieuses du coeur, qui vous aspirent, énergie! de leurs ventouses
insondables" (spongy putrifications of the heart, which suck at you,
energy! with their limitless mouths; *E.M.*, 11). The end of the
rains brings the trade winds or *Alizés,* a period of fair weather but
also a period which demands renewed activity on the part of the
leader and his people—the farmers, fishermen and herders whose
labor he glorifies with his song. The Harmattan, a drying wind,
brings yet another type of challenge, but eventually trees flower
and Senghor describes a period of renewal corresponding with the
Easter season: "Que meure le vieux nègre et vive le Nègre nouveau! /
Et l'esprit est descendu parmi nous dans la pourpre des flamboyants"
(Let the old negro die and the New Negro live! / And the spirit
has descended among us in the purple of the flamboyants; *E.M.*,
18). Before the rains begin again, the tall dry grasses must be burned
and new seeds selected to be sown: "Nous choisirons des semences
de choix / De telle dilection, semences des longues méditations"
(We will choose choice seeds / With such tender love, seeds of long
meditations; *E.M.*, 18). Here, as elsewhere in the poem, the surface
description of a cultivator planning carefully for next year's crop
only barely hides what must surely be the poet's true intention: to
depict the activities of the new nation's planners and administrators
as they prepare carefully for its future. The last stanza brings the
writer back to the beginning of the seasonal cycle and runs in rapid
succession through the events which are to come, many of which—
the tornadoes, Toussaint, the harvests—have already appeared in
the poem's earlier description of the rainy season and the coming
of the trade winds. The poem concludes in the anticipation of the
returning *Alizés.*

In certain respects, *Elégie des Alizés* resembles the previous elegies.
There are distinct similarities of style and of tone: we continue to
be aware of the poet as an individual and of the heavy burden of

responsibilities which weighs on him. There is in the later poem, a complete structural pattern somewhat different from preceding poems in that it is not composed of a crisis and resolution, but of a repetition of the seasonal cycle which might conceivably recur indefinitely. While each season brings its various challenges, the poet appears to have been caught up in the rhythm of nature and to have found a certain harmony within that rhythm. The advent of the *Alizés* logically marks the high point of the cycle since they accompany the end of the rainy season and bring a period of favorable weather. Senghor gives their arrival added significance by associating them, in the fourth stanza, with memories of the childhood paradise, and in the sixth stanza, with images of night, both ideas being closely linked elsewhere with the narrator's sense of his own Negritude. Because they occur at about the time when All Saints' Day is celebrated, they also have some association with the Dead, the Ancestors who consistently symbolize the poet's African heritage throughout his poetry. The connection between the *Alizés* and Easter in the eighth stanza gives them a spiritual dimension, and there are also implications here of a bond between the image of the *Alizés* and the narrator's love for his wife, a relationship to be more precisely defined in *Lettres d'hivernage*. It is possible to see in the Alizés the creation of a new and powerful image, an important addition to the poet's vocabulary capable of containing within itself the essence of Senghor's previously established ideals.

In *The Myth of the Eternal Return*, Mircea Eliade contends that in traditional civilizations there is constant imitation of the archetypes that he interprets as an attempt to abolish time and to return to the primordial era. This can be accomplished either by the repetition of the paradigmatic gestures and periodic ceremonies or through a single regeneration anticipated in the future.[4] Throughout the first works of Senghor, there is a conscious attempt to create a myth with the implications of the second method: the poet continually looks forward to the restoration of the "Royaume d'enfance," the childhood kingdom that, in his cosmogony, represents his own primordial era. With independence and statehood achieved and the kingdom symbolically restored, it is not surprising that in this later poem the poet, for the moment, perceives time as cyclic rather than linear as he looks forward to the annual return of the trade winds with the memories of childhood they evoke and with their messages of divine and human love. Hubert de Leusse, one of the few critics to treat this poem and who wrote on only the unfinished version consisting of the first four stanzas, was especially struck by the hope and optimism implict in the poem's perspective with respect to time: "But, like the *Alizés,* this poem also brings us the freshness of a hope . . . The hour no longer belongs to the nostalgia for a past, regardless of how beautiful it might have been! . . . The hour belongs to the certainty of marvellous tomorrows . . ."[5]

Lettres d'hivernage

Among those associations which seem to crystallize around the image of the trade winds as Senghor develops it in the *Elégie des Alizés,* we find a number of references to the poet's wife and to his love for her. The best developed instance in which they are linked occurs in the second to the last stanza where, as the rainy season begins, the poet seeks comfort in evoking the woman he loves: ". . . . sous tes yeux je serai, soufflera sur ma fièvre le sourire de tes yeux alizés / Tes yeux vert et or comme ton pays, si frais au solstice de Juin" (. . . under your eyes I will be, the smile of your tradewind eyes will cool my fever / Your eyes green and gold like your country, so fresh at the June solstice; *E.M.,* 19). But, in point of fact, the loved one is not actually present: "Où es-tu donc, yeux de mes yeux, ma blonde, ma normande ma conquérante? Chez ta mère à la douceur vermeille?" (Where are you therefore, eyes of my eyes, my blond, my Norman, my conqueror? At the home of your mother with its vermilion sweetness?; *E.M.,* 19). Finally he repeats his references to the trade winds in a last line which emphasizes her absence and his longing for her: "Mais chante sur mon absence tes yeux de brise alizés, et que l'Absente soit présence" (But sing over my absence your tradewind eyes of breeze, and let the Absent Woman be presence; *E.M.,* 19). The network of imagery that the poet develops, in which the woman's absence is linked to the rainy season and her presence is represented by the return of the trade winds, is not only poetically effective, but also has some basis in the cycle of the writer's personal life. During his presidency he and his wife customarily vacationed in her native Normandy. (The reference in the above lines to the conqueror recalls the family history of Colette Hubert whose Norman forebears fought with William at the battle of Hastings.[6]) The period of these visits normally coincided with the rainy season *(hivernage)* in Senegal, and in both *Elégies de Alizés* and *Lettres d'hivernage,* it becomes clear that on some occasions the president, with his official duties, was unable to be with his spouse. Her absence tends to render the humid period of the rains even more depressing and her return contributes to his anticipation of the arrival of the trade winds in October. This same separation also justifies the epistolary poetry of *Lettres d'hivernage* (1973), a collection of 30 poems in the form of intimate letters from the poet to his wife. The passage of time through the rainy season to the return of the trade winds—and the return of the woman—provides a coherent structural device strongly supported by nature imagery appropriate to the changing seasons.

In addition to endowing the annual cycle of nature with a certain personal symbolism, Senghor makes it obvious that another cycle, the one which coincides with the life span of a single human being, must also revolve until it too comes at last to its own autumn or *hivernage.* In the "Argument," the poet's prefatory statement, he explains that the term *hivernage* denotes the rainy season, which in Senegal begins in June and ends around the second week in October. The word, he tells us, was coined by the colonial army, which "wintered" during this time of the year. He then specifies that this season is that of summer and the beginning of autumn and adds that "il y a aussi l'hivernage de la *Femme*" (there is also the *hivernage* of the Woman; *Poèmes,* 218). The woman addressed in the poems has reached a certain maturity, a certain season of her life, but there is only one poem in the entire work which deals specifically with the theme: in "Tu parles" ("You speak"), the narrator offers assurances of continued love and admiration to his companion in her anxiety that she is growing older. Senghor does not belabor the point, and although the novelty of a cycle of love poems destined not for a first love or a new love but for a wife of some fifteen years of marriage has an undeniable charm and contributes much to the character of the volume, the reference to the woman's age might best be regarded as a reflection on the poet himself and as a part of a whole set of ideas which identify these poems as stemming from the early autumn of his life, his *hivernage.* A comparison between the vision depicted in earlier love poems and these later pieces readily reveals the poet's own maturity and his awareness of himself as a man of middle years. This change in perspective is evident in the writer's depiction of both space and time and in the modification of various features of the narrator's self-image.

Orpheus in Mid-Life.[7]   Even the choice of setting distinguishes these poems from the previous cycles dedicated to women. Whereas "Chants pour Signare" takes place largely within an exotic, pastoral framework and "Epîtres à la Princesse" drew upon the glamour of both Europe and Africa in the middle ages in order to depict a Scandinavian princess and her royal African lover, *Lettres d'hivernage* situates the narrator in the realistic setting of modern-day Dakar. This contemporary, urban setting—unusual for Senghor—is hardly more than mentioned but exists nevertheless as an important backdrop for the presentation of the letters. The rural, tropical landscape so often used in previous works was characterized by its innocence and evoked a way of life in harmony with nature and atune to the mysteries of hidden forces; in Senghor's inner cosmogony, it clearly represented Eden. The city, on the other hand, has far different connotations for the poet. He describes its buildings "humming with power and ambition," its "impatient villas," and its "monstrous medinas" (*Poèmes,* 226). He often seeks escape from his surroundings either by casting his gaze out to sea or by visits to his weekend villa a few miles away from Dakar at Popenguine, which he associates with Joal, his childhood home and the prototype for his personal notion of paradise:

Contre le désespoir, mon refuge mon seul, le royaume d'Enfance.
Je marche sur la plage, à Joal-Popenguine
Le sable sous la paume de mes pieds: le baiser de la terre maternelle.

(Against despair, my refuge, my only refuge, the kingdom of Childhood
I walk along the beach, at Joal-Popenguine
The sand under the sole of my feet: the kiss of the maternal earth.)

(*Poèmes,* 237)

In the same poem, he longs for a return to a simpler time in history or, perhaps, merely a less complicated time in his own life: "Qui me rendra les plateaux d'Ethiopie, où le pâtre sur un pied se / Repose à l'ombre de sa flute? (Who will give me back the plateaux of Ethiopia, where the shepherd on one foot / Reposes in the shadow of his flute?; *Poèmes,* 238). The entire collection is laced with a similar nostalgia.

Other verses underscore the collection's modernity, for in contrast with the lover of earlier poems, the poet no longer speaks with the voice of a medieval knight who would ride off with his lady on the back of a Tuareg steed, nor of a nomad Prince of one of the great African Empires. The poem "Vertige" ("Vertigo") is written from an airplane, and "Retour de Popenguine" ("Return from Popenguine") appears to have been composed during a helicopter ride. In "Ta lettre, ma lettre" ("Your letter, my letter"), there are references to the red telephone and to communications satellites. Such allusions, which provide the appropriate decor for a contemporary head of state, occur only infrequently but enough to place the work unquestionably in the poet's present and to identify the writer in terms of his office. The romantic idealism of youth gives way to the more realistic outlook of the adult.

The realism that characterizes the setting in *Lettres d'hivernage* and makes it different somehow in tone from the other love poems also adds a new dimension to the narrator's persona. With the primary exception of the poem "Toujours 'Miroirs' " ("Forever 'Mirrors' "), where the poet is transported into the past either in a dream or in his imagination, the role which the narrator plays is largely straightforward and unallegorical, although references to personal details— the presidential palace, its vast parks, his official duties—subtly create an awareness of the stature of the speaker, a device which in a sense, is fully as dramatic as the imaginary masks donned in earlier romances. In spite of these occasional reminders of the poet's political identity, the emphasis is generally on those activities which identify the speaker as an ordinary husband and father who likes to take his tea at five o'clock, enjoys his Sundays and vacations by the sea, often strolls along the beach or takes a swim, and has a rather sophisticated knowledge of botany.

As it is true that the woman to whom and of whom he writes has reached her middle years, it is also true for the poet. Characteristic of a man of that age, he seems to concentrate less on goals for the future, as he often did in earlier works, and to emphasize instead his past accomplishments and his regrets. A case in point is the poem "Toujours 'Miroirs' " that, once the element of fantasy is pierced, seems to be a recitation of just such past achievements:

Général et commandant ses armées, j'ai tendu les ressorts de sa grandeur
J'ai conseillé leurs mouvements, paré d'or et d'ivoire ses triomphes, couronné de plumes d'autruche.
Dites-moi qui a volé le secret de la Parole; au tréfonds des cavernes, la vérité des formes?

Forgé l'ordonnance des rites et la matrice des techniques?
Car des mots inouïs j'ai fait germer ainsi que des céréales nouvelles, et
    des timbres jamais subodorés
Une nouvelle manière de danser les formes, de rythmer les rythmes.

(Poèmes, 243)

(General and commanding its armies, I extended the jurisdiction of its
    grandeur
I advised their movements, decorated with gold and ivory its triumphs,
    crowned with ostrich plumes.
Tell me who stole the secret of the Word; in the depths of the caverns,
    the truth of forms?
Invented the order of the rites and the matrix of technical skills?
For I brought forth unheard-of words as well as new cereals and never-
    suspected timbres,
A new manner of dancing forms, of creating rhythms.)

Despite the metaphorical language, the poet is clearly depicting
himself in the role of innovator or as a new Prometheus. What is
significant is his use of the past tense. Compare this poem to those
of *Chants d'ombre* which use the future tense or dreams of the future
to outline what will be the task of the poet. In such a scene in the
eighth part of *Que m'accompagnent kôras et balafong,* he describes his
aspirations: "Ah! me soutient l'espoir qu'un jour je coure devant
toi, Princesse, porteur de ta récade à l'assemblée des peuples" (Ah!
I am sustained by the hope that one day I may run before you,
Princess, your sceptor-bearer in the assembly of nations; *Poèmes,* 32).
In these lines he anticipates the mission which he will have fulfilled
by the time he writes *Lettres d'hivernage.* A similar expression of his
looking towards the future occurred in the poem "Par delà Éros":
"Mon âme aspire à la conquête du monde innombrable et déploie
ses ailes, noir et rouge / Noir et rouge, couleurs de vos étandards!"
(My soul aspires to the conquest of the innumerable world and
deploys its wings, red and black / Black and red, colors of your
standards!; *Poèmes,* 43). The writer vows to the Ancestors the future
conquests which in "Toujours 'Miroirs' " he describes as a *fait accompli.*
    A man of middle-age not only has successes to remember but
also, inevitably, a few regrets. In Senghor's case, one particularly
poignant regret concerns the choice he was obliged to make at one
point in his life between politics and poetry. In "Je repasse" ("I
ponder"), he dramatizes the consequences of his decision by per-

sonifying the poetry which he might have written as a daughter which he never had:

Où est donc la fille de mon espoir défunt, Isabelle aux yeux clairs ou
   Soukeïna de soie noire?
Elle m'écrirait des lettres frissonnant d'ailes folles
D'images coloriées, avec de grandes bêtes aux yeux de Séraphins
Avec des oiseaux-fleurs, des serpents-lamantins sonnant des trompettes
   d'argent.
Car elle existe, la fille Poésie . . .

(Poèmes, 224–25)

(Where, therefore, is the daughter of my defunct hope, Isabelle with the
   bright eyes or Soukeïna of black silk?
She would write letters to me quivering with mad wings
With colored images, with great Seraphim-eyed beasts
With flower-birds, and serpent-manatees sounding silver trumpets.
For she exists, the daughter Poetry. . . .)

This disappointment at having to abandon poetry appeared earlier in the poem "Chaka," in which the Zulu chief bemoans the circumstances that require him to sacrifice the maiden Nolivé, the incarnation of his poetic instinct, in order to lead his people more effectively: "Un politique tu l'as dit—je tuai le poète—un homme d'action seul" (A politician, you said—I have killed the poet—a man of action alone; *Poèmes*, 120). That Senghor represents poetry as a child—his own child—in these later verses rather than as a mistress, as in "Chaka," points to yet another development in his perception of himself. In growing older, he must naturally begin to think less in terms of what he alone, a finite being, can accomplish and more of how his influence might best endure. In "Je repasse," the nostalgia for his unfulfilled vocation for poetry, the daughter, arises in association with thoughts of his son: "Je songe à mon enfant dernier, l'enfant de l'avenir" (I am dreaming of my last child, the child of the future; *Poèmes*, 224). This reference, which must surely indicate the poet's third son and his only child by Colette Hubert, reflects back on the poet by virtue of its orientation toward the future and identifies him as a man who has come to the time in life where he contemplates the inevitability of one day yielding to the next generation. Fatherhood is a new role for the narrator in the poems.

Structure and imagery. The theme of age and references to the cycle of life have less bearing on the actual structure of the work than does the cycle of seasons which governs the poet's separation and reunion with the woman. The first letters introduce the rainy season and the basic theme of the woman's absence. Gradually, the climate changes and at the end of the collection, the arrival of the trade winds announces the woman's return. Beyond the passage from one season to the next and the unifying focus on the woman's absence, the arrangement of the poem appears to have no apparent internal logic, no plot.[8] The work begins with a poem lamenting the woman's departure, and in subsequent poems, the poet describes his longing for her, at first with restraint and later—in the poems "Et le sursaut soudain" ("And the sudden start") and "Mon salut" ("My greeting") and in the initial lines of "Les Matins blonds de Popenguine" ("The Blond Mornings at Popenguine")—with the intense emotions of great suffering and anguish. In "J'aime ta lettre" ("I like your letter"), he describes the onslaught of the rainy season which is itself a motif in other poems, but about two-thirds of the way through the collection, beginning with "Tu te languis" ("You are pining"), he starts to contemplate the return of the trade winds and the woman, a dual theme which occurs intermittently throughout the rest of the collection. In addition to the notions of departure and return, there are also several poems built around the idea of separation. Among these would be classed the poems which feature references to ships or ports: the garland of white ships in "C'est cinq heures" ("It is five o'clock") that are departing both for the rivers of the South and for the northern fjords; the lights that come up on the cargo tankers in "Ton soir mon soir" ("Your evening my evening") and infuse the poet with the desire to be gone; and, in "Car je suis fatigué" ("For I am tired"), the departing boats which remind the waiting lover that he is indeed tired:". . . fatigué / De n'aller nulle part quand me déchire le désir de partir" (. . . tired of going nowhere when the desire to leave is tearing me apart). Whereas in "Chants pour Signare" the questing hero was always on the move, *Lettres d'hivernage* assigns him a static, waiting role, one which is visibly and continually frustrating. His eyes invariably gaze out to sea as if in an attempt to ignore his immediate environment and to broach the distance, if only in revery, between himself and the beloved.

Other poems strive to show the extent to which the woman occupies the poet's thoughts: he describes his memories of her and of other women who remind him of her; he dwells on their mutual attraction for one another; he dreams of her and fantasizes about her. Even when his thoughts have apparently strayed to other subjects, he inevitably returns to thinking of her. The overriding importance of this single emphasis is best stated by the poet himself in a poem which comes about a third of the way into the collection:

Je pense à toi quand je marche je nage
Assis ou debout, je pense à toi le matin et le soir
La nuit quand je pleure, eh oui quand je ris
Quand je parle je me parle et quand je me tais
Dans mes joies et mes peines. Quand je pense et ne pense pas
Chère je pense à toi!

(Poèmes, 228)

(I think of you when I walk I swim
Seated or standing, I think of you morning and evening
At night when I cry, ah yes, when I laugh
When I talk, I talk to myself and when I am silent
In my joys and my sorrows. When I think and don't think
Dear I think of you!)

Although in other poems the poet touches on a variety of topics, he never wanders very far from this single axis, the woman who is the recipient of the letters.

The principal mechanism in the poems involves the passage, through various associations, from some stimulus in the poet's immediate environment to an image involving the woman. The technique, reminiscent of Baudelaire's, often involves a tortuous journey through the imagination that sometimes entails travelling full circle to arrive back again at the starting point. The spark which sets the poet off varies from poem to poem but one of the most frequently used devices elaborates on a sensation. In "J'aime ta lettre," this pattern revolves around a fragrance; in "Sur la plage" ("On the beach"), a sensation of rhythm; in "Il a plu" ("It rained"), the thunder and lightning of a rainy night; in "Le Salut du jeune soleil" ("Greeting of the young sun"), the light of the sun. For two poems, "Que fais-tu" ("What are you doing") and "A quoi comment" ("Of what how"), the poet's springboard is the fiction that he is responding to her letters, which of course we are not privileged to read. Her letters and the poet's feelings about them constitute additional ways of focusing the images in various other poems. In eleven of the pieces, there is an explicit use of the word "letter" to refer to her letters to him, and in other poems references to her letters can be assumed. The letter is frequently mentioned near the beginning of a poem and often provides the basis for the initial comparison that activates the poet's imagination. At tea time, for example, the letter is fresh bread; elsewhere it is described as being sweeter than Saturday afternoons or than hysop. In a moment of anguish, the letter is likened to the flame that draws the moth but scorches its wings or to the fatal song of the siren. The letter itself is the subject of the poem "Ta lettre sur le drap" ("Your letter on the sheet") where it is associated with a series of life-sustaining elements: salt, air, milk, bread, rice, and sap. In "Ta lettre, ma lettre," it introduces a poem on the subject of communication. At one point the letter is tremulation and fever, but soon after, it is a blossoming of roses in an anticipation of floral images. Finally, the letter radiates light announcing the homecoming of the beloved whose return is bathed in light imagery appropriate to the end of the rainy season and in keeping with the poet's joyful mood. The letter, in short, evolves into a talisman capable of evoking the woman and of stirring the lover's emotions.

Although the poems are letters addressed to her and they deal with the poet's thoughts of her, the woman herself remains elusive and even less concrete in some respects than in her conventionalized, allegorical role of the Princess in "Epîtres à la Princesse." Her presence in the poet's thoughts is usually conveyed by figurative language and through various associations. Much of the imagery evokes previous Senghorian women, especially the depiction of the Princess for whom Mme Senghor was also a model. In the same way that Senghor's landscapes often exhibit feminine features, his women tend to reflect the landscape. The Princess, in tribute to Colette Hubert's Norman ancestry or perhaps as a device to clarify the dichotomy between North and South, seems vaguely Scandinavian and is frequently depicted in terms of a seascape. In *Lettres d'hivernage,* the woman also has affinities with the sea. In "Je repasse," the sea is compared to her eyes; in "Tu parles" ("You Speak"), her eyes are compared to the sea at dawn. Contemplating the sea often brings her to the lover's mind as in "Ton soir, mon soir" in which the sea at his feet reminds him of her standing before a sea of wheat. In "Trompettes des grues couronnées" ("Cries of Crested Cranes"), a description of the sounds, sights, and smells of the sea at dawn is entirely transformed into a vision of the beloved. Unlike the careful contrast between the African desert and the glacial fjords of the Vikings which polarized "Epîtres à la Princesse," the sea which brings to mind the woman in this instance and the one which is used to describe her is that of the port city of Dakar or of the beach at Popenguine. In this new configuration, far from being a part of the set of images which distinguish Europe from Africa, the sea is closely linked to Africa and home.

As another device for conveying the spiritual and physical charms of the woman, the writer has frequent recourse to floral images and the rose becomes her special emblem. In "Ton soir, mon soir" he visualizes the beloved on another continent surrounded by roses; in "Il a plu" he transforms a reference to Tinchebray roses, bright with dew, into a memory of her sparkling eyes. The letter of "Ta lettre" ("Your Letter") brings to mind the perfume of roses and thoughts of the woman, and she is described in "Tu parles" as having hands like rose petals. The flower is especially appropriate because of its traditional association with love and feminine beauty and because it is a typical European plant in contrast with the flamboyant which flourishes in the tropical setting—even in the absence of the beloved. The rose, buffeted by storms, fades at the beginning of the rainy season as if in sympathy with the departure of the woman.

In addition to being an ideal source of images for depicting the woman in the poems, the poet's references to nature help to signal the changing seasons that constitute the central organizing device for the arrangement of the work. The effect the weather has on various plants and animals establishes the necessary time-frame within which the poet tells his story. Specifically, the first rains damage the tender European plants in the garden, the laurel roses which are described with reason as "Signares à la fin du bal" (Signares at the end of the ball; *Poèmes,* 222). (Like Proust, Senghor often relates women to flowers and vice versa.) The rains also bring the scent of black vipers, a menacing image which foreshadows the lover's suffering in the absence of his mistress. At the end of the collection, the new budding of wild mint predicts the arrival of the gentle trade winds and with them, the return of the woman: "Mais déjà tu t'es annoncée aux marées de Septembre / Forte houle d'odeurs du côté des menthes sauvages" (But you are already announced in the September marshes / Heavy swelling of odors from the direction of the wild mint; *Poèmes,* 240). The last lines in the collection refer again to the odor of wild mint associated with her coming and to the perfume of the lily, a flower from the temperate zone with connotations of rebirth drawn from its connection with Easter. Just as the initial fading of the roses parallels the perfume of the lily in full bloom at the end of the collection, the vipers of the rainy season give way to images of dragonflies. The tempests of the rainy season are in perfect harmony with the poet's predominently low mood during the absence of the beloved; the anticipation of fair weather provides a fitting exteriorization of the poet's joy on her return.

In previous works inspired by women, the poems have generally served on some level to illustrate an aspect of Senghor's philosophy. In "Chants pour Signare" the questing figure of the early Negritude poetry becomes the questing lover whose mistress incarnates Negritude. In "Epîtres à la Princesse" the romance permits the poet to dramatize Africa's ability to contribute to the betterment of civilization. The apparent absence of any didactic or allegorical element in *Lettres d'hivernage* has proved extremely bothersome to Senghor's critics, who naturally expect to uncover yet another elaboration of his cultural and political ideas. In a lengthy article, R. J. Sherrington refuses categorically to interpret the collection as merely a series of verses for an absent loved one and emphasizes instead the various unresolved ambiguities of theme and structure in the work as a new technique for presenting the notion of culture conflict: ". . . the division between Black and White, Africa and Europe, which has always constituted a primordial leitmotif in Senghor's work . . . is no longer perceived simply at the rather fundamental level of explicit themes, but henceforth takes root in the very depths of the poem, is revealed but is hidden everywhere, ceases to be its subject in order to become the marrow."[9] Senghor seems to place less emphasis on questions of race in these poems and ambiguity and ambivalence figure importantly in his technical repertoire, but why relegate to the background the clearly stated subject of the collection: the woman and her absence? Hubert de Leusse admits the dominant role accorded to the theme of love in *Lettres d'hivernage* but he cannot help suggesting that human love is intended here to serve as a reflection of spiritual love: "This terrestrial and impassioned love leads us to 'the ultimate Reality'; to the supreme Beauty, which it symbolizes, victorious even over the terrors of Death."[10] Since Senghor occasionally uses religious vocabulary and motifs, especially references to rebirth, and since the *Alizés* are explicitly associated with Easter and with God in *Elégie des Alizés,* Leusse's idea has some justification, although it is equally plausible to interpret the mystical imagery conversely as a poetic expression of human love. As is characteristic of Senghor's writing, the poetry remains sufficiently ambiguous to allow a variety of interpretations, but there is something disturbing about the inability of those long familiar with the poet to accept what one critic has justly called the work's "noble simplicity."[11] Senghor himself has described this as "an entirely personal poetry."[12] Taken on that level alone, *Lettres d'hivernage* contains some very fine poems and stands up quite well against other works and other writers that have set out to chronicle the universal experience of love.

Chapter Ten
Elégies majeures

Elégies majeures, containing a republication of *Elégie des Alizés* (1969) and five additional poems, first appeared in 1978 in an edition illustrated by various artists and again in 1979 without illustrations in a volume including the essays entitled "Dialogue sur la poésie francophone" ("Dialogue on Francophone Poetry"). The latter contains essays on Senghor's poetry by the French poets Alain Bosquet and Jean-Claude Renard, a poem to Senghor by Pierre Emmanuel, and Senghor's response, "Lettre à trois poètes de l'hexagone" ("Letter to Three Poets of the Hexagon"), which outlines many of his own poetic theories. While *Lettres d'hivernage* consisted almost entirely of love poems of a highly personal nature, the selections in *Elégies majeures* are again the works of the public figure treating subjects that directly or indirectly emanate from issues of national or even global significance. These include memorial poems for three figures whose deaths would naturally elicit the attention of Senegal's head of state: a young member of France's equivalent of the American Peace Corps; a former French president, Georges Pompidou; and the American civil rights leader, Martin Luther King. The other two previously uncollected poems continue to repeat and develop themes long associated with Senghor and advance his concepts of Negritude and the Universal Civilization. In spite of their uniformly political inspiration and in keeping with the lyric quality inherent in the elegy as a genre, these works also manage to express something of the writer's own sentiments and furnish still other dimensions to the portrait of the narrator as he changes and matures throughout the years.

Three Memorials

With age, men show an increasing proclivity to consider the subject of death, and while the theme has often appeared in Senghor's writing, it undergoes considerable development in a volume appearing after the poet had reached his seventies. No longer an abstract phenomenon, it touches the narrator personally by taking the lives of three men whose destinies have, in different ways, been associated with his. As he feels his own death approaching, we see him taking stock of his life and reflecting on the nature of what may lie beyond the grave. In his review of the collection, Jacques Chevrier calls these elegies "poems about death, but also poems against death,"[1] and all of them deny the final dominion of nothingness. Equally important are the messages proclaimed to the living.

In "Elégie pour Jean-Marie," Senghor mourns the passing of a young *coopérant,* a member of the French contingent that provides needed expertise in areas such as education, agriculture, and technology for parts of the developing world. As he earlier lauded the contributions of the nurse Emma Payelleville, so the writer praises the selfless contributions of the young man whose untimely death joins in grief both black and white mourners with the funeral traditions of both races. By emphasizing Jean-Marie's European attributes—his appearance, his cultural heritage, and his technical skill—the poem reiterates Senghor's message of intercultural dependence and harmony between the races. As a head of state whose people profit from the contributions of cooperation, Senghor eulogizes a martyr, but in what could have remained essentially a piece of official poetry, the writer has also managed to insert some strikingly personal elements. He obviously knew the young man and held him in high esteem. In the third stanza, he describes an encounter with the youth in which the two share their thoughts of Africa, the younger man with his illusions and the older one with his memories. Although the writer does not give us his subject's family name and the poem is dedicated very broadly to the *coopérants* of the contingent, the lines lose still more of their circumstantial veneer when we learn that Jean-Marie is the son of Paul Flamand, the poet's friend of long standing and the editor who first helped prepare his poetry for presentation to the world.[2] Much of the poem is addressed familiarly to the deceased, but in the last two stanzas the poem becomes a prayer. As if the death of one close to him has reminded the poet to put his own soul in order, he prays for God's pity and blessing, but the last lines, while acknowledging a willingness to obey God's will and to accept what he ordains, show the extent to which he has been personally touched by the death of one so young: ". . . s'il faut que Tu tonnes Tu frappes ma maison sans paratonnerre . . . Frappe ce chef grisonnant et sec comme une meule de foin"

(. . . if Thou must thunder Thou must strike my house without lightening-rod . . . Strike this head graying and dry like a haystack; *E.M.,* 27). These lines become all the more touching in view of the death of one of Senghor's own sons not long after the composition of this poem.

In contrast with the preceding lines, the second eulogy in the collection presents the more rhetorical voice of the poet. Senghor's elegy for Martin Luther King both memorializes the great American Black leader and reinterprets King's assassination in such a way as to place the poet's own meaning on the events of that decade. Following a few prefatory remarks that help to set the scene, we learn in the second stanza that the date of King's death, 4 April, coincides with Senegal's national holiday, and the poet is reminded of the tragedy a year later by its association with the national celebration. The next part of the poem seeks to explain the coincidence of the two dates. Senghor does this by linking two of the decade's worst crises together: for Africa, the period from 1968 to 1974 was marked by the great Sahelian drought; for the United States, this was the era of its participation in the Vietnamese war. Senghor considers the former a punishment from God because Africa did not act on King's behalf to support his antiwar stance. The poet describes the assassination, and finally, in a vignette inspired by the famous "I have a dream" speech, he envisions an American paradise where black and white heroes rejoice together in the presence of God.

In addition to presenting several particularly memorable passages—Africa in the grip of the drought, the assassination scene, the concept of an interracial American Valhalla—the poem also offers us a symphony on the contrasting themes of violence and peace. Since "Epîtres à la Princesse," Senghor has expressed his fear of a world war with its potential for nuclear death and his insecurity in the face of the destructive power wielded by what he calls the "Super-Greats." In "Elégie des Eaux," he used the magic power of the poet's voice to counter such forces, but in the opening lines of "Elégie pour Martin Luther King," even the powers of the Word seem to fail. He tells us: ". . . les mots comme un troupeau de buffles confus se cognent contre mes dents / Et ma voix s'ouvre dans le vide" (. . . words like a herd of buffalo beat against my teeth / And my voice opens up into the void; *E.M.,* 34). Despite his prestige and his position of leadership, all of the speaker's acts must be performed under the constraints imposed by a century threatened by atomic war and restricted by hate and violence. In the first stanza, he evokes the nuclear standoff "quand tout pouvoir est poussière toute force faiblesse, que les Sur-Grands / Tremblent la nuit sur leurs silos profonds de bombes et de tombes . . ." (when all power is dust all force weakness, that the super powers / Tremble at night over their silos, deep in bombs and tombs; *E.M.*, 33). Later in the poem, he deplores the post-colonial war in Vietnam "où les Sur-Grands vous napalment par parents interposés" (where the super powers napalm you indirectly through your relations; *E.M.*, 37). Such conditions are, of course, diametrically opposed to the black values of love and peace advocated in other poems and attributed here to King. The American's role as civil rights advocate and his contributions towards improving conditions for his race are underplayed by the poet, who appears to be most deeply grieved by the loss of one of the world's great peacemakers. In fact, written in capital letters at the end of the second stanza is the line: MARTIN LUTHER KING LE ROI DE LA PAIX. Senghor's depiction of the final scene on the motel balcony, the confrontation between James Earl Ray and his victim, provides a further and more moving variation of the poem's unifying themes of violence and peace, and finally, in the Senghorian vision of the resurrection that concludes the poem, the African joins his voice to that of the slain black leader in order to weave a song of hope for America: "Je chante l'Amérique transparente, où la lumière est polyphonie de couleurs / Je chante un paradis de paix" (I sing America transparent, where light is polyphony of colors / I sing a paradise of peace; *E.M.*, 42). In spite of his initial misgivings, the poet once more puts his prophetic powers to work preparing a future in which the forces of hostility will be overcome.

In "Elégie pour Georges Pompidou," Senghor laments the passing of the French president and commemorates an extraordinary friendship between two men of different worlds. Students together at the Lycée Louis-le-Grand, the two future presidents become close friends. Elsewhere, Senghor describes their relationship as follows: "We really began to feel a fraternal affection for one another. It was more than friendship. I spent ten summer vacations at the home of Pierre Cahour, his father-in-law, at Château-Gontier."[3] In the years that followed, the two were not always on the same side politically, but the relationship endured. Senghor also tells us how he hesitated to write an elegy on Pompidou's death because of the political implications, but a month later as he was travelling in China, he proceeded with the first stanza.[4] The allusion in that stanza to his reluctance towards writing the poem seems to represent his state of mind at the time and not to be merely a rhetorical device. Any assumption on the part of the reader that this is purely a ceremonial poem that fulfills an official obligation disappears in the second stanza as he recounts his last interview with his former schoolmate. He tells how the latter, so visibly close to death, joked about his illness and how he himself pretended not to know how serious it was: "Je jouais à ne pas savoir, nous jouions au qui perd gagne de l'amitié" (I would play at not knowing, we would play at friendship's game of winners losers; E.M., 55). Throughout the remainder of the poem, the writer embroiders on various subjects associated with death: he lauds the Frenchman's struggle against his illness figuratively depicted as a many-headed dragon, he reflects on the nature of paradise, and he describes a visit to the cemetery on a beautiful spring day bursting with the message of renewal. The dominant theme in the last stanzas of the poem is love. In Senghor's imagination, the essential feature of heaven will be love, and in the name of that love, he beseeches his friend to pray for him so that he, the poet, might have the courage to face his own dragons and to pray for all the peoples of the earth. What follows is a typically Senghorian collage of races and ethnic groups, including the super powers, "avec leurs super-bombes et leur vide, et ils ont besoin d'amour" (with their super-bombs and their emptiness, and they have a need for love; E.M., 57).

Begun during Senghor's visit to the Far East, this poem is dated Peking-Madras, 1974, and bears the notation "for symphonic orchestra, including an organ and some Indian, Chinese, and Negro-African instruments." Within the work, the Eastern images and references sound a little out of place at first but provide the basis for at least two very effective images. A bare mention of the Great Wall in the first stanza gives specific visual and political dimensions to the initial lines of the second stanza alluding to the hatreds of race and ideology walls. Finally, in the last stanza, the poet compares his own poem to another memorial for another type of love, the Taj Mahal, of which he says: ". . . je l'ai trouvé splendide / Et je l'ai dédaigné, si froid pour un amour si grand" (. . . I found it splendid / And I disdained it, so cold for such a great love; E.M., 59). For his friend, Senghor offers a more human remembrance in a poem about a relationship between two men who would have not even met each other in the atmosphere of the colonial mentality that scarred the previous generation, a poem which, like the Indian mausoleum, stands as a monument to love in a world otherwise confounded by hate and separated by walls. In his review of the collection, Raymond Darricau calls this selection one of the high points of the volume and fits it into the long tradition of great texts on the subject of friendship from Aristotle to Mauriac.[5]

A Universal Civilization:
The Berber and Arabic Contributions

Senghor's use of the elegy is not limited to poems mourning the dead. Dated First Tunis Colloquium, 1975, and addressed to Habib Bourguiba, the "Elégie de Carthage" recalls the proud history of that ancient city. After a brief introductory stanza that serves as an invocation to his muse, the poet revives the exploits of three legendary Carthaginians: Dido, the queen abandoned by Aeneas; Hannibal, the general defeated in his ambitious European adventures; and Jugurtha, the Berber chieftain who, failing in his attempt to revive the kingdom of his forefathers in the face of Roman occupation, was taken to Rome in 105 B.C. to be imprisoned and to die of starvation. It is probably no coincidence that Senghor has chosen three stories in which Carthage clashed with Europe as a prelude to the final stanza where he salutes the courage and accomplishments of a modern-day hero in Habib Bourguiba, the president of Tunisia who helped to bring independence to his nation. Senghor's selection of Tunisia as subject may stem in part from his own personal admiration for Bourguiba. When asked a few years before his retirement from office which African leaders, living or dead, he felt the closest to, he named Bourguiba, Nyerere, and Sadat, but qualified his response by saying that, especially in terms of political ideology, he felt closest to the Tunisians.[6] The inclusion of an elegy commemorating the historic grandeur of North Africa is also a logical addition to the collection in the light of Senghor's interests both in African unity and in the concept of mutual ties within the French-speaking world. Taken together with the Portuguese culture represented in "Elégie des *saudades*" of *Nocturnes* and the Arab and Ethiopian heritage alluded to in "Elégie pour la reine de Saba," the final selection in *Elégies majeures,* this poem dedicated to the cultural contribution of the Berbers constitutes part of a growing tribute to the diversity and magnificence of the continent and helps to break down the previously bipartite nature of the Universal Civilization which at first seemed composed almost entirely of black Africans and Frenchmen.

A reading of the "Elégie pour la Reine de Saba" inevitably recalls previous Senghorian love poems inspired by the beauty of black women—poems such as "Femme noire," "Chants pour Signare," and "L'Absente." Senghor proclaims this most recent work an attempt to improve on the previous ones: "I wanted in this elegy, to sing better than I had done in 'Femme noire,' what represents for me, the Black Woman."[7] Both the woman and the love story in the elegy, as in several of the earlier works, can be interpreted symbolically to convey the idea of a mystical marriage with special significance within the framework of Senghor's thought. Such an allegorical reading seems to be invited by the direct citation before the beginning of the poem of a line from the Biblical *Songs of Songs:* "Moi, noire et belle . . ." (I am black but beautiful . . .). The erotic imagery of these scriptures has often been interpreted analogically by theologians for whom the use of human love as an image of man's relationship to God provides the basis for the tradition of mysticism. Similarly, Senghor tells us that his poem can be treated on several levels with the Ethiopian Queen representing at the same time Black Africa, femininity, Poetry, and Love.[8]

The poem, in five parts, begins with the narrator's memory of the beloved. Assuming for himself the role of Solomon, he sets out through the power of memory to recall his encounter with the Queen of Sheba. Part two tells of how the news of her beauty reached him through the nomads whose caravans entered his kingdom and of how the two first exchange communications until at last she accepts his proposal of marriage. In part three, the poet describes the lavishness of her entourage and the festivities and dancing in her honor. The last two sections of the poem, a passionate duet danced by the bride and groom and a physical description of the woman in her lover's embrace, rank among the poet's most sensual verses. Even in this brief synopsis, which in no way conveys the effects of music and imagery so important to the beauty of the poem, there is already obvious elaboration on the Biblical tale where a marriage between Solomon and the Queen is not mentioned and only a rich imagination can even find evidence of intimacy. In Ethiopian tradition, the royal family claims descent from the seduction of the Queen by Solomon, but, in Senghor's poem, the queen is clearly referred to as the betrothed, and a marriage is celebrated. The Koran also contains a variation of the celebrated encounter; while the notion of a marriage does not appear in that account either, it does occur in literary elaborations on the Islamic version.[9] Senghor takes pride in his familiarity with Arabian literature and when asked once which five books he would consider his favorites, he included the Arabian *Chants d'Amour et de Guerre d'Islam*. He also mentioned *The Book of the Dead* as translated into French by J. C. Mardrus.[10] He might therefore conceivably be familiar with the Mardrus translation of the Sheba legend. In addition to describing an actual marriage of the two monarchs, it shares so many elements in common with Senghor's poem that it or some variant of the Arabian legend must surely have provided the poet with his historical background.[11] Senghor's choice of an Arabian source is especially appropriate in the light of one of his expressed purposes for the poem: the celebration of the Negro-Semitic biological and cultural crossbreeding.[12] As such, the elegy reflects the statesman's interest in establishing a greater rapport between Black African and Arab-African peoples, a relationship elaborated on his essay entitled *Les Fondements de l'Africanité où Négritude et Arabité (The Foundations of "Africanité" or "Négritude" and "Arabité").*[13] Considering the poet's symbolic intentions, it is important to note that contemporary historians—and indeed the Mardrus translation—locate Sheba not in Ethiopia, but at the tip of the Saudi Arabian peninsula.[14] Senghor is aware of the distinction but explicitly ignores it when describing the origins of the queen: ". . . fille de l'Ethiopie pays d'opulence, de l'Arabie heureuse / Je ne sais plus. . . ." (. . . daughter of Ethiopia, country of opulence, of fortunate Arabia / I no longer know. . . .; *E.M.*, 66). Far from detracting from the poem, the confusion arising from the woman's origins aids in developing the various levels of symbolism.

The Place of *Elégies majeures* in Senghor's Work

At the end of our discussion of Senghor's first volume of poetry, *Chants d'ombre,* we anticipated that the two quest themes introduced in that volume—the search for the bride and the initiation quest dedicated to the father—would continue to be important structural devices in Senghor's writing, and to some extent most of his work

can be placed in one or the other category. The first emerges in the
more intimate poems in which the poet's ideals are incarnated in
the beloved; the second finds the narrator effecting important changes
in the real world in accordance with the mission he earlier pledged
to the Ancestors, and in such cases his objectives tend to be largely
political. *Elégies majeures* contains additional examples of both: "Elégie pour la Reine de Saba" provides yet another depiction of the
writer's inner quest as a union of two lovers. The other elegies
discussed here develop still further Senghor's concept of a Universal
Civilization where the uniqueness of each culture will be recognized
and all men will live together in harmony. This vision appeared as
early as 1945 in "Prière aux masques," but in most of the previous
collections, the dream of solidarity is subordinated to other objectives whose accomplishment must necessarily precede it: the themes
of racial equality in *Hosties noires,* the problems of pre-independence
politics in *Ethiopiques,* and the birth pangs of nationhood in *Nocturnes.* This hope for a new world order is never lost entirely, and
in each of the preceding collections, there are important poems that
announce its realization: "Prière de la paix," "Epîtres à la Princesse,"
"A New York," and "Elégie des Eaux" all predict the eventual
dawning of a new day in which all cultures will participate and
where the contributions of Africa, hitherto disparaged, will at last
come into their own.

Nowhere are other cultures depicted in such diversity as in *Elégies
majeures.* The recognition of the special relationship existing between
Senegal and the French has not diminished, as we see first in a work
dedicated to the French *coopérants* and then in a eulogy for France's
president. The poet's notion of African culture is expanded appre-
ciably in poems that do homage to both the Berber and Semitic
civilizations. But the poet's imagination is drawn far beyond his
two customary sources of inspiration, Africa and France, in the
"Elégie pour Georges Pompidou," which honors the two great civilizations of China and India. At the same time that the poet manifests his admiration for the positive contributions of these various
peoples to the heritage of mankind, he also castigates the forces that
risk man's destruction. The primary thrust of the "Elégie pour
Martin Luther King" is to condemn the violence of the nuclear
powers—and especially the United States—as a threat to the creation of a harmonious new world order. The expansion of the statesman's field of interest that was suggested earlier in "Elégie des

saudades" reasserts itself in *Elégies majeures* where the head of state, realizing that the ideal he has envisioned for his people cannot be created in isolation from the rest of the world, adapts his personal quest to yet another stage, this time a global one.

Of the new themes introduced in *Elégies majeures,* the most interesting is that of death. It provides two of the most touching passages in Senghor's entire opus, first in the meditations of the elder statesman on the death of the young *coopérant* and secondly in the description of the last reunion of the writer with his colleague, Georges Pompidou. There are also attempts on the poet's part to anticipate what life will be like after death. Interestingly, these views of heaven are, in two instances, merely transpositions of the writer's own earthly ideals. The association between paradise and childhood that has long dominated Senghor's view of history returns again in the "Elégie pour Georges Pompidou," although the idea is not entirely new. The earlier "Elégie de Minuit" had already expressed the desire to return in death to Joal, his childhood home and the source of his life's inspiration, if only to be buried there. This same notion occurs in one of the versions of his own epitaph: "Quand je serai mort mes amis, couchez-moi sous Joal, l'Ombreuse" (When I am dead, my friends, make me to lie down beneath Joal, the Shady.)[15] A second vision of heaven appears in "Elégie pour Martin Luther King," where Senghor depicts a cross-cultural, interracial paradise that dramatizes his ideal in yet another way—as a variation on his dream of a Universal Civilization. *Elégie majeures* implies a further elaboration on the poet's search for the Kingdom of Childhood by equating it with heaven and man's final reunion with God.

Chapter Eleven

Conclusion

From his student days in Paris to his retirement from office, the works by Léopold Sédar Senghor represented here span forty years or more, a considerable period of productivity that, under any circumstances, would accompany the creator through significant changes.[1] For Senghor, these changes are especially vivid and radical in as much as they closely reflect the exceptionally dynamic motion of his continent within that era: the decline of colonialism, the struggle for racial equality and nationhood, and the emergence of the Third World onto the global political scene. As a member of French-speaking Africa's educated elite, as Senegal's representative to France, and then as the president of his country, Senghor was officially a part of those political events that influenced, to a large extent, the direction of his life, but that, in turn, came to bear the stamp of his own special vision. On one hand, the poetry provides a privileged view of these eventful years as seen from the African perspective, but for the writer who regards his songs as a form of verbal magic, these works must also be considered an active force, itself contributing to those changes. Senghor recognized this dimension of his writing in choosing as a title for his book-length interview with Mohamed Aziza the phrase "poetry of action," and the narrator in the poems is constantly aware of the potency of his ideas in their spoken and written form. They are explicitly intended to effect change—in the poet's attitude, in the minds of political decision-makers, and in the overall relationships between men and between men and things.

To frame these optimistic visions of the future and to counter the prevailing negative stereotypes depicting his race, the writer effectively devised his own exceptionally creative map of the universe. Within this view, time began with the Kingdom of Childhood, an image growing out of the nostalgia of his expatriate status in France and including everything positive in his experience of Africa and its culture. Having discovered, as he records it in *Chants d'ombre,* that merely returning to Africa does not suffice to restore the kingdom, he envisions his adult goal as its re-establishment by other means. On one level, this implies the political rehabilitation of Africa eventually associated with Senegalese independence and, beyond nationhood, the creation of a new cultural configuration that he refers to as a Universal Civilization. But Senghor's kingdom has never been limited exclusively to a political concept. More than that, it also represents the composite values of the writer as an individual and includes his own serenity. Throughout his works, he has, in addition to his political efforts, also sought access to the kingdom through other means, especially through the medium of a woman who, in some way, could reflect this more personal aspect of his quest. Elsewhere, the Kingdom of Childhood becomes linked to the Kingdom of God and emerges in yet another form as an unattainable state not to be realized in this life.

Senghor's view of time and history reflects his own needs and his own experiences. In our discussion of the poetry, we have consistently pointed out its broader implications for unique as the narrator's story most certainly is, it may also be perceived as somehow representative, and we become aware that through one man's eyes, we are in essence participating in the story of a people and a continent, a role that Senghor self-consciously accepts time and again. In describing himself, the writer repeatedly draws on the archetypal patterns traditionally associated with the universal hero who, in his various roles as lover, warrior, nation-builder, or leader of the people, has established a place for himself in the national epics of peoples throughout the world. These archetypal elements supply additional evidence that the first-person experience narrated in the poems involves considerably more than the destiny of a single individual, and steeped in the idiom of oral poetry and tied so strongly to the racial and national issues that normally constitute the matter of epic, Senghor's poetry exhibits the essential features needed to be considered a modern African epic, a contemporary racial myth.

Senghor acknowledges the mythic elements in his work as long as the term "myth" is identified in the sense of "a symbolic story translating an essential reality."[2] In the theoretical essay appended to *Elégies majeures,* he describes the nature of the myth that he perceives as animating his poetry:

Still on the benches of the *Cours secondaire* in Dakar, I lived the essential myth of Africa. On one hand, Africa, crucified, like Christ, for five

centuries by the Slave Trade and colonization, but Africa redeemed and,
by its sufferings, ransoming the world, coming back to life to bear its
contribution to the germination of a panhuman civilization; on the other
hand, Africa Black Africa, Femininity, Love, Poetry, which appears here,
in the last of the *Elégies majeures,* in the person of the Queen of Sheba,
with whom I have lived in adoration for years. (*E.M.,* 101)

In the above passage, the writer concisely sums up the two major
threads of his work, the objects of his own outer-directed and inner-
directed quests.

Because of his strategic situation at the very origins of modern
African literature in French, Senghor has emerged as a factor to be
reckoned with in the criticism of that literature. Rare is the contemporary African writer who does not feel obliged to take some
stand on the philosophy of Negritude or who does not in some way
position his own ideas with respect to those of Senghor, and it is
difficult to imagine an introductory course on African writing, either
in French or English, that would fail to include some reference to
his work. In years to come, he will undoubtedly maintain his place
in histories of African literature, for his work chronicles an important
period in black history as experienced by one of its heroes and
constitutes a worthy celebration of the awakening of black racial
consciousness. Apart from their historical role, Senghor's poems have
other enduring qualities. As the memory of the colonial era fades,
the circumstantial and rhetorical works will probably find less favor
with the general reader than the more intimate pieces: the self-
conscious early verses of *Chants d'ombre,* the love poems from *Chants
pour Naëtt* through *Lettres d'hivernage,* and some of the more poignant
passages of the elegies. In these works especially, the poet has
succeeded in capturing with words something universally appealing
in his own emotions.

Notes and References

Chapter One

1. The actual date of birth is uncertain. According to Senghor, the baptismal certificate gives 15 August whereas civil records show 9 October; see his book-length interview with Mohamed Aziza, *Léopold Sédar Senghor: La Poésie de l'action* (Paris: Editions Stock, 1980), p. 33. Biographers who supply this information usually indicate the discrepancy but give 9 August as the date on the baptismal certificate; see also Jean Rous, *Léopold Sédar Senghor: La Vie d'un président de l'Afrique nouvelle* (Paris, 1967), p. 12; Ernest Milcent and Monique Sordet, *Léopold Sédar Senghor et la naissance de l'Afrique moderne* (Paris, 1969), p. 11; and Sylvia Washington Bâ, *The Concept of Negritude in the Poetry of Léopold Sédar Senghor* (Princeton, 1973), p. 5.

2. Senghor notes that his type A blood supplies additional proof of possible Portuguese ancestry; see Aziza, *La Poésie*, p. 32. The frequency of type A blood is relatively low in sub-Saharan Africa but high in Portugal as indicated in A.E. Mourant, Ada C. Kopec, and Kazimiera Domanieska-Sobczak, *The Distribution of the Human Blood Groups and Other Polymorphisms*, 2d ed. (London: Oxford University Press, 1976), pp. 70, 109.

3. Bâ, *Concept of Negritude*, p. 5. In his interview with Aziza (p. 31) Senghor gives slightly different interpretations: "Qui n'a pas honte" (He who is not ashamed) or "qu'on ne peut humilier" (he who cannot be humiliated).

4. *Liberté I: Négritude et humanisme* (Paris, 1964), p. 269.

5. *Poèmes* (Paris, 1973), pp. 55–56.

6. Ibid., pp. 26–35.

7. Senghor in Aziza, *La Poésie*, p. 37.

8. *Liberté I*, p. 269.

9. These poems were not included in either the 1964 or 1973 editions of Senghor's collected works but are available in Armand Guibert's *Léopold Sédar Senghor* (Paris, 1969), pp. 171–75.

10. For an extensive discussion of the relationship between education and assimilation, see Jacques Louis Hymans, *Léopold Sédar Senghor: An Intellectual Biography* (Edinburgh, 1971), pp. 9–11.

11. Hymans, *Biography*, p. 13. Hymans corroborates both incidents through interviews with Senghor and his brother, Charles Diène Senghor. Elsewhere, the two encounters are presented without the direct cause-effect relationship. See Bâ, *Concept of Negritude*, pp. 8–9; Milcent et Sordet, *La Naissance*, p. 29; and Rous, *La Vie d'un président*, p. 16. In Aziza, *La*

Poésie, p. 52, Senghor attributes his being discouraged from entering the priesthood to his "caractère difficile."

12. *Liberté I*, pp. 403–6.

13. Bâ, *Concept of Negritude*, p. 10. See also Guibert, *Senghor*, p. 23.

14. Interview with Abdoulaye Ly referred to in Hymans, *Biography*, p. 18. An interesting qualification of this contention appears in a letter from Senghor appended in Hymans, *Biography*, p. 269: "Although I do not like to make confidences, the one or two amorous deceptions of which one of your informers spoke did not come from white society, but from black society. As I have said elsewhere—and you have reproduced my words—in this period of exalting *négritude* I found the white woman to be savourless."

15. Letter from Senghor to the author appended in Hymans, *Biography*, pp. 263–64.

16. For a well-documented account of this period, see Robert Cornevin, *Littérature d'Afrique noire de langue française* (Paris: Presses Universitaires de France, 1976), pp. 144–55.

17. *Liberté I*, p. 116.

18. For an analysis of the intellectual origins of Negritude, see Lilyan Kesteloot, *Les Ecrivains noirs de langue française: Naissance d'une littérature* (Brussels, 1965).

19. Rous, *La Vie d'un président*, p. 19. Although the importance and general tone of *L'Etudiant noir* tend to be agreed on by critics and historians, the actual review appears rather elusive. Kesteloot, who devotes a chapter to it, was unable to obtain copies (p. 91) and M. a M. Ngal, in his biography of Césaire, affirms that no copies exist; see M. a M. Ngal, *Aimé Césaire: Un Homme à la recherche d'une patrie* (Dakar: Nouvelles Editions Africaines, 1975), p. 60.

20. Senghor in interview with Aziza, *La Poésie*, p. 83.

21. Ibid., p. 84.

22. Ibid., p. 149.

23. For background on Senghor's role in the making of Senegalese foreign policy, see W.A.E. Skurnik, *The Foreign Policy of Senegal* (Evanston: Northwestern University Press, 1972), especially the chapter entitled "Léopold Senghor's Personality," pp. 275–84.

24. Further details on Senghor's years as president can be found in Sheldon Gellar, *Senegal: An African Nation Between Islam and the West* (Boulder, Colo.: Westview Press, 1982).

Chapter Two

1. Sylvia Washington Bâ, *The Concept of Negritude in the Poetry of Leopold Sédar Senghor* (Princeton, 1973); S. Okechukwu Mezu, *Léopold Sédar Senghor et la défense et illustration de la civilisation noire* (Paris, 1968); Barend

v. D. Van Niekerk, *The African Image (Négritude) in the Work of Léopold Sédar Senghor* (Capetown: A.A. Balkema, 1970); Hubert de Leusse, *Léopold Sédar Senghor: L'Africain* (Paris, 1967); Gusine Gawdat Osman, *L'Afrique dans l'univers de Léopold Sédar Senghor* (Dakar, 1978); Marcien Towa, *Léopold Sédar Senghor: Négritude ou servitude?* (Yaoundé: Editions CLE, 1971).

2. Jean Paul Sartre, *Black Orpheus*, trans. S. W. Allen (Paris: Présence Africaine, 1963), pp. 16–18.

3. Irving Leonard Markovitz, *Léopold Sédar Senghor and the Politics of Negritude* (New York, 1969), p. 49.

4. Sartre, *Orpheus*, pp. 20–21.

5. L. V. Thomas, "Senghor et la recherche de l'homme Nègre," *Présence Africaine*, no. 49 (2nd Trimester 1965), p. 9.

6. Ibid., pp. 10–11.

7. Markovitz, *Politics of Negritude*, pp. 49–58.

8. For an analysis of the poem, see Towa, *Négritude ou servitude*, pp. 14–19.

9. Thomas, *Senghor et la recherche*, pp. 16–19.

10. Sartre, *Orpheus*, p. 15.

11. Ezekiel Mphahlele, *The African Image* (London: Faber and Faber, 1962), pp. 25–39.

12. Frantz Fanon, *The Damned*, trans. Constance Farrington (Paris: Présence Africaine, 1963), pp. 171–72.

13. The way in which Senghor's concept of Negritude changed during this period receives a very thorough treatment in Jacques Louis Hymans, *Léopold Sédar Senghor: An Intellectual Biography* (Edinburgh, 1971).

14. Towa, *Negritude ou servitude*, pp. 79–80.

15. Ibid., p. 115.

16. Ezekiel Mphahlele, "Negritude and Its Enemies: A Reply," in *African Literature and the Universities*, ed. Gerald Moore (Ibadan: Ibadan University Press, 1965), p. 25.

17. *Pierre Teilhard de Chardin et la politique africaine*, Cahiers Pierre Teilhard de Chardin, no. 3 (Paris: Seuil, 1962), p. 21.

18. Ernest Milcent and Monique Sordet, *Léopold Sédar Senghor et la naissance de l'Afrique moderne* (Paris: Seghers, 1969), pp. 248–49.

19. Markovitz, *Politics of Negritude*, pp. 56–60, has some reservations about the validity of this distinction.

20. Ibid., p. 28.

21. For a lengthy discussion of "prospective" Negritude, see Thomas, *Senghor et la recherche*, pp. 19–29.

22. *Teilhard*, p. 64.

23. Daniel Ewande's *Vive le Président* as described by Dorothy S. Blair, *African Literature in French* (Cambridge: Cambridge University Press, 1976), p. 152.

24. *Liberté I: Négritude et humanisme* (Paris, 1964), p. 9.

25. Negritude in the thought and works of Aimé Césaire receives a thorough treatment in A. James Arnold, *Modernism and Negritude: The Poetry and Poetics of Aimé Césaire* (Cambridge: Harvard University Press, 1981).

26. Anthologized in *Liberté I*, pp. 252–86.

27. Ibid., p. 255.

28. Ibid., p. 259.

29. Ibid., p. 259.

30. Ibid., p. 260.

31. Ibid., p. 24.

32. Sartre, *Esquisse d'une théorie des emotions*, cited in *Liberté I*, p. 262.

33. *Liberté I*, p. 264.

34. Ibid., p. 278.

35. For a very good treatment of Negritude in Senghor's poems, see Bâ, *Concept of Negritude*.

36. Hymans, *Intellectual Biography*, pp. 60–70, provides a discussion of the influence of various anthropologists on the theory of Negritude.

37. See Towa, *Négritude ou servitude*, pp. 114–15.

38. Mphahlele, "Negritude and Its Enemies," p. 25.

39. Mphahlele quoted by Bernard Fonlon, "The Kampala Conference," in *Negritude: Essays and Studies*, ed. Albert H. Berrian and Richard A. Long (Hampton, Va.: Hampton Institute Press, 1967), pp. 107–8.

40. Fanon, *The Damned*, pp. 179–80.

41. Sartre, *Black Orpheus*, p. 40.

42. Henry A. Murray, "The Possible Nature of a 'Mythology' To Come," in *Myth and Mythmaking*, ed. Henry A. Murray (New York: George Braziller, 1960), p. 319.

43. Ibid., p. 345.

44. Ibid., p. 345.

Chapter Three

1. *Liberté I: Négritude et humanisme* (Paris, 1964); *La Parole chez Paul Claudel et les Négro-Africains* (Dakar: Nouvelles Editions Africaines, 1973); *Elégies majeures* (Paris, 1979), pp. 85–124.

2. See Hubert de Leusse, *Léopold Sédar Senghor, L'Africain* (Paris, 1967), p. 169; and Abiole Irele, ed., *Selected Poems of Léopold Sédar Senghor* (Cambridge, 1977), pp. 23, 29.

3. Barend v. D. Van Niekerk, *The African Image (Négritude) in the Work of Léopold Sédar Senghor* (Capetown, 1970), pp. 104, 109.

4. W. E. Abraham cited in Irving Leonard Markovitz, *Léopold Sédar Senghor and the Politics of Negritude* (New York, 1969), p. 78.

5. Janis S. Pallister, "Léopold Sédar Senghor: A Catholic Sensibility?" *French Review* 53 (1980), pp. 670–73.

6. Senghor has provided us with an eloquent defense of the French language in his essay "Le Français, langue de culture," *Liberté I*, pp. 358–63.

7. Jahnheinz Jahn, *Muntu: An Outline of the New African Culture*, trans. Marjorie Grene (New York: Grove, 1961), p. 124.

8. ". . . fécondé par la parole d'Amma . . . ." *Claudel*, p. 13.

9. Jahn, *Muntu*, p. 135.

10. *Liberté I*, pp. 341–42. ". . . l'Homme est un être 'cosmique.' . . . Il vit dans et par le monde. Or, sous son apparence de chaos, le monde est ordre harmonieux. Pour vivre, matériellement et spirituellement, l'Homme doit démêler cet ordre. Pour s'y conformer ou, s'il est troublé, le rétablir par la Parole. Mythologie de la Parole dans les civilisations traditionnelles. Je laisse la matière aux polytechniciens. Au Poète, appartient l'Esprit. Homme privilégié parmi les hommes, le Poète est l'Ordinateur et l'Ordonnateur: il est, tout à la fois, le Père, le Prêtre, le Magicien."

11. Ibid., p. 171.

12. Jahn, *Muntu*, p. 125.

13. Henri Lemaître quoted in Geneviève Lebaud, *Léopold Sédar Senghor ou la poésie du Royaume d'enfance* (Dakar, 1976), p. 89.

14. Quoted in *Claudel*, p. 31.

15. *Claudel*, p. 14. "Comme dans la doctrine catholique et son interprétation première par Claudel, on trouve la création, la faute et son châtiment. Mais on y trouve autre chose: essentiellement, l'homme achevant, par la parole, la création du monde et s'accomplissant en même temps."

16. *Liberté I*, p. 279.

17. ". . . le premier don du poète négro-africain soit le don de l'image." *Liberté I*, p. 161.

18. Irele, *Selected Poems*, p. 23.

19. "Elle [l'image] n'a pas pour fonction de décrire, ni de cerner d'un contour aux traits précis. . . ." Lebaud, *La Poésie*, p. 81.

20. *Liberté I*, p. 200.

21. See Breton quoted by Senghor, *Liberté I*, p. 164, and also the response from Senghor which follows.

22. *Elégies majeures*, p. 106.

23. R.J. Sherrington, "La Femme ambiguë des 'Lettres d'hivernage,' " in *Hommage à Léopold Sédar Senghor, homme de culture*, ed. Présence Africaine (Paris: Présence Africaine, 1976), pp. 278—99.

24. Glossaries for the unfamiliar African expressions in the poetry can be found at the end of the volume of collected works; in Sylvia

Washington Bâ, *The Concept of Negritude in the Poetry of Léopold Sédar Senghor* (Princeton, 1973), pp. 281–89; and in Gusine Gawdat Osman, *L'Afrique dans l'univers poétique de Léopold Sédar Senghor* (Dakar, 1978), pp. 229–51. Another valuable source, especially for proper names and place names, is Lucille Gallistel Colvin, *Historical Dictionary of Senegal*, African Historical Dictionaries, no. 23 (Metuchen, N.J.: Scarecrow Press, 1981).

25. *Liberté I*, p. 220. "Quand nous disons *kôra, balafong, tam-tam,* et non harpe, piano et tambour, nous n'entendons pas faire pittoresque; nous appelons 'un chat un chat.' "

26. For a lengthy discussion of Senghor and surrealism which includes ample references to scholarship on the subject, see Daniel Garrot, *Léopold Sédar Senghor: Critique littéraire* (Dakar: Nouvelles Editions Africains, 1978), pp. 71–105.

27. *Elégies majeures,* p. 87.

28. Further similarities between Baudelaire and Senghor are discussed in Alfred Joseph Guillaume, Jr., "The Primitivist Impulse in the Poetic Vision of Baudelaire and Senghor" (Diss., Brown University, 1976). See also his "Conversation with Léopold Sédar Senghor on His Poetry and Baudelaire's," *French Review* 52, no. 6 (May 1979):839–47.

29. *Liberté I*, p. 221.

30. Most of the major studies on Senghor's poems treat the subject of rhythm in some depth; it is the principal focus in Renée Tillot, *Le Rythme dans la poésie de Léopold Sédar Senghor* (Dakar: Nouvelles Editions Africaines, 1979).

31. *Liberté I*, p. 226.

32. For a reference to the event, see Lilyan Kesteloot, *Les Ecrivains noirs de langue française: Naissance d'une littérature,* 3d ed. (Bruxelles, 1965), p. 197.

33. *Liberté I*, pp. 211–2.

34. Ibid., pp. 208–9.

35. Ibid., p. 212.

36. Leusse, *Senghor, l'African,* p. 120.

37. *Claudel,* p. 8.

38. For a treatment of the Biblical influence on Claudel's verset, see Elfrieda Dubois, " '. . . La prosodie me fut enseignée par les psaumes . . .': Some Reflections on Claudel's *verset"* in *Claudel: A Reappraisal,* ed. Richard Griffiths (London: Rapp and Whiting, 1968), pp. 112–30.

39. *Claudel,* p. 55.

40. *Liberté I*, p. 334.

41. Ibid., p. 337.

42. Senghor in a letter quoted by Bâ, *Concept of Negritude,* p. 131.

43. Kesteloot, *Les Ecrivains,* p. 200.

44. *Liberté I*, p. 335.

45. Bâ, *Concept of Negritude,* p. 128.
46. Irele, *Selected Poems,* p. 34.
47. Jean Rousselot cited in Armand Guibert, *Léopold Sédar Senghor: L'Homme et l'oeuvre* (Paris, 1962), p. 158.

Chapter Four

1. G.-E. Clancier, *Paysage Dimanche,* 2 Sept. 1945, as quoted in Armand Guibert, *Léopold Sédar Senghor: L'Homme et l'oeuvre* (Paris, 1962), p. 156. ". . . alors il nous fera pénétrer vraiment dans un univers poétique, qui est original et d'une riche humanité."
2. Pierre Emmanuel, *Temps Présent,* 3 Aug. 1945, as quoted in Guibert, p. 155. ". . . pour évoquer le continent noir dans son étrangeté magique."
3. Armand Guibert, *Cahiers du Sud,* no. 293, as quoted in Guibert, p. 157. ". . . une poésie qui rend sensible la face charnelle du continent de la passion et l'éternelle gésine de la Nuit."
4. Pierre Testas, *L'Université Syndicaliste,* 10–25 June 1945, as quoted in Guibert, p. 155.
5. The concept of the solar hierarchy is developed in Sartre's *Black Orpheus,* trans. S. W. Allen (Paris: Présence Africaine, 1963), pp. 26–30.
6. Hubert de Leusse, *Léopold Sédar Senghor, L'Africain* (Paris, 1967), pp. 174–75.
7. Jonathan A. Peters, *A Dance of Masks: Senghor, Achebe, Soyinka* (Washington, D.C., 1978), pp. 17–18.
8. Marcien Towa, *Léopold Sédar Senghor: Négritude ou servitude* (Yaounde: Editions CLE, 1971), p. 8. *"Joal* traduit un amour du terroir exacerbé par l'hostilité d'une terre étrangère."
9. Geneviève Lebaud, *Leópold Sédar Senghor ou la poésie du Royaume d'enfance* (Dakar, 1976), p. 27. See also the first note, pp. 38–39.
10. Leusse, *Senghor, Africaine,* pp. 127–29.
11. Abiola Irele, ed., *Selected Poems of Léopold Sédar Senghor* (Cambridge, 1977), pp. 31–33.
12. Ibid., p. 95.
13. Ibid., p. 96.
14. Barend v. D. Van Niekerk, *The African Image (Négritude) in the Work of Léopold Sédar Senghor* (Capetown, 1970), p. 40.
15. A thorough discussion of Joal, its definition and symbolism, appears in Gusine Gawdat Osman, *L'Afrique dans l'univers poétique de Léopold Sédar Senghor* (Dakar, 1978), pp. 184–217.
16. S. Okechukwu Mezu, *Léopold Sédar Senghor et la défense et illustration de la civilisation noire* (Paris, 1968), p. 61. "Joal, comme la Beauce de Péguy, comme la terre angevine de Du Bellay, représente tout ce qui

est cher dans la vie de Senghor: foyer, famille, enfance et pays natal."
Mezu's study incorporates an interesting analysis of "Joal" in terms of the
contrast between Christian and animist ritual as represented in the poem,
pp. 59–66.

17. For an analysis of accent and rhythm in "Femme noire," see
Sylvia Washington Bâ, *The Concept of Negritude in the Poetry of Léopold Sédar
Senghor* (Princeton, 1973), pp. 132–35.

18. Irele, *Selected Poems*, p. 9, suggests that the "color of life" in the
poem might alternatively be green, the color associated with nature.

19. Mezu, *La civilisation noire*, p. 74. "Ce poème n'est ni très per-
sonnel ni très inspiré. C'est un beau tableau un peu froid, merveilleusement
imagé, mais dans lequel l'artiste a mis peu de lui-même."

20. Van Niekerk, *African Image*, p. 48.

21. Peters, *Dance of Masks*, pp. 25–26.

22. Towa, *Négritude ou servitude*, p. 24.

23. Collected in his *Liberté I: Négritude et humanisme* (Paris, 1964),
pp. 22–38.

24. Peters, *Dance of Masks*, p. 30.

25. For a structural analysis of "Le Totem" using the techniques of
Roman Jakobson, see Sunday O. Anozie, *Structural Models and African
Poetics* (London: Routledge and Kegan Paul, 1981), pp. 169–87.

26. *Oeuvres completes*, Bibliothèque de la Pléiade (Paris: Galimard,
1961), pp. 70–71.

27. See Lebaud, *la poesie du Royaume d'enfance*, pp. 13–15, for further
remarks on the relationship between this poem and the works of Baudelaire.

28. Baudelaire, *Oeuvres complètes*, pp. 54–55.

29. Mezu, *La civilisation noire*, p. 66.

30. This poem contains numerous African references, most of which
are explained by Irele, *Selected Poems*, pp. 102–6.

31. Peters, *Dance of Masks*, p. 18.

32. Mezu, *la civilisation noire*, p. 67. "On associe toujours l'innocence
à l'enfance. Ainsi, dans ce poème, Senghor transfère cette qualité humaine
au continent africain toute entier . . . Comme si l'Adam et l'Eve noirs
n'avaient jamais péché et vivaient toujours au paradis noir en toute
innocence."

33. Joseph Campbell, *The Hero with a Thousand Faces* (New York:
The World Publishing Co., 1966), p. 136.

34. Lebaud, *la poesie du Royaume d'enfance*, pp. 68–69, discusses the
importance of ritual bathing in Serer ceremonies.

35. Mezu, *la civilisation noire*, p. 82.

36. Lebaud's study of Senghor's poems devotes an entire chapter to
the writer's use of the initiating quest pattern, pp. 41–71.

Chapter Five

1. Gaëtan Picon, *Panorama de la nouvelle littérature française* (Paris: Editions Gallimard, 1976), pp. 234–35.

2. S. Okechukwu Mezu, *Léopold Sédar Senghor et la défense et illustration de la civilisation noire* (Paris, 1968), pp. 89–90.

3. Ibid., p. 101.

4. See Marcien Towa, *Léopold Sédar Senghor: Négritude ou servitude?* (Yaoundé: Editions CLE, 1971), pp. 7, 15–19.

5. Abiola Irele's dating of the situation in this poem from Senghor's 1932 vacation trip is inconsistent with the Almeria incident. We know that the poet also returned to Dakar in 1937, the same year as the bombardment, and if he went by sea, this experience would seem to be the more likely source of inspiration. As additional confirmation, we note that the place and date of composition given for the poem are Dakar, 1938. For Irele's discussion of "Méditerranée," see his *Selected Poems of Léopold Sédar Senghor* (Cambridge, 1977), pp. 109–10.

6. *Liberté I: Négritude et humanisme* (Paris, 1964), p. 77. "Plus importants que les devoirs envers le prochain sont ceux envers soi-même. Il ne s'agit pas seulement d'exiger et de recevoir des marques de *téranga,* mais encore et surtout d'affirmer et de protéger sa *personne.* Celle-ci s'affirme essentiellement par le *courage* et la *générosité* qui sont vertus nobles. Mais la personne peut être offensée et, parfois, le Destin nous empêche toute riposte efficace. Nous n'avons alors qu'une solution: abandonner notre souffle vital pour sauver notre vie personnelle, notre âme. *Le suicide est l'exigence dernière de la Susceptibilité, fille de l'Honneur.*"

7. The only source to our knowledge which explicitly makes de Gaulle the subject of this poem is Jean Rous, *Léopold Sédar Senghor: La Vie d'un président de l'Afrique nouvelle* (Paris, 1967), p. 21. The context of the poem, its place in the collection and its date, September 1940, seem to leave little question about the poet's intent.

8. Barend v.D. Van Niekerk, *The African Image (Négritude) in the Work of Léopold Sédar Senghor* (Capetown, 1970), p. 58.

9. Mezu, *la civilisation noire,* p. 99. He is citing from "Poème liminaire" (*Poèmes,* 53).

10. Irele, *Selected Poems,* p. 115, suggests that the dedication to a "young black girl with a pink heel" is intended for Senghor's first wife.

11. Our source for the historical incident which probably inspired the poem is Lamine Diakhate, *Lecture libre de "Lettres d'hivernage" et d' "Hosties noires"* (Dakar: Nouvelles Editions Africaines, 1976), pp. 62–63. Another poem inspired by the event is Keita Fodeba's "African Dawn."

12. See Towa, *Négritude ou Servitude,* pp. 60–74.

13. Mezu, *la civilisation noire,* p. 101.

14. Gerald Moore, *Twelve African Writers* (Bloomington: Indiana University Press, 1980), pp. 31–32.

15. *Liberté I,* p. 11–21.

16. Ibid., pp. 36–39.

17. Mezu, *la civilisation noire,* p. 98.

Chapter Six

1. Senghor quoted in Mohamed Aziza, *Léopold Sédar Senghor: la poésie de l'action. Conversations avec Mohamed Aziza* (Paris: Stock, 1980), p. 152. "Je brûlerais tous mes textes en prose pour sauver un seul de ces poèmes d'amour."

2. Lloyd W. Brown, *Women Writers in Black Africa,* Contributions in Women's Studies, no. 21 (Westport, Conn.: Greenwood Press, 1981), p. 8.

3. *Liberté I: Négritude et humanisme* (Paris, 1964), p. 269. "La femme parce que 'permanente' de la famille et donneuse de vie, a été promue en source de force vitale et gardienne de la maison, c'est-à-dire dépositaire du passé et garante de l'avenir clanique."

4. *Liberté I,* p. 117. "Car la Femme est, plus que l'Homme, sensible aux courants de la vie et du cosmos, plus perméable à la joie et à la douleur."

5. For a comparison of the images of women in works by both Baudelaire and Senghor, see Alfred Joseph Guillaume, Jr., "The Primitivist Impulse in the Poetic Vision of Baudelaire and Senghor" (Diss., Brown University, 1976), p. 217.

6. *Liberté I,* p. 274. "Tout d'abord l'animisme negro-africain fait, de la *Terre* . . . une personne, un génie. L'Ancêtre du clan, le permier défricheur et occupant, a conclu, avec ce génie, un pacte sanctionné par un sacrifice rituel."

7. Jean-Paul Sartre, *Black Orpheus,* trans. S.W. Allen (Paris: Présence Africaine, 1963), pp. 44–45.

8. Sylvia Washington Bâ, *The Concept of Negritude in the Poetry of Léopold Sédar Senghor* (Princeton, 1974), p. 52.

9. Senghor quoted in Aziza, *la poésie de l'action,* p. 155.

10. Barend v. D. Van Niekerk, *The African Image (Négritude) in the Work of Léopold Sédar Senghor* (Capetown, 1970), p. 76.

11. Bâ, *Concept of Negritude,* p. 288.

12. Northrop Frye, *Anatomy of Criticism: Four Essays* (New York: Atheneum, 1966), pp. 199–200.

13. See Armand Guibert, *Léopold Sédar Senghor: L'Homme et l'oeuvre* (Paris, 1962), pp. 77–86, for explications of "Ton visage . . ." and "Etait-ce une nuit . . ."

14. Gerald Moore, *Twelve African Writers* (Bloomington: Indiana University Press, 1980), p. 32.

15. Jonathan Peters, *A Dance of Masks: Senghor, Achebe, Soyinka* (Washington, D.C., 1978), p. 83.

16. Ibid., p. 84.

17. Ibid., p. 84.

18. Hubert de Leusse, *Léopold Sédar Senghor, l'Africain* (Paris, 1967), p. 77.

19. Peters, *Dance of Masks,* p. 60.

20. S. Okechukwu Mezu, *Léopold Sédar Senghor et la défense et illustration de la négritude* (Paris, 1968), p. 119. "Les vers sont riches, charnels et voluptueux à l'encontre de la sécheresse et de l'abstraction de 'Femme Noire.' "

Chapter Seven

1. Michael Crowder, *Senegal: A Study in French Assimilation Policy* (New York: Oxford University Press, 1962), pp. 36, 39, as indicated in Ernest Milcent and Monique Sordet, *Léopold Sédar Senghor et la naissance de l'Afrique moderne* (Paris, 1969), p. 117.

2. John Reed and Clive Wake, introduction to *Léopold Sédar Senghor: Selected Poems* (New York: Atheneum, 1969), p. xiv.

3. Jonathan A. Peters, *A Dance of Masks: Senghor, Achebe, Soyinka* (Washington, D.C., 1978), p. 57.

4. For an introduction to studies on the ritual origins of myth, see K. K. Ruthven, *Myth,* The Critical Idiom, 31 (London: Methuen, 1976), pp. 35–38.

5. Barend v. D. Van Niekerk, *The African Image (Négritude) in the Works of Léopold Sédar Senghor* (Capetown, 1970), p. 82.

6. Papa Gueye N'Diaye, *Ethiopiques: Poèmes de Léopold Sédar Senghor. Edition critiquée et commentée* (Dakar: Nouvelles Editions Africaines, 1974), p. 10. "Dans les sociétés guerrières, l'Homme n'accède à sa condition d'Homme, c'est-à-dire à la virilité, au sens étymologique du terme, et à la sociabilité, qu'après avoir fait son initiation: tuer un animal réputé dangereux."

7. Ibid., p. 10. "Le poète se fait contemporain d'Adam, qui regarde naître le monde. Poème de la Pensée domptant une Création hostile, il contient un triple symbole, avec l'émergence de l'Homme hors de l'animalité et celle de la Raison hors de l'instinct. Mais cette émergence semble s'être faite en Afrique même, où l'Homme a fait, pour la première fois, son apparition."

8. Jonathan Ngate, "'L'Homme et la Bête' de Senghor: son thème et sa portée," *Proceedings of the Pacific Northwest Conference on Foreign Languages* 27, no. 1 (1976): 48. ". . . le poème de Senghor nous offre le spectacle d'un initié générique en train de franchir l'une des étapes de la vie . . ."

9. Ibid., p. 48. ". . . il terrasse 'la Bête' de l'ignorance."

10. Sylvia Washington Bâ, *The Concept of Negritude in the Poetry of Léopold Sédar Senghor* (Princeton, 1973), p. 140. See also her scansion of "L'Homme et la Bête," pp. 136–37.

11. For additional discussion of the initiation quest, see Geneviève Lebaud, *Léopold Sédar Senghor où la poèsie du Royaume d'enfance* (Dakar, 1976), pp. 41–66.

12. Peters, *Dance of Masks*, p. 82.

13. Van Niekerk, *African Image*, p. 80.

14. See Van Niekerk, *African Image*, p. 83, and N'Diaye, *Ethiopiques*, p. 17.

15. Gusine Gawdat Osman, *L'Afrique dans l'univers poétique de Léopold Sédar Senghor* (Dakar, 1978) p. 250.

16. N'Diaye, *Ethiopiques*, p. 37.

17. Mircea Eliade, *Myths, Dreams and Mysteries* (New York: Harper Brothers, 1960), p. 197.

18. *Liberté I: Négritude et humanisme* (Paris, 1964), p. 52.

"Dans le Royaume du Sine et, en général, chez les Sérères, les *classes d'initiés* ont remplacé les classes d'âge, conformément à l'évolution naturelle des sociétés négro-africaines. Ces classes se forment au moment de la circoncision, cérémonie qui a lieu autour de la puberté. En réalité, la circoncision n'est que l'occasion d'une véritable éducation. Il s'agit de préparer les jeunes gens à leur fonction d'homme. Plutôt, il s'agit d'une véritable initiation religieuse, avec épreuves, ascèse, rites et cérémonial, d'une initiation qui repose sur le mystère de la Mort-Renaissance."

19. Eliade, *Myths Dreams*, p. 197.

20. David P. Gamble, *The Wolof of Senegambia*, Ethnographic Survey of Africa (London: International African Institute, 1957), p. 65.

21. Armand Guibert, *Léopold Sédar Senghor: L'Homme et l'oeuvre* (Paris, 1962), p. 69. ". . . la Victoire politique, à la fois proche et à longue échéance; la Femme aimée, décrite physiquement, avec ses charmes et ses joyaux; la Négritude, proclamée comme une force mystique; et enfin la Poésie, forme suprême de la culture.

22. Bâ, *Concept of Negritude*, p. 54.

23. N'Diaye, *Ethiopiques*, p. 25.

24. Bâ, *Concept of Negritude*, p. 54.

25. Eliade, *Myths Dreams,* p. 174–75.
26. Ibid., p. 175.
27. See Donald Burness, *Shaka, King of the Zulus, in African Literature* (Washington, D.C.: Three Continents Press, 1976).
28. Armand Guibert, *Léopold Sédar Senghor,* Poètes d'aujourd'hui, 82 (Paris, 1969), p. 71. "Sans méconnaître le droit du poète à l'invention, on peut estimer qu'il valait mieux créer le mythe de toutes pièces plutôt que de travestir Gilles de Rais en Vercingétorix."
29. *Liberté* I, p. 141. "On sait que l'attitude de l'Homme devant la Nature est le Problème par excellence, dont la solution conditionne le destin des hommes. L'Homme devant la Nature, c'est le *sujet* en face de l'*objet.* Il est question, pour l'Européen, *Homo faber,* de connaître la Nature pour en faire l'instrument de sa volonté de puissance: de l'*utiliser.* Celui-ci la fixera par l'analyse, en fera une chose morte pour la disséquer. Mais comment, d'une chose morte, faire de la Vie? C'est, au contraire, dans sa subjectivité que le Nègre, 'poreux à tous les souffles du monde', découvre l'objet dans sa réalité: le *rythme.* Et le voilà qui s'abandonne, docile à ce mouvement vivant, allant du sujet à l'objet, 'jouant le jeu du monde'."
30. Alain Baudot, "Ré-écouter 'A New York,' " *Présence Francophone* 8 (1974), p. 111.

Chapter Eight

1. "Keeping It Dark: Negritude in a Changing World," *Times Literary Supplement* (London), 21 September 1962, p. 703, quoted in S. Okechukwu Mezu, *Léopold Sédar Senghor et la défense et illustration de la civilisation noire* (Paris, 1968), p. 141.
2. Jonathan A. Peters, *A Dance of Masks: Senghor, Achebe, Soyinka* (Washington, D.C., 1978), p. 85.
3. Ibid., p. 86.
4. The term is used figuratively although Senghor did supply the lyrics for the Senegalese national anthem.
5. For our analysis of Senghor's political ideas prior to independence, we have drawn primarily from Jean Rous, *Léopold Sédar Senghor: La Vie d'un président de l'Afrique nouvelle* (Paris, 1967), pp. 23–46.
6. Abiola Irele, ed., *Selected Poems of Léopold Sédar Senghor* (Cambridge, 1977), p. 21.
7. Ibid., p. 132.
8. Gerald Moore, *Twelve African Writers* (Bloomington: Indiana University Press, 1980), p. 35.
9. Mezu, *la civilisation noire,* p. 139. ". . . rien en ce monde n'est éternel, rien ne peut apaiser la soif de l'homme."
10. John Reed and Clive Wake, introd. and trans., *Léopold Sédar Senghor: Selected Poems* (New York: Atheneum, 1969), p. xvi.

11. Armand Guibert, *Léopold Sédar Senghor: L'Homme et l'oeuvre* (Paris, 1962), pp. 91–92.

12. Senghor interviewed in Mohamed Aziza, *La Poésie de l'action: conversations avec Mohamed Aziza* (Paris: Stock, 1980), p. 18.

13. Guibert, in his explication of "Elégie de minuit," p. 91, identifies the Father Cloarec mentioned in the poem as R.P. Jouan, the priest who baptized Senghor.

14. Senghor defines the term "lamarch" as "landowner—from Serer *lamane,* landowner, and Greek *archos,* ruler." See the glossary in Léopold Sédar Senghor, *Nocturnes,* trans. John Reed and Clive Wake (London: Heinemann, 1969), p. 60.

15. Irele, *Selected Poems,* p. 133.

16. Peters, *Dance of Masks,* p. 85.

17. Senghor interviewed in Aziza, *La Poésie de l'action,* p. 351.

18. Barend v.D. Van Niekerk, *The African Image (Négritude) in the Works of Léopold Sédar Senghor* (Capetown : A.A. Balkema, 1970) p. 129, n. 314.

19. Peters, *Dance of Masks,* p. 84.

20. Reed and Wake, Introd., *Nocturnes,* p. xi.

21. Ibid., p. xii.

22. See the glossary to Reed and Wake's translation of *Nocturnes,* p. 60.

23. Peters, *Dance of Masks,* p. 84.

24. See Senghor's interview with Aziza, *La Póesie de l'action,* pp. 324–35, for a short discussion of the role of the Portuguese in Africa.

Chapter Nine

1. Hubert de Leusse, *Léopold Sédar Senghor: L'Africain* (Paris, 1967), pp. 245–49.

2. *Elégies majeures* (Paris, 1979), p. 13. All other citations from this collection will be taken from this edition and indicated in parentheses in the text.

3. David P. Gamble, *The Wolof of Senegambia,* Ethnographic Survey of Africa (London: International African Institute, 1957), p. 28.

4. See Mircea Eliade, *The Myth of the Eternal Return,* trans. Willard R. Trask, Bolingen Series, 46 (New York: Pantheon Books, 1954).

5. Leusse, *L'Africain,* p. 243. "Mais, comme les Alizés, ce poème nous apporte aussi la fraîcheur d'un espoir. . . . L'heure n'est plus à la nostalgie d'un passé si beau fût-il! . . . L'heure est à la certitude de lendemains merveilleux . . ."

6. See Senghor interviewed in *La Poésie de l'action: Conversations avec Mohamed Aziza* (Paris: Stock, 1980), p. 150.

7. For many of the ideas related to the perspective of the writer in mid-life, we are indebted to Sharan B. Merriam, *Coping with Male Midlife: A Systematic Analysis Using Literature as a Data Source* (Washington, D. C.: University Press of America, 1980).

8. For a discussion of the inter-relationships of the poems within the volume see R. J. Sherrington, "La Femme ambiguë des *Lettres d'hivernage,*" *Hommage à Léopold Sédar Senghor: Homme de culture* (Paris: Présence Africaine, 1976), pp. 279–84.

9. Sherrington, *La Femme ambiguë,* p. 279. ". . . le déchirement entre Noir et Blanc, Afrique et Europe, qui constitue depuis toujours un leitmotiv primordial chez Senghor . . . ne se perçoit plus simplement au niveau assez primaire des thèmes explicites, mais s'enracine désormais jusqu'au plus profond du poème, se révèle mais se dérobe partout, cesse d'en être le sujet pour en devenir la moëlle."

10. Hubert de Leusse, *Des "Poèmes" aux "Lettres'd'hivernage": Senghor* (Paris, 1975), p. 95.

11. Marcel Schaettel, *Léopold Sédar Senghor: Poétique et poésie* (Lyon: L'Hermes, 1977), p. 9. Although devoted exclusively to *Lettres d'hivernage,* this little study provides some interesting comments on Senghor's poetic style.

12. Senghor, quoted by Pierre Klein, "Présentation des *Lettres d'hivernage* de L. S. Senghor,*" *Le Soleil,* n.d., as cited by Leusse (1975), p. 14.

Chapter Ten

1. Jacques Chevrier, "Le Testament poétique," *Jeune Afrique,* 17 Oct. 1979, p. 61.

2. Concerning the relationship between writer and editor, see Paul Flamand, "Hommage à Léopold Sédar Senghor," in *Hommage à Léopold Sédar Senghor: Homme de culture* (Paris: Présence Africaine, 1976), p. 137.

3. Senghor interviewed in *La Poésie de l'action: Conversations avec Mohamed Aziza* (Paris: Stock, 1980), p. 64. "Nous nous sommes vraiment pris d'affection fraternelle l'un pour l'autre. C'était plus que de l'amitié. J'ai passé dix grandes vacances chez le docteur Pierre Cahour, son beau-père, à Château-Gontier."

4. Senghor, interviewed in Aziza, *La Poésie de l'action,* p. 65.

5. Raymond Darricau, "Les 'Elégies majeures' du Président Léopold Sédar Senghor," *Revue Française d'histoire du livre,* 25 (1979), 859.

6. Senghor, interviewed in Aziza, *La Poésie de l'action,* p. 135.

7. Ibid., pp. 152–53. "J'ai voulu, dans cette élégie, chanter, mieux que je ne l'avais fait dans *Femme noire,* ce que représente, pour moi, la Femme noire."

8. "Lettre à trois poètes de l'hexagone," in his *Elégies majeures* (Paris: Le Seuil, 1979), p. 101.

9. Our reference for the several versions of the Sheba myth is James Pritchard, ed., *Solomon and Sheba* (London: Phaidon, 1974).
10. Senghor, interviewed in Aziza, *La Poésie de l'action*, p. 354.
11. For an English version of J. C. Mardrus' translation of the Arabic tale, see E. Powys Mathers, *The Queen of Sheba* (London: Westminster Press, n.d.).
12. Senghor, interviewed in Aziza, *La Poésie de l'action*, p. 153.
13. Senghor's speech by this title, delivered at the Unversity of Cairo on 16 Feb. 1967, has appeared in English as *The Foundations of "Africanité" or "Negritude" and "Arabité"* (Paris: Présence Africaine, 1971).
14. See Gus W. van Beek, "The Land of Sheba," in Pritchard, *Solomon and Sheba*, pp. 40–63.
15. Gusine Gawdat Osman, *L'Afrique dans l'univers poétique de Léopold Sédar Senghor* (Dakar, 1978), p. 74. For a reproduction of three versions of the epitaph and a detailed analysis of the texts, see Osman, pp. 73–84.

Chapter Eleven

1. Uncollected works not treated in this volume include the poems "Chant pour Jackie Thompson" and "Chant pour Yacine Mbaye" as well as poems for an unfinished collection, *Chansons du Farba Kaymôr*, referred to in the catalog for the Bibliothèque Nationale exposition in 1978, p. 108.
2. Senghor quoted in Daniel Garrot, *Léopold Sédar Senghor: Critique littéraire* (Dakar: Nouvelles Editions Africaines, 1978), p. 148. ". . . une histoire symbolique traduisant une réalité essentielle. . . ."

Selected Bibliography

PRIMARY SOURCES

1. Poetry

Chants d'ombre. Paris: Editions du Seuil, 1945.

Hosties noires. Paris: Editions du Seuil, 1948.

Chants pour Naëtt. Paris: Editions Pierre Seghers, 1949.

Ethiopiques, Paris: Editions du Seuil, 1956.

Nocturnes. Paris: Editions du Seuil, 1961.

Elégie des Alizés. Paris: Editions du Seuil, 1969.

Lettres d'hivernage. Paris: Editions du Seuil, 1973.

Elégies majeures. Génève: Editions Regard, 1978. Reprinted with "Dialogue sur la poésie francophone" by Editions du Seuil, 1979.

Poèmes. Paris: Editions du Seuil, 1964. Included works published by that date with the exception that *Chants pour Naëtt* appeared only in its revised form as "Chants pour Signare."

Poèmes. Paris: Editions du Seuil, 1973. A re-edition of previous *Poèmes* with the addition of *Lettres d'hivernage.*

Poèmes. Paris: Editons du Seuil, 1984. Along with previously collected works, Senghor has included the *Elégies majeures* and an elegy composed on the death of his son, Philippe Maguilen.

2. Selected Prose Works

Liberté I: Négritude et humanisme. Paris: Editions du Seuil, 1964.

Liberté II: Nation et voie africaine du socialisme. Paris: Editions du Seuil, 1971.

Liberté III: Négritude et civilisation de l'Universel. Paris: Editions du Seuil, 1977.

3. Other Works

Anthologie de la nouvelle poésie nègre et malgache de langue francaise. Paris: Presses Universitaires de la France, 1948.

La Poésie de l'action: Conversations avec Mohamed Aziza. Paris: Stock, 1980. A book-length interview that provides considerable background on the poet's life and thought.

4. Translations

Léopold Sédar Senghor: Prose and Poetry, ed. and trans. John Reed and Clive Wake. London: Oxford University Press, 1965. Reprinted in Heinemann's African Writers Series, 1976.

Léopold Sédar Senghor: Selected Poems, trans. and introd. John Reed and Clive Wake. London: Oxford University Press, 1964. Reprinted in New York: Atheneum, 1969.

Nocturnes, trans. and introd. John Reed and Clive Wake. London: Heinemann, 1969.

Selected Poems/Poèsies Choisies: A Bilingual Text with English Translations and an Introduction by Craig Williamson. London: Rex Collings, 1976.

SECONDARY SOURCES

Bâ, Sylvia Washington. *The Concept of Negritude in the Poetry of Léopold Sédar Senghor.* Princeton: Princeton University Press, 1973. Defines Negritude in terms of African philosophy and studies its appearances in the poetry. Good biographical chapter and very fine translations of Senghor's poems including "Elégie pour Martin Luther King," in the appendix.

Guibert, Armand. *Léopold Sédar Senghor.* Poètes d'aujourd'hui, No. 82. Paris: Seghers, 1969. Early biographical study of poet with general comments on poems. Essential reading.

Hymans, Jacques Louis. *Léopold Sédar Senghor: An Intellectual Biography.* Edinburgh: Edinburgh University Press, 1971. Well-documented, historical study of intellectual currents influencing the development of Senghor's concept of Negritude. Useful biographical information.

Irele, Abiola, ed. *Selected Poems of Léopold Sédar Senghor.* Cambridge: Cambridge University Press, 1977. Generally fine, detailed commentaries of poems selected.

Kesteloot, Lilyan. *Les Ecrivains noirs de langue française; Naissance d'une littérature.* 3rd ed. Bruxelles: Editions de l'Institut de Sociologie de l'Université Libre de Bruxelles, 1965. An important source for the history of the Negritude movement with a chapter on *Chants d'ombre* and *Hosties noires.*

Lebaud, Geneviève. *Léopold Sédar Senghor ou la poésie du Royaume d'enfance.* Dakar: Nouvelles Editions Africaines, 1976. A short thematic study emphasizing archetypal imagery, the quest theme, and the role of the poet as magician. No index.

Leusse, Hubert de. *Léopold Sédar Senghor: L'Africain.* Paris: Hatier, 1967. An interesting thematic study of works through *Elégie des Alizés.* Some especially insightful comments on Senghor's use of rhythm. No index.

———. *Des "Poèmes" aux "Lettres d'hivernage": Senghor.* Paris: Hatier, 1975. A summary of previous study updated by a comprehensive analysis of *Lettres d'hivernage.* One of the few extensive studies of that collection.

Markovitz, Irving Leonard. *Léopold Sédar Senghor and the Politics of Negritude.* New York: Atheneum, 1969. Primarily a historical study which analyzes the political implications of Negritude.

Mezu, S. Okechukwu. *Léopold Sédar Senghor et la défense et illustration de la civilisation noire.* Paris: Librairie Marcel Didier, 1968. A chronological study of the poems through *Nocturnes.* Interesting chapters on sources.

Milcent, Ernest and Monique Sordet. *Léopold Sédar Senghor et la naissance de l'Afrique moderne.* Paris: Seghers, 1969. A study of Senghor's life and political career up to the presidency with an interesting chapter on Negritude and its development. Good chronology.

Osman, Gusine Gawdat. *L'Afrique dans l'univers poètique de Léopold Sédar Senghor.* Dakar: Nouvelles Editions Africaines, 1978. A thematic study through *Lettres d'hivernage* that includes the categories of emotion, rhythm, imagery, nature, women, and the village. No index.

Peters, Jonathan A. *A Dance of Masks: Senghor, Achebe, Soyinka.* Washington, D.C.: Three Continents Press, 1978. Although Peters is especially interested in mask images, this is an extremely perceptive analysis of the different volumes of poetry studied in sequence through *Nocturnes.*

Rous, Jean. *Léopold Sédar Senghor: La Vie d'un président de l'Afrique nouvelle.* Paris: Editions Jean Didier, 1967. A biography of Senghor written by a political advisor with chapters on his philosophy and on his daily life.

Tillot, Renée. *Le Rythme dans la poésie de Léopold Sédar Senghor.* Paris: Nouvelles Editions Africaines, 1979. Especially interesting for its reproduction and comparisons of prior versions of both published and unpublished works.

Van Niekerk, Barend v. D. *The African Image (Négritude) in the Work of Léopold Sédar Senghor.* Capetown: A.A. Balkema, 1970. Interesting sequential study of the poems. Although this is in many respects a more balanced assessment of the poetry than is to be found elsewhere, an attentive reader might have some reservations about the South African perspective.

Index